Miller Cornfield
— at —
Antietam

Rare 1861 photograph of the Marion County, Texas men of Company D (Star Rifles), First Texas Infantry Regiment. Seven Oliver boys served in Company D, First Texas. In this photograph, Absalom C. Oliver (*center*) and Henry Oliver (*right*) are seen standing above three seated family members: John Oliver, William A.T. Oliver and Thomas F. Oliver. *Jefferson Historical Society and Museum, Jefferson, Texas.*

Miller Cornfield at Antietam

The Civil War's Bloodiest Combat

Phillip Thomas Tucker, PhD

Published by The History Press
Charleston, SC
www.historypress.net

Cover images: Lower image on front from author's collection.

First published 2017

Manufactured in the United States

ISBN 9781625858658

Library of Congress Control Number: 2017931818

To the First Texas.

To the young men and boys on both sides who made the supreme sacrifice at Antietam.

Many people deserve special thanks in helping to make this book possible over a period of more than two decades. The author is very grateful to them all.

Contents

Introduction

America was never the same after the bloodiest day of not only the Civil War but also American history: a decisive Wednesday, September 17, 1862. Lasting more than a dozen hours, this epic clash of arms between the Army of Northern Virginia and the Army of the Potomac on a beautiful, late-summer day in western Maryland resulted in an unprecedented slaughter on a single day. To decide a nation's destiny and fate, an unparalleled number of Americans were cut down on this day of surreal carnage on a scale previously unseen in America in the most decisive battle in the most decisive theater during the war's most decisive year, 1862.

Antietam (a Delaware Indian word meaning "swift current") was a name derived from the clear waters of picturesque Antietam Creek. Fought with an unprecedented savagery just outside the sleepy farming community of Sharpsburg, Maryland, the climactic showdown at Antietam was a major turning point in American history. Quite simply, the course of the Civil War was never the same after this horrific battle (called Sharpsburg by the mostly rural Confederates, unlike their mostly urban Northern counterparts, who named Civil War battles after natural landmarks like Antietam Creek) amid the fertile, pristine farmlands drained by Antietam Creek.

Here, the Confederacy's high tide in the eastern theater crested during General Robert Edward Lee's first Northern invasion. Never were Confederate military and political ambitions or prospects higher than in the late summer of 1862. On the war's most nightmarish day, more than twenty-three thousand Americans became casualties, littering the fields, farm lanes and autumn-hued woodlots around Sharpsburg in overwhelming numbers—more than seven times American losses (killed and wounded) in the Japanese surprise attack on Pearl Harbor, Hawaii, on December 7, 1941, and more than four times the American losses inflicted by Adolf Hitler's Wehrmacht during the Allies' landing on the beaches of Normandy, France, on D-day, June 6, 1944.

This titanic clash of arms and sacrifice of thousands of soldiers in this deluge of bloodletting occurred precisely because so much was at stake. Because Antietam's slaughter left lengthy burial trenches piled high with so many young men and boys from across America, the repulse of Lee's first invasion north of the Potomac River became the North's most important strategic and political victory of the war.

Indeed, this hard-earned success in stopping Lee's seemingly invincible army amid the lush farmlands of Washington County, Maryland, provided the long-awaited opportunity for President Abraham Lincoln to deliver his most important political stroke. Lincoln signed the historic document that set the North's war effort on an entirely different course. To take advantage of the opportunity provided by the costly success at Antietam, the sixteenth president gained the moral high ground for the Union when he issued the Emancipation Proclamation to transform the Northern war effort into a great moral crusade to end slavery's curse and America's greatest paradox. President Lincoln bestowed the war-weary North with a much-needed moral and psychological boost to prosecute the conflict to the bitter end.

The most important phase of this climactic showdown at Antietam took place in the most unlikely and serene of places in the middle of nowhere. The first phase of the battle swept through an obscure thirty-acre cornfield with an unprecedented fury, taking lives at a rate not seen before in this war. Ironically, this nearly ripe cornfield, owned by farmer David R. Miller and located west of Antietam Creek and north of Sharpsburg, served as one of the war's most dramatic stages on the morning of September 17. Here, the best combat troops of opposing armies sought to destroy each other with a ferocity seldom seen. In this broad cornfield just east of the Hagerstown Road, which led to Sharpsburg to the south, the lives of thousands of young men were consumed with an unprecedented rapidity during the grimiest harvest seen on the war's bloodiest day. As fate would have it, no soldiers suffered more severely in this unprecedented slaughter of the fatal cornfield than members of the elite Texas Brigade, especially the First Texas Confederate Regiment.

It was hardly before the sun had risen on September 17 that the mighty First Corps, Army of the Potomac, launched its most powerful offensive effort by attacking south from north of Sharpsburg in a bid to smash through Lee's weak left flank, capture the town and gain Lee's vulnerable rear to ensure the destruction of the Army of Northern Virginia—a climactic showdown that determined if the South's primary eastern army was to survive.

And at no single place on the battlefield's twelve square miles during a dozen hours of combat was the contest more lethal than in the Miller Cornfield. To determine the destinies of two republics, no combat during the war's four years compared to the sheer intensity of the brutal struggle that raged throughout the cornfield. Here, on a battleground that was transformed into a hell on earth for the common soldiers in blue and gray, the best combat unit of the Army of Northern Virginia, the Texas Brigade, rose to the challenge to save the day for Lee's reeling army. In Antietam's most high-stakes showdown, the Texas Brigade battled the best combat unit of the Army of the Potomac, the Iron Brigade. It was truly an epic clash of arms between the two finest fighting units of their respective armies in the Miller Cornfield.

With the outnumbered Rebels facing their greatest no-win situation during what looked like certain annihilation for the South's primary army, Lee was very fortunate in one crucial regard. At the moment of greatest crisis, he possessed one last strategic reserve, his ace in the hole in this showdown at Antietam: Brigadier General John Bell Hood's Division (including the Texas Brigade), which was in the ideal position to unleash a desperate bid to reverse the day's fortunes. But this was no accident, as Lee had hoped to exploit any tactical vulnerability in order to launch a counterattack in an attempt to reap a decisive victory that might alter the war's course by garnering foreign recognition for the Confederacy from England and France and strengthening the North's antiwar peace party. Therefore, for a host of reasons, the counterattack of Hood's Division was launched to reverse the tide of not only the battle but also the war itself.

In attacking north through the Miller Cornfield's very heart and then beyond its northern edge while driving back one victorious Union command (including the hard-fighting Iron Brigade) after another, the Texas Brigade accomplished one of the war's most remarkable combat performances—an unprecedented tactical feat in reversing the tide of an all-important battle and saving Lee's Army from an early death. In the nightmarish close-range combat that swirled through the tasseled green cornstalks that stood high before being cut down by projectiles, the First Texas Confederate Regiment lost more than 82 percent, a frightful sacrifice that surpassed the losses of any regiment, North or South, on a single day during the four years of war.

A long-standing debate among Civil War historians has been the controversy regarding which regiment or brigade comprised America's best combat troops. This often-heated discussion has long focused not only between troops from North and South but also from east and west. The historic "east versus west" debate was actually more appropriate because east/west rivalries on multiples levels, including political and economic, had existed far longer throughout American history, extending to the colonial period.

Not surprisingly, this historic east/west rivalry continued to exist unabated between Civil War soldiers on both sides from 1861 to 1865. Thanks to the powerful Virginia press (influential newspapers centered in the Confederacy's capital of Richmond) and an Army of Northern Virginia dominated by Old Dominion leadership and blatant cronyism at all levels, full recognition of battlefield accomplishments (overly embellished by the Richmond press) by Virginia troops only too often came at the expense of non-Virginia troops, especially those units from the west.

However, what the Texans accomplished at Antietam simply could not be ignored or glossed over even by the influential Richmond newspapers. Indeed, one non-Virginia unit of Lee's Army, the Texas Brigade, emerged to exceed all others (including Virginia troops and even the famed Stonewall Brigade) in terms of the unparalleled battlefield accomplishments without the usual support of regional backers, favoritism and a home state press (the Texans served more than one thousand miles from home).

What the Texas Brigade demonstrated on September 17, 1862, was that the finest combat troops of the Army of Northern Virginia hailed from a distinctive Southwest frontier region located the greatest distance from Richmond. Hailing from a historical evolutionary process and a struggle of survival of the fittest in a harsh, untamed land, the Texans evolved into crack combat troops partly from the Trans-Mississippi and frontier experiences—an environmental forge that created inordinately tough, resilient and resourceful fighting men—while the much-celebrated Virginians were far removed from the western frontier experience by comparison. Ironically, both on and off the battlefield, Virginia's finest soldiers certainly looked like the army's elite troops compared to the rough-hewn Texans, who cared nothing about outward appearances. But the truth was quite the opposite, and this was fully demonstrated in the Texans' fierce counterattack through the Miller Cornfield and beyond.

Indeed, the Texas Brigade early proved to be a superior fighting machine to even Virginia's famed Stonewall Brigade, whose record has been long embellished and romanticized by generations of Virginia historians. At Antietam, the Stonewall Brigade (which primarily gained its reputation by way of the achievements of its legendary commander, Major General Thomas Jonathan "Stonewall" Jackson, who served as Lee's dependable right arm) was smashed by Union attackers north of Sharpsburg on the early morning of September 17, before the Texans' counterattack reversed the tide and saved the day for Lee's Army.

Commanding the Fifteenth Alabama Confederate Infantry, Colonel William Calvin Oates, who had lived on the prewar Texas frontier, revealed one of the Civil War's forgotten truths regarding the factors that were most responsible for forging elite combat units. Most importantly, he intimately understood the key correlation between hard-fighting qualities and the western experience. This knowledgeable Alabamian emphasized that "the men from the Cotton States [including Texas] were better soldiers and harder fighters [because of] the difference between the frontiersmen and the citizen of more refined and regular habits of the older States," including Virginia. Oates also maintained, correctly, how the Confederacy's best combat troops hailed from regions farthest west. To fully support Colonel Oates's keen observations and insights, the Confederacy's farthest point west was the Southwest frontier of Texas. The colonel certainly knew what he was talking about. Oates served in the same division (under Major General John Bell Hood of Lieutenant General James Longstreet's First Corps in 1863) as the hard-fighting Texas Brigade during the Gettysburg Campaign.

In agreement with Colonel Oates's astute analysis, the annals of Civil War historiography have fully demonstrated that the Civil War's best combat troops indeed hailed from regions farther west—an often-overlooked correlation that applied to both sides from 1861 to 1865. Regarding the Army of the Potomac, the superior battlefield performance (including at the David R. Miller Cornfield) of the famed Iron Brigade of Wisconsin, Michigan and Indiana troops has also revealed as much. The famous sobriquet of the Iron Brigade referred specifically to this elite command's sterling qualities and combat prowess on the battlefield. Although not generally realized today by the American public and even historians, Civil War soldiers on both sides at the time intimately understood this close correlation between the toughening process of the western frontier experience and superior combat qualities. As proven repeatedly in the eastern and western theaters, the Confederacy's finest combat units hailed from the West, including the Texas Brigade, the Orphan Brigade of Kentucky and the First Missouri Brigade (the last two fought in the western theater).

But the very best example of this unique phenomenon was in the case of the Texas Brigade, which hailed from the Confederacy's westernmost and most frontier region. As its record of impressive battlefield successes has repeatedly demonstrated from beginning to end, the Army of Northern Virginia's finest combat unit consisted of fighting men from the Southwest frontier. The slashing counterattack of the Texas Brigade, especially the First Texas Infantry Regiment, which surged through the tall, tasseled stalks of the Miller Cornfield, was the most magnificent attack of the day and a significant offensive effort at Antietam regarding overall results.

Paradoxically, the surreal slaughter in the Miller Cornfield mocked the picturesque setting and natural beauty of this bountiful agricultural region in Washington County. This dramatic stage of unprecedented slaughter was located just west of the bluish-hued ranges of South Mountain, which was the easternmost extension of the Appalachians. The Miller Cornfield was situated on fertile ground nestled amid an agrarian paradise, fed by the Antietam's clear waters that flowed south to enter the Potomac River just below Sharpsburg. A mild climate, rich soil and plentiful amounts of rainfall made this attractive region especially productive for industrious farmers (mostly Germans), who never imaged that their well-manicured farmlands of plenty would become the center of the war's most terrible storm.

On a hot, humid morning in the midst of a beautiful Indian summer, the Miller Cornfield was transformed into a scene of unparalleled carnage during some of the war's most bitter fighting, especially the dramatic showdown between two of the best combat units of their respective armies, the Iron Brigade and the Texas Brigade. Appropriately, these two elite fighting machines of hardy westerners—especially the "Ragged First" Texas versus the "Black Hats" of the Iron Brigade—gave undeniable validity to the geographical correlation between combat superiority and western origins.

When everything was at stake, this epic confrontation in the Miller Cornfield pitted the best fighting men of both armies against each other in a brutal slugfest between the only all-western brigade of the Army of the Potomac and the only all-western brigade of Lee's Army. These environmental, geographic and cultural distinctions of the Iron and Texas Brigades fueled a heightened combat prowess among these crack westerners in blue and gray (mostly young farm boys of middle-class origins) when they met for the first time on Antietam's great killing field.

As demonstrated by its sweeping counterattack that turned the tide north of Sharpsburg, the best combat regiment of "Lee's Grenadier Guard" was the elite First Texas. These battle-hardened veterans again demonstrated their lethality in spearheading the Texas Brigade's attack north through the high-standing cornstalks, including against the Iron Brigade. The dramatic story of the Texans' splendid combat performance certainly deserves greater recognition today, as this severe contest represented a major turning point of the Civil War.

With the Army of the Potomac on the verge of achieving a decisive victory (the war's most important to date) and systematically destroying Lee's Army after smashing through initial Confederate resistance north of Sharpsburg, the Texans' counterattack through the Miller Cornfield ensured that Lee's crumbling left flank would not be completely turned and his army destroyed. Quite simply, the Army of Northern Virginia was never more vulnerable than at this critical moment in the early morning hours of September 17, when Hood's Division was unleashed. A relatively small number of Texans saved Lee's Army in a truly remarkable tactical feat that ensured that the Battle of Antietam later shifted to sectors farther south, where Lee's troops possessed better defensive ground and more favorable chances for holding firm in good defensive positions than in the open farmlands like at Miller Cornfield.

Without the Texas Brigade's counterattack and unparalleled sacrifice in the cornfield, Lee's Army would have been vanquished, and an open road to Richmond would have beckoned to the victorious Army of the Potomac. The war's entire course, therefore, was very much determined by what happened there. These young soldiers on both sides seemed to instinctively realize what was at stake on the morning of September 17: nothing less than America's fate and future destiny. The dramatic story of the vicious struggle for possession of the Miller Cornfield is truly one of the most unforgettable and significant chapters of the Civil War.

To pay a proper tribute and honor to so many young men on both sides who fought and died in the Miller Cornfield on the most awful morning in September, this book will focus primarily on the personal experiences of the common soldiers, bringing their remarkable personal stories to life through letters, memoirs and diaries. This approach is important to illuminate one of the greatest battlefield tragedies that ever befell one of America's finest combat units: the decimation and sacrifice of the Texas Brigade in saving the day. Most of all, this is the tragic story of the surreal holocaust that consumed the Miller Cornfield and the lives of so many soldiers caught in the epicenter of Antietam's nightmarish struggle, when America's fate was determined on a mid-September morning in Washington County, Maryland.

Chapter 1

THE ILL-FATED INVASION OF MARYLAND

No army in the annals of American history had been more successful on the battlefield than the Army of Northern Virginia by the late summer of 1862. Richmond, the Confederacy's capital on the James River, had been saved by only a narrow margin from the clutches of the mighty Army of the Potomac during the Peninsula Campaign. All the while, Brigadier General John Bell Hood's Texas Brigade was evolving into the shock troops of the South's primary eastern army under the aggressive leadership of General Robert Edward Lee. The Texas Brigade had spearheaded the hard-hitting assaults that secured a dramatic victory outside Richmond's gates on the Virginia Peninsula during the Seven Days.

But Lee's stirring victories in Virginia had been replete with indecisive results and were nothing more than Pyrrhic successes. Therefore, Lee needed to win a decisive success on Northern soil to eliminate the strategic stalemate in Virginia that was gradually dooming the young Confederacy to a slow death. Lee's victory at Second Manassas over General John Pope's Army of Virginia at the end of August 1862 finally bestowed the long-awaited opportunity to gain the strategic initiative by launching his invasion of Maryland. Here, the Texas Brigade had played a key role in reaping Lee's most brilliant tactical success to date by charging through one Federal unit after another in overrunning strategic Chinn Ridge. After the disastrous loss at Second Manassas, Pope's beaten army retired northeast to the safety of the massive ring of fortifications surrounding Washington, D.C. The way was now open for a vigorous Confederate

A native Kentuckian who resigned from the United States Army in April 1861 to cast his fate with the Confederacy, Brigadier General John Bell Hood became one of General Robert Edward Lee's hardest-hitting division commanders of the Army of Northern Virginia. During one of the most dramatic attacks of the war, the veterans of Hood's crack division, including the famed Texas Brigade, nearly reversed the course of the battle of Antietam on the morning of September 17, 1862, during the war's bloodiest single day. *Author's collection.*

push north and across the Potomac River for the fulfillment of Southern dreams.

Without the possibility of forcing a decisive engagement with what remained of Pope's defeated army—as he had wisely refused to commit the folly of attacking the Federals in their powerful Washington, D.C., fortifications and endorsing the Maryland invasion plan long espoused by his top lieutenant, Major General Thomas Jonathan "Stonewall" Jackson—Lee eyed the promised land of "My Maryland."

As he informed President Jefferson Davis on September 3 by letter, Lee was determined to retain the initiative and offensive momentum to not only exploit his most recent success at Second Manassas but also reap greater gains in the "Old Line State" (a sobriquet for the Maryland Continental Line of the American Revolution) to bring the beleaguered Confederacy the much-needed foreign recognition from Great Britain and France. Lee also wanted to affect the fall midterm elections, bolstering the strength of the peace party (Northern Copperheads) and perhaps even gain a negotiated settlement to ensure a new nation's independence—if an important victory could be won. As Lee reasoned in the same letter to President Davis, "[T]hough weaker than our opponents in men and military equipments, [we] must endeavor to harass, if we cannot destroy them" in western Maryland, where the Army of the Potomac would be more vulnerable.[1]

General Robert E. Lee, the South's most successful commander, risked the life of his Army of Northern Virginia by deciding to make an audacious defensive stand at Antietam against immense odds. Despite his best efforts, Lee's first invasion of the North (which was to have continued into Pennsylvania) was thwarted at Antietam, but he saved his army to fight another day—a rather remarkable tactical achievement that kept the dream of Southern independence alive. *Library of Congress.*

In fact, Lee was far too ambitious considering his army's reduced capabilities after his devastating losses in the bloody summer of 1862. He was already thinking about pushing through Maryland and then on into Pennsylvania. Nevertheless, as Lee admitted to President Davis, his army was "not properly equipped for an invasion" of the North.[2]

Major General Thomas Jonathan Jackson, a Mexican-American War veteran and former professor at the Virginia Military Institute, was Lee's most able top lieutenant. "Stonewall" Jackson was a West Pointer who had emerged as a popular hero across the South. Jackson and Lee formed the most dynamic and formidable leadership team in America by the time of the dramatic showdown at Antietam. *Library of Congress.*

Like Davis, Lee was eager to take the war north of the Potomac because this increasingly brutal war of attrition was slowly dooming the Confederacy to an early death. Most of all, he knew that a decisive victory had to be won as soon as possible for his nation's survival. Consequently, Lee prepared to advance even before receiving official approval from Davis. Since July and reflecting the desires of the Southern people, the strategically astute president from Mississippi had seen the strategic wisdom of invading Union soil. He now believed that the summer of 1862 was the best opportunity to attempt to regain the strategic initiative. Richmond newspapers, like the influential *Richmond Whig*, had long denounced Davis's defensive policies.

But the Army of Northern Virginia's veterans had been marching, fighting and maneuvering almost continuously for nearly four months to considerably diminish overall war-waging capabilities. Indeed, the Peninsula and the Second Manassas Campaigns actually formed a single bloody summer campaign. Nevertheless, Lee prepared to launch his most ambitious undertaking to date without allowing his worn troops adequate recuperation from a spring and summer of intense combat and long-distance marching.[3]

Indeed, the initial thrust northward had actually begun after Lee repulsed General George Brinton McClellan's Army of the Potomac to save Richmond during the summer of 1862. Making the most of the opportunity, Lee had then swung north to strike Pope's Army of Virginia far outside Washington, D.C., and where the Battle of First Manassas had

Major General George Brinton McClellan, a Mexican-American War veteran and military intellectual, was known across the North as the "Young Napoleon." However, his lofty reputation and Napoleonic image were largely a creation of the popular media and an overly inflated ego. An excellent organizer and administrator, McClellan was far less capable on the battlefield. He missed one of the best opportunities of the war to destroy the Army of Northern Virginia at Antietam. *Library of Congress.*

been fought in July 1861. However, these Confederate successes, including Second Manassas, in a relatively short time had taken a severe toll on the common soldiers' morale regarding advancing beyond the South's borders. Quite simply, Lee's Army was unfit for launching the war's most ambitious invasion to date. Lee himself lamented that his army "lacks much of the material of war…and the men are poorly provided with clothes, and in thousands of instances are destitute of shoes."[4]

Lee's other pressing concern was how to supply his troops once they entered Maryland. Most of all, this struggle was a modern war based on logistical considerations, especially during a Northern invasion. The resource-short Confederate nation was unable to adequately support a far-flung army in Northern territory. Because this was the Confederacy's first attempt in the eastern theater to take the conflict beyond Virginia's borders, logistical experience for an invasion was sadly lacking for the extensive challenges that lay north of the Potomac River.

Thinking about the glory days of the Mexican-American War during the march of General Winfield Scott's army from the Gulf of Mexico (the port of Vera Cruz) across the Central Valley to Mexico City, Major General James Longstreet, who commanded what would become the First Corps (by the time of the Battle of Gettysburg), Army of Northern Virginia, was optimistic for success. He convinced Lee that the army could live off Maryland's bountiful land like Napoleon Bonaparte's and Scott's armies. Napoleon had moved long distances to outmaneuver his opponents while subsisting on the natural bounty of the best cultivated agricultural areas in central Europe. Longstreet emphasized, "I related my Mexican War experiences [when troops subsisted on] roasting ears and green oranges, and said that it seemed to me that we could trust to the fields of Maryland, laden with ripening corn and fruit, to do as much as those of Mexico; that we could in fact subsist on the bounty of the fields" of Maryland. Ominously, there was then no ripe corn standing in Maryland's fields as in Mexico's lush Central Valley, as harvest time came much later.[5]

Lee's "Old War Horse" from Georgia was overly optimistic. Like other veterans of Scott's 1847 campaign, he was still living in a past fondly remembered. One theory that has sought to explain Southern defeat has espoused that the Confederacy died because of an overreliance on the successful offensive tactics of the Mexican-American War.[6] Lee agreed with Longstreet's analogy that an invading American army could live off the land north of the Potomac. The logistical lesson of the triumphant march to Mexico City in the summer of 1847 (symbolically, that successful campaign had ended in another balmy mid-September, when the Battle of Antietam was also fought) convinced Lee that this seemingly time-proven logistical concept could be accomplished in Maryland and Pennsylvania. Having served under him with distinction, Lee had been a great admirer of General Scott, who had conquered Mexico City to hasten the war's end.[7]

Clearly, Scott's remarkable 250-mile march along the same route (through Mexico's Central Valley, which abounded with foodstuffs, including ripe fruit), like Don Hernán Cortés when he and his Spanish conquistadors and Indian allies had conquered the Aztec Empire, significantly influenced Lee's logistical thinking. Consequently, those lessons of 1847 were not lost on Lee in September 1862, nor were the Napoleonic teachings of West Point—dual legacies that propelled Lee's Army north with confidence. Lee fully embraced Longstreet's analogy of what had proved a successful formula in Mexico: a relatively small army of American troops traveling light and living off the land in a wide-ranging campaign in hostile territory, even though it was outnumbered and far from supply bases, could succeed.[8]

But what Lee overlooked was the significant fact that the 1847 campaign across central Mexico embraced far more achievable strategic objectives than his Maryland invasion. Lee's vision of his upcoming campaign north of the Potomac River initially included no plans to capture any important cities in Maryland, such as Baltimore. Lee more readily incorporated the logistical lessons of Scott's campaign rather than the strategic. Lee wisely ruled out advancing on the heavily fortified capital. Ironically, this type of strategic thinking was unlike that of Lee's top lieutenant, Thomas J. Jackson. "Old Blue Light" Jackson had long advocated the launching of a Northern invasion, but with a clear strategic objective of capturing a major Northern city, such Baltimore or Philadelphia. Even Confederate common soldiers later became convinced that "Lee would dictate terms of peace in Independence Square, Philadelphia."[9]

The North had early taken the pressure off Washington, D.C., by targeting Richmond in the spring of 1862. In a letter to the home folks, a confident Lieutenant Robert "Billy" Hugh Gaston, a young officer of Company H (Texas Guards), First Texas Confederate Infantry, in which his two brothers also served, bragged to his "Pa & Ma" how "Lincoln has said that he would dine in Richmond, before long. We would all be glad to see him & would give him a very warm reception."[10]

Initially without a key strategic objective such as a major Northern city, Lee's Maryland incursion actually more resembled a raid than a proper invasion. Lee described his advance north as "an expedition into Maryland" but still envisioned pushing into Pennsylvania if the opportunity existed. The

Maryland invasion evolved into an advance away from northeastern cities, largely to allow the replenishing of the supply-short army in a countryside unspoiled by the war's devastation like Virginia.

General Lee initially possessed no strategic objective, such as Washington, D.C. Lincoln's capable chief of staff, Henry W. Halleck, was puzzled by what seemed to him merely a raid launched by the Rebels. Instead, Lee planned to move across territory of relatively little real strategic value so that his army could subsist by living off the land.

General Lee remained pragmatic, understanding that he had to cross the Potomac because of pressing political objectives. But his short-term logistical considerations of supplying his army (instead of long-term considerations of establishing a supply line to the fertile Shenandoah Valley, the Army of Northern Virginia's vital breadbasket) negated the all-important long-term strategic objectives, including the capture of Washington, D.C.; Baltimore; or Philadelphia. Without initially establishing a targeted strategic objective in a too hastily conceived plan of striking north of the Potomac River with the summer drawing to an end, the Confederate offensive effort into Maryland was largely doomed to failure from the beginning. Lee planned to invade the North, avoid a major confrontation in order to not risk a decisive defeat that would prove catastrophic for the Confederacy, and recruit eager Marylanders in a war of liberation to replenish his army. Most of all, Lee now needed men, materiel and supplies that were increasingly unattainable in a war-ravaged Virginia.[11]

In reality, however, the decision to invade Maryland was one of Lee's worst strategic decisions, as Scott's march on Mexico City could not be resurrected a decade and a half later north of the Potomac. Consequently, this audacious decision to take the war across the Potomac would shortly prove nearly fatal to not only the Army of Northern Virginia's life but also the Confederacy.

Lee's first Northern invasion was launched with high expectations but without the fundamental ingredients necessary for decisive success. Indeed, "despite the extraordinary nature of the undertaking, no logistical forethought had been given to the expedition" into Maryland. Ironically, the Confederacy would have had a much better chance of winning foreign recognition had Lee captured Baltimore or Washington, D.C. Realizing as much, experienced Union leadership was convinced that once in Maryland in what was essentially a feint, Lee then planned to eventually turn southeast toward Washington, D.C.[12]

President Lincoln and Chief of Staff General Henry Halleck perhaps realized early on that the Army of Northern Virginia possessed little chance for reaping a decisive success on such an overly ambitious undertaking north of the Potomac. Meanwhile, Lee's logistical concerns steadily mounted. From near Dranesville, Virginia, Lee wrote to President Davis on September 3, explaining that "what occasions me most concern is the fear of getting out of ammunition."[13]

In addition, Lee was not entirely sure of the exact numbers of soldiers he commanded. Even worse, he overestimated the stamina and capabilities of his men for an invasion's unprecedented challenges. Just northwest of Washington, D.C., during the first week of September, the Rebel army prepared to cross the wide but relatively shallow Potomac. Cutting through densely wooded hills, this picturesque river served as the natural boundary between Virginia and Maryland. With cheers and waving red battle flags decorated with the names of past victories across Virginia, thousands of Lee's soldiers began to cross the Potomac River on September 4 at White's Ford, just northeast of the Leesburg, Virginia area.

However, this spirit of elation among the invaders was badly misplaced. The Potomac was the river of no return for thousands of Lee's men. Ominously, many common soldiers remained far behind in Virginia, after having left ranks and voted their disapproval for a Northern invasion with their feet—unofficially boycotting Confederate leadership decisions in their own way. For largely regional and moral reasons, many Rebels believed that they signed up only to defend the Confederacy's borders and not to invade an enemy's homeland. Consequently, the Army of Northern Virginia was fundamentally more of an unmatched defensive fighting machine on Southern soil rather than an effective offensive force when far away from Southern territory.

With expectations of reaping future victories while the late summer sunshine made the Potomac's waters sparkle, the Texas Rebels waded across the river's cold waters of White's Ford on September 6. The Texans were in a festive mood, yelling and laughing while wading toward the Maryland shore. Despite one of the driest summers on record, Lee's men believed that destiny awaited them in Maryland. The brass band of the Fourth Texas Infantry played, "Maryland, My Maryland" to inspire confidence. Other Confederate brass bands struck up "Dixie," "The Girl I Left Behind" and even "Yankee Doodle" to mock their often-defeated opponent. Described by one man as "ragged, dirty, sun-browned and careworn," these battle-hardened soldiers of the First, Fourth and Fifth Texas (the army's only Lone Star State regiments) were "bent on effacing the print of the 'despot's heel' from 'Maryland's shore'" and perhaps even in Pennsylvania.[14]

However, the lengthy push north from central Virginia's depths had continued to exact a heavy toll. Broken down by disease and exhaustion, large numbers of Southerners steadily fell out of ranks. Meanwhile, the summer heat sapped the strength of other soldiers. Thousands of veterans failed to continue marching north. Corporal Orlando Thacker Hanks, Company K (Texas Invincibles), First Texas, described how "[w]e are undergoing as hard or harder force march as we ever accomplished. The men are taxed, almost beyond human endurance; would think they could go no further, and then still go on."[15]

The silk Lone Star flag of the First Texas was carried onto Maryland soil for the first time by a remarkable color guard member. Born on Galveston Island on January 5, 1843, Color Corporal George A. Branard had worked as a mechanic for the firm of Close and Cushman before the insanity of war changed his life forever. During the first battle of the Texas Brigade at Eltham's Landing on the Virginia Peninsula early during the 1862 Peninsula Campaign, Branard had made a name for himself. When the color sergeant fell wounded, Branard grabbed the regimental colors and sprinted ahead of the regimental line. When he advanced too far before the regiment, shouts erupted from his comrades for Branard to return. Despite a bleeding wound when a bullet grazed his head, an angry Branard turned back and shouted that he would not return. Instead of a stalled offensive effort, regimental members were inspired by his defiant example before the ranks. Consequently, the entire First Texas surged forward with Rebel Yells. The feisty color guard corporal won a promotion to a color sergeant's rank.

Despite being barefoot and with sore feet like so many other Lone Star State soldiers, Branard, formerly a corporal of Company L (the Lone Star Rifles, consisting of men from the Gulf of Mexico port of Galveston), First Texas, held the regiment's flag on the Maryland side in a symbolic gesture. He had been appointed color sergeant on May 11, 1862, and never relinquished rank or that responsibility (considered the highest honor among regimental members), until disabled by a series of wounds.

In high spirits, the Texans swarmed into the promised land of Maryland with renewed confidence for success. Lee's boldest thrust north was not the first invasion of "foreign" soil for some Texas Brigade men. Some brigade soldiers (older officers, unlike the many teenagers in the ranks) had invaded

Mexico with General Winfield Scott or had battled Mexican guerrillas after crossing the Rio Grande to carry the war against an ancient opponent.[16]

As ragged and dirty as Lee's troops appeared to the astonished Marylanders, Lee's most shoddily attired soldiers were the First Texas Rebels. The Lone Star State soldiers, wrote Corporal Orlando Thacker Hanks—who had been born in 1844 in St. Augustine, in the pine and prairie country of east Texas, and was a member of Company K (Texas Invincibles), First Texas—now wore parts of Yankee uniforms and equipment taken from the dead. Private Joseph Benjamin Polley, Company F (Mustang Grays), Fourth Texas, described the situation of the Texas boys, who were farther away from their beloved Lone Star State than ever before: "No clothing or shoes had been furnished [to Hood's Division] since it left Richmond, and in a month and a half of hard marching and harder fighting hundreds of the men had become ragged and barefooted, while lack of provisions forced them to subsist on green corn and green apples" from Maryland's fields and orchards that seemed like an agricultural paradise compared to war-devastated Virginia.[17]

This Maryland invasion "has electrified the nation," wrote the Richmond editor of the *Southern Illustrated News*. However, this long march north was considered far less glorious by half-starved soldiers, who raided so many cornfields that they dubbed this the "green corn campaign."[18]

Stripped Maryland cornfields were visual evidence of a rapidly deteriorating situation in the invading army. However, this logistical breakdown was even more severe among the Texans at this time. They suffered more than any of Lee's troops because of harsh strategic and geographic realities. Because these western frontier exiles hailed from west of the Mississippi River (controlled mostly by the Union navy) and because they were farther from home (more than one thousand miles) than any other Southern troops, adequate supplies from Texas were not forthcoming. Ironically, while these men fought and died representing the Lone Star State on the war's major battlefields, Texas (under threat of Union invasion) was unable to provide support to the Texas Brigade soldiers so far away from home.

As if pausing for breath before continuing farther into western Maryland, Lee and his army rested before the heavily forested South Mountain, a northern extension of the Blue Ridge of Virginia, at Frederick, about forty-five miles northwest of Washington, D.C. Here, in the well-cultivated valley of the Monocacy River, the Texas soldiers learned that their reputations for ferocity had preceded them. Corporal Hanks described how when "passing through Frederick, a beautiful little city [it seemed that all of the] people appeared awe stricken [and] One little fellow was perched on the fence and asked if these were Texians. On being told, yes, he remarked 'Oh, Mama, they look just like our folks.' Another one was heard to say: 'Here comes the Bonny Blue Flag now, come and see it.' It was a large Lone Star flag carried by the first Texas regiment."[19]

Many of Lee's veterans believed that they were engaged in a righteous war of liberation for pro-Southern Marylanders. In an emotional letter to his "little Sis," one South Carolina Rebel explained his sense of righteousness because the oppressors' "iron heel is upon the neck of poor Maryland, and when I thought of the fact that our army, with hearts burning with sympathy on account of her oppressed condition, had entered her territory to tear the tyrant's yoke from her bleeding neck, how could I otherwise than breathe a prayer to the Almighty to assist us in the glorious work?"[20]

At Frederick, Lee realized that one of his central objectives was already doomed to failure: the flocking of thousands of western Marylanders to swell his army's ranks never occurred as anticipated by Richmond's armchair political optimists. Unfortunately, Southern leadership knew nothing of the nuances of Maryland's demographics and sentiments. While Baltimore and southern Maryland, where slavery thrived, were pro-Confederate, western Maryland had been settled largely by Germans, who were decidedly pro-Union. Lee and the Confederate government never fully understood the demographic realities of western Maryland. This was a largely wheat-growing and pro-Union region located just below the Pennsylvania border and even included a good number of free black farmers.

In fact, far more serious problems infected the very core of the Army of Northern Virginia. Georgian Colonel Edward Porter Alexander, one of Lee's best artillery officers despite being only in his twenties, realized that this self-destructing invading army of ill-supplied Rebel soldiers was already in deep trouble. He wrote how "we laid there [at Frederick] & took a much needed rest for man & beast for four days [but] even that was scarcely enough, for stragglers were lining the roads, &, what with these & the killed & wounded at Second Manassas, divisions had sunk to little more than brigades & brigades nearly to regiments."[21] At this time, at least half of the army was absent. Desertions had increased with each mile Lee had pushed north to fulfill his ambitions.[22]

Two critical factors had combined to doom Lee's Maryland invasion almost from the start. Maryland's expansive fields supplied only green corn, and fruit orchards provided a limitless supply of green apples that ravaged the bowels and health of the common soldiers. This epidemic of sickness swept through the ranks. Regarding logistical and supply considerations near summer's end, one Confederate sorely regretted that Lee's timing could not have been worse, as the corn in the field was unripe. Unfamiliar with the nuances of climate north of Virginia, Lee overlooked the slight, but significant, differences in seasons between Maryland and Virginia: crops and fruit ripened later than in Virginia.

Unrealized by bureaucratic officials in Richmond, the precise timing of the army's invasion, which was crucial for success, was off. While the American army's march west from the port of Vera Cruz to Mexico City had benefited from a mild tropical climate and fertile countryside that supplied plenty of food and fodder, thanks to Central Mexico's long growing season and almost ceaseless sunshine, the Maryland invasion had been launched too early in early September before crops had ripened. The hard, forced marches, hot weather, lack of regular supplies and extremely harmful effects of attempting to live off the land led to widespread suffering and indiscipline, effectively sapping the army's strength.

With the combined effect of mass straggling and an epidemic of desertions, this slow disintegration of the army had soared to unprecedented levels with each passing mile in western Maryland. Without the sturdy moral, emotional and psychological foundations of a righteous defense of the Southern homeland, this disastrous psychological and logistical situation resulted in the steady dissolution of Lee's Army. Instead of gaining strength as it advanced into Maryland, as Lee envisioned by drawing multitudes of Maryland recruits, the army actually grew weaker and combat capabilities steadily decreased with each passing day.

While the invasion into Union territory was a new experience for the most successful American army to date, such liabilities were not unusual for an invading army when penetrating into enemy territory, especially in unfamiliar regions and when far from support. In the history of warfare, logistical failures had led to more campaigns being lost than from enemy counteroffensives. The 1862 Maryland campaign was no exception. In launching his first invasion, Lee lacked the necessary experience to fully understand the many subtle logistical realities that so widely separated the Mexican-American War experience from the existing situation in western Maryland fifteen years later.[23] Young Private Valerius Cincinnatus Giles,

Company B (Tom Green Rifles), Fourth Texas, described the march north of the Potomac as nothing more than Lee's "first raid into Maryland."[24]

Additionally, Lee was not aware of how quickly the Army of the Potomac had advanced north from Washington, D.C., between September 5 and 7. Other aspects of the Lee's plans also unraveled. Lee's decision to occupy Frederick had been calculated to force the evacuation of the Union garrisons at Harpers Ferry and Martinsburg to the west—a case of wishful thinking. On September 9, Lee decided that Harpers Ferry and its eleven thousand men must be captured because they loomed as a potential threat in his army's left flank. Also, the supply line to the Shenandoah Valley could be opened with Harpers Ferry's capture, allowing the possibility for the army to remain for an extended period north of the Potomac if necessary. The capture of Harpers Ferry, where abolitionist John Brown had made his October 1859 raid to polarize the nation, became a top priority. Therefore, for a continuation of a march beyond Frederick and farther into western Maryland, Lee decided to divide his army into wide-ranging columns in order to reduce the Harpers Ferry and Martinsburg garrisons to eliminate these threats along his communications line to the Shenandoah Valley, gain supplies and safeguard his withdrawal route back to Virginia.

Lee's risky decision to divide his forces in the face of the advance of a rejuvenated Army of the Potomac (morale was high because it now defended home soil), which continued to march northwest, was largely Napoleonic in conception. As taught at the United States Military Academy as one of Napoleon's basic principles of waging war, Lee's plan of dividing his already diminutive army was also based on logistical considerations. Lee now hoped that his columns, moving on their own along different routes, would provide greater opportunities for his men to forage over a wider area. Most importantly in terms of a historical lesson now ignored, however, General Scott had not divided his forces on the march to Mexico City. The sage War of 1812 veteran of imposing physical presence had early decided not to take the considerable risk of a self-inflicted divide-and-conquer strategy while deep in Mexico.[25]

Generals Jackson and James Longstreet opposed Lee's risky plan of operation. They desired to ignore Harpers Ferry and keep Lee's small army (growing weaker with each passing day) concentrated at all costs. Instead, Jackson favored a defensive stand at Frederick to confront the advancing Army of the Potomac. Likewise, General Longstreet was worried by the troops' overall poor condition. He, therefore, advocated against a division of force so deep in enemy country and a lengthy, difficult march of two-thirds of the army to South Mountain's other side (west) to subdue Harpers Ferry. Longstreet, known as Lee's "Old War Horse," considered the movement too risky.

But General Lee thought otherwise. Orders went out from his Frederick headquarters on September 9 to split his small army into four columns for the push into unfamiliar territory. Three of the four columns, under Jackson, who now reluctantly embarked on his risky assignment, were ordered to descend on Harpers Ferry. Lee also now wanted to proceed farther west to place the imposing South Mountain between him and the now-approaching Army of the Potomac. He then planned to re-concentrate the Army of Northern Virginia amid the open country of western Maryland beyond and west of the mountains and just north of the Potomac to provide a retreat route to Virginia if necessary. But if Major General George Brinton McClellan's Army of the Potomac advanced more rapidly than usual—which was completely unexpected at Lee's headquarters—then the scattered Southern forces could be caught when most vulnerable, before uniting their already seriously reduced strength.[26]

If successful in cutting the enemy's communications lines (rail and canal) and if developments proved favorable, Lee only now decided that he would then "turn my attention to Philadelphia, Baltimore, or Washington, as may seem best for our interests."[27] Ironically, Lee should have early planned on this all-important objective of capturing a strategic city rather than making this belated decision on the fly at Frederick, after his army's capabilities had been dramatically reduced.

Lee now possessed far too few troops (fewer than forty thousand men) at hand. Additionally, too much time had been already wasted, especially at the ever-seductive picturesque town of Frederick. The extent of the logistical breakdown had already made the possibility of gaining an important strategic objective of a major Northern city virtually impossible by this time. Unfortunately, for Southern fortunes, thousands of the Army of Northern Virginia's most experienced soldiers, including officers, never reached Frederick. Instead, they had remained behind along the dusty roads leading from Virginia to recuperate and sit-out Lee's most ambitious campaign to date. These veterans almost seemed to sense that disaster lay ahead for the diminutive army that had ventured too far from home. Worst of all for Lee's ambitions, McClellan's resilient troops were highly motivated and eager to repel the invaders from sacred Union soil.

Lee's surviving veterans nevertheless pushed west over green (an early autumn hue had not yet descended on western Maryland) rolling hills from Frederick and toward the Blue Ridge Mountain on September 10 with expectations of easy success. The army's separation into widely divided columns in the march westward was a dangerous undertaking, however. This situation was made worse when Lee's campaign plans (dated September 9) to split his army into four parts were accidentally lost in the now vacated Southern encampments at Frederick and then fell into Union hands on September 13, after the Army of the Potomac had gained possession of the town.

Now with a concentrated Union army of more than eighty thousand troops (more than double the size of Lee's Army) from the combined might of Pope's Army of Virginia and the Army of the Potomac, "Little Mac" McClellan now possessed a golden opportunity to advance rapidly to catch and then destroy the widely scattered Confederate army, because of Lee's ill-fated decision to capture Harpers Ferry. Ironically, and not realizing that his detailed campaign plan was in McClellan's hands, Lee still felt that he had plenty of time to eventually confront McClellan, who was well known for his caution, after taking Harpers Ferry. Meanwhile, a jubilant McClellan telegraphed the good news to President Lincoln and promised to "send you trophies" of his upcoming victory over Lee's Army.[28]

McClellan was now moving faster than expected because of his newly gained knowledge of Lee's tactical plans, including the army's separation into far-flung columns. In addition, Lee had underestimated the overall quality of the boys in blue. They were not demoralized after their summer setbacks. Instead, McClellan's men were incensed that the Rebels had marched with impunity across Northern soil. One Southerner wrote how "it must be admitted, however, that McClellan had displayed unexpected energy and boldness in his movements [because] he put his army in motion as soon as possible after we crossed into Maryland, and moved boldly on our track."[29]

Meanwhile, the Confederates continued to trudge deeper into western Maryland. Soldiers from Louisiana, Georgia, North and South Carolina and other Deep South states continued to depart the ever-thinning ranks to forage off the land out of necessity, leading to additional desertions. Even worse, the steady diet of green apples and green corn, especially when combined with hot weather and poor drinking water, continued to cause greater sickness for the army. For many miles, worn-out and ill soldiers lined the sunbaked roads of western Maryland by the thousands in this most ill-fated of Confederate invasions that continued to lose more momentum and strength with each passing day. The ravages of disease, poor discipline, foraging, straggling and desertions slowly but methodically eroded the army's combat capabilities long before its first engagement erupted on Maryland soil.[30]

By September 12, Lee had informed President Davis of the shocking new developments—the army had been reduced as much as one half—that were systematically destroying the army's strength more effectively than the Union army. All the while, the already low chances of Confederate success north of the Potomac continued to rapidly diminish like the hot summer that was gradually fading away. Lee never realized that McClellan possessed a copy of his campaign plans (Special Order No. 191). Especially in forcing his way through the vital Turner's and Fox's Gaps of South Mountain after fierce resistance from diehard defenders on September 14 to continue the pursuit of the one-third of Lee's Army that had not gone to Harpers Ferry, McClellan's sudden assertiveness came when Lee's force was now only a mere shell of its former self. That hard-hitting fighting machine that had won so many improbable victories across Virginia now only existed on paper. Without a choice in a crisis situation, Lee was forced to retreat to the west side of South Mountain and regroup into the fertile valley of Antietam Creek.

For the final showdown between the two armies in the lush farmlands of western Maryland, fewer than forty thousand Rebel troops were about to confront the mighty Army of the Potomac of more than eighty-five thousand Federals west of South Mountain. Perhaps as many as twenty thousand Confederates were now absent from the army's thinning ranks just before a climactic showdown. Ironically, what had been recently envisioned with unbounded optimism as a glorious campaign north of the Potomac to rescue the Confederacy had been suddenly transformed by fate, green corn and hubris into a march to folly.[31]

Meanwhile, Lee attempted to concentrate his widely scattered and divided forces to make a defensive stand at Sharpsburg, before it was too late. He decided to make a bold stand to confront McClellan's army along the west side of Antietam Creek. He made his decision with less than half his troops and with the Potomac River to his rear after finally learning of Jackson's belated capture of Harpers Ferry on September 15.

Like a high-stakes player at a poker table, Lee gambled that Jackson would be able to march his troops the seventeen miles from Harpers Ferry to Sharpsburg in time to meet the inevitable assault of McClellan's powerful army. Of course, making a defensive stand on mostly open ground of rolling farmlands was extremely risky, especially with a fast-flowing river to Lee's back. The Potomac was a formidable barrier to the army's escape and retreat to Virginia. Quite simply, if Lee's audacious gamble failed to pay off, then his army, now at its most vulnerable, might be destroyed in Washington County, Maryland.

Merely to survive his ill-advised defensive stand amid the open, rolling farmlands around Sharpsburg, Lee hoped to concentrate his widely scattered forces as rapidly as possible, before "Little Mac" struck with overpowering might. Displaying his trademark audacity in the face of even the greatest danger, Lee now based everything on a hasty (almost improbable) emergency concentration of his widely flung units in time to face the Army of the Potomac's overwhelming might. Here, at a small agricultural village, Sharpsburg, whose setting could not have been more idyllic, the destinies of two republics was about to be decided.

Lee gambled that Jackson, who received the surrender of the large Harpers Ferry garrison on the morning of September 15 and needed to complete all necessary arrangements of the capitulation before pushing north for Sharpsburg, would arrive in time to reinforce his thin defensive lines situated along a line of gently rolling hills behind, or west of, Antietam Creek. As part of the urgent concentration of all available troops, the worn Texas Brigade soldiers were on the move early on the warm morning on September 15. With Enfield rifles on right shoulders, they marched in sweat-stained uniforms through the rising clouds of dust to reach the Antietam's fertile valley as soon as possible. Thanks to sturdy stone bridges, constructed skillfully by Irish immigrants across the clear watercourse, Lee's troops easily crossed Antietam Creek to reach the relative safety of its west side. Here, Lee had decided to make his bold defensive stand so that a creek flowed between him and his powerful opponent, who now possessed his best chance of destroying the Army of Northern Virginia.

After McClellan's forces had pushed aside the stubborn Rebels defending the gaps of South Mountains, tens of thousands of bluecoats poured down the mountain's western slopes. They now headed toward the stately stone bridges that spanned across the Antietam's blue waters, which nourished the valley. By mid-September 1862, in this productive land now ravaged by a severe drought, a dramatic showdown amid the flowing fields around Sharpsburg was rapidly taking shape. Amid this land untouched by the war's devastation, thousands of men in blue and gray were about to be sacrificed at a rate heretofore unseen in America's most murderous war. On this great upcoming clash of arms in the midst of this picturesque countryside hung the futures of two neighboring republics that looked to the same God for deliverance and preservation: the United States, born of an earlier people's revolution, and the Confederacy, born of the latest revolution on American soil. As one Connecticut soldier correctly penned in a letter, the Antietam was about to become "the creek of death."[32]

Chapter 2

The Texas Brigade's Supreme Challenge on America's Bloodiest Day

While pushing steadily westward since the early morning of September 15, the Texans trudged along the dusty National Pike from Boonsboro, Maryland, just west of South Mountain. Under the searing sun, the Lone Star State soldiers then pushed southwest toward Sharpsburg and the Antietam's quiet valley, while serving as Lee's dependable rear guard. As so often in the past, this honored rear guard assignment was a compliment to the command's proven dependability and fighting prowess.

The battle-hardened soldiers of Lieutenant Colonel Philip Alexander Work's First Texas Infantry Regiment basked in the recognition of having been assigned by Lee to this coveted position of honor. They hoped that a successful Northern invasion might reverse the war's course away from a disastrous war of attrition that the manpower-short South could never win, while also taking pressure off the Texas homeland under threat of Union invasion from multiple directions.

The Texans had not been issued any new clothing since the bitter fighting outside Richmond during the Peninsula Campaign. With the first cold snaps of autumn on the horizon—although the weather was still summer-like and the hardwood forests were donned in thick summer foliage—the Texans' long hair and beards made them look like impoverished beggars from the dirty streets of New York City or Philadelphia. Nothing about them revealed that these young men were crack soldiers, but outward appearances were deceiving.

Hood's Texans had good reason to be proud and cocky. Helping to buy precious time in a crisis situation, the Texans' most recent success came on

September 14 during the Battle of South Mountain, where they had held the Yankees at bay for an extended period. As if fighting on the Southwest frontier, the Texas Brigade's soldiers were not content to remain simply on the defensive. Instead, they had launched a bayonet charge to repel an advancing line of Federal skirmishers. The attack was also born of frustration. Lieutenant Colonel Work and his First Texas had played no leading role in South Mountain's defense, where the rear guard Rebels of Major General Daniel Harvey Hill's Division had attempted to stop McClellan's effort to gain Lee's vulnerable rear.[33]

Boding well for the upcoming challenge at Antietam, Work handled the First Texas as a well-oiled machine. Born on the Ohio River's south bank at the commercial town of Cloverport, Breckinridge County, Kentucky, on February 17, 1832, Work was a rising star of the Texas Brigade. He was the promising son of Dr. John Work, who served as the assistant surgeon of the First Texas from October 1862 to July 1864: a rare father-son team functioning at such a high level. Philip's family had moved to the port town Velasco, Texas, which had been founded only seven years before and located on the Brazos River's east side in southeast Texas several miles from the Gulf of Mexico, migrating from the Kentucky Blue Grass in 1838. The Work family eventually established roots in another Texas community of commercial promise, Town Bluff. This small town was located at the head of navigation of the Neches River and a longtime river crossing point. Philip Alexander Work then became a lawyer in Woodville, Texas, in 1853. He was about to face his greatest challenge during the upcoming dramatic showdown at Antietam, which was shaping up to be one of the most climactic battles of the war.[34]

Throughout the morning of September 15, Major Generals James Longstreet's and Daniel H. Hill's troops had marched west toward Sharpsburg along the dusty Boonsboro-Sharpsburg Road, after crossing the Middle Bridge spanning the Antietam. Resistant to heavy flooding as designed, this stately stone structure was distinguished by three majestic arches. Weary Rebel troops were then turned south and deployed along the slight ridges, open and devoid of timber for farming and grazing purposes, on the west side of Antietam Creek, which meandered lazily toward the Potomac. In a most vexing tactical dilemma, Lee felt relief that he now had this fast-flowing creek, which looked too deep to be forded, between him and the fast-approaching Army of the Potomac. On Lee's right flank, the Lower Bridge, also known as the Rohrbach Bridge, which crossed the Antietam, was held by Georgia Brigade veterans, of Longstreet's Command, under General Robert "Bob" Toombs, a hardheaded former Georgia politician who was about to make a name for himself on September 17.

On the early afternoon of September 15, with temperatures rising, the Texas Rebels finally reached the placid creek nestled in the picturesque valley just west of South Mountain. While marveling at the sight of the fertile lands around them, the Lone Star State soldiers marched slowly across the graceful stone structure (the Middle Bridge opposite Sharpsburg). Quite unlike the non-stone structures back in the piney and scrub oak woods of east Texas, where rickety wooden bridges were primitive and often washed away by spring flooding, this stone structure was elegant, with three stately Roman arches, and all but indestructible. The bridges had long greatly facilitated the transportation of crops, especially wheat, to Baltimore, from where flour was then shipped around the world—an early boon to the economy. These beautiful stone bridges that spanned the meandering Antietam had been built by expert Irish stonemasons and workmen in the mid-1830s. Fortunately for the beleaguered Rebels, the stone bridges (the Upper, Middle and Lower Bridges) across the Antietam proved a God-send, providing easy access for troops, artillery and wagons to the creek's west side.

With well-worn Enfield rifled muskets on shoulders, the Texans continued marching west toward Sharpsburg and then moved up gently rising ground before finally aligning in the fields of late summer located just south of the Boonsboro Road, which led into the town's east side. Now on the Antietam's west side and just east of Sharpsburg, the Texans faced east toward the expected Federal advance from South Mountain, which loomed on the distant horizon like a blue-hued tower. Lieutenant Colonel Work described how Longstreet's Command was now deployed "in position and battle array on a ridge between Sharpsburg on the West and Antietam creek on the East [and] the position of the Texas Brigade was almost immediately between Sharpsburg and the only bridge across the Antietam" at this defensive point.[35]

Ironically, for its greatest challenge to date, the Texas Brigade was now commanded not by a Texan but a Georgian of relatively little military experience. Much like General Toombs, the commander was more of a Georgia politician than professional fighting man, although he possessed ample experience, including from the Mexican-American War. Leading the Texas Brigade only because he was now the command's senior colonel, Colonel William Tatum Wofford, age thirty-nine, was about to prove that he was an excellent leader. Wofford formerly commanded the Eighteenth

Georgia Infantry. Under his able command, the Eighteenth Georgia had compiled a solid combat record.

A dynamic man of varied talents, Wofford was a product of Cassville, Georgia, where Generals William T. Sherman and Joseph E. Johnston were destined to clash at the heads of their respective armies in the spring and summer of 1864 during the Atlanta, Georgia Campaign. The heavily bearded colonel excelled at various endeavors before the war, including law, agriculture, journalism and government. Wofford managed a fine plantation—his pride and joy—and was a large slave owner. He had needed the laborers to make his lands productive, but he now found himself in a more highly cultivated region of many free blacks. Part of his appeal to the boys in the ranks, Wofford was more of a self-made man of middle-class means rather than a privileged member of the elitist planter aristocracy.[36]

Before the war, Colonel Wofford also had been more of a Unionist than a secessionist. He had remained true to his personal convictions and pro-Unionism even in the heart of the Deep South, going against popular sentiment—a true profile in moral courage of an independent-minded man. He had been a longtime confirmed bachelor until marrying the woman of his dreams in the summer of 1859. Therefore, Wofford was now very much still a novice as both a new husband and the Texas Brigade's leader. Wofford became the Texas Brigade's commander when General John Bell Hood, who originally had been the Fourth Texas's colonel before he became the Texas Brigade's leader, took command of the division in late July 1862.[37]

A native Kentuckian and revered West Pointer, Hood was a rising star of the Confederacy and Richmond high society for his hard-hitting ways and past successes. More than anyone else, Hood had been most responsible for having transformed the Texas Brigade into an elite "fighting machine" second to none in this revolutionary army.[38]

Wofford won respect among the Texas Rebels as the capable leader of the Eighteenth Georgia, which the Texans viewed as worthy comrades in arms (adopted Texans, in essence). By the time of the Antietam Campaign, Colonel Wofford was a great favorite of the Texans. Among this Peach State regiment were seasoned companies like the Rowland Highlanders, the Davis Invincibles, and the Newton Rifles. As if ordained by a strange fate, this lone Georgia regiment became part of the Texas Brigade quite by accident. Because the Georgians had been encamped near the Texas

Rebels at Dumfries, Virginia, located just north of Fredericksburg, during the winter of 1861–62, they had been officially brigaded with the Texans, cementing a relationship that resulted in a very good combat team.[39]

In part because of Colonel Wofford's leadership skills, the Eighteenth Georgia had evolved into a dependable regiment that made a most worthy addition to the Texas Brigade. In fact, this Georgia regiment even earned the highly prized distinction as the so-called Third Texas, given by the Texans themselves—the highest compliment ever bestowed on non-Texas troops. These Peach State veteran soldiers, who hailed from central and west Georgia, carried a colorful battle flag on which they had sworn to live or die in its defense. They had fought beside the Lone Star State men at Eltham's Plantation. Here, nestled between the York and James Rivers during the early stages of the 1862 Peninsula Campaign, the attacking Texas and Georgia Rebels had forced the Yankees to run during the Texans' baptismal fire. The Texas Rebels had played a key role in thwarting McClellan's attempt to cut off the Southern withdrawal from Yorktown and toward Richmond, while winning the first Confederate success on the Virginia Peninsula.[40]

By the time of the Antietam Campaign, the Texas troops saw these Georgians as kindred spirits. Corporal William David Henderson Pritchard, Company I (Crockett Southrons, which had been named in honor of Alamo defender David Crockett), First Texas, wrote:

> [A]*t a time when the Georgia brigades were all full, they were attached to us; being thus thrown with men who already had a reputation, they felt the importance of their position and determined to maintain their honor. This they did, and amid the many perilous scenes of our early campaign, they were ever with us. Where the shot fell thickest, where death's frightful carnival was highest, the gallant Col. Wo*[f]*ford with his noble men could be found; they shrank from no duty, quailed at no danger. When the battle raged the hottest, when the hope seemed most forlorn, we could look to the right and always find "Georgia"* [and those] *gallant Goober Grabblers....Ever ready at the bugle call, they feared no foe. As fierce in fight as the Couger that roams in the western hills. The*[y] *charge like the blizzard that sweeps the boundless plains* [and] *carried everything before it.*[41]

Knowing that the bonds of comradeship led to superior battlefield performances, General Hood explained how his Texas boys "had become warmly attached" to the Georgians, who had "in every emergency had proved itself bold and trusty; it styled itself, from a feeling of brotherhood, the Third Texas."[42] The affectionate feeling was fully returned by the Eighteenth Georgia men. In a late March 1862 letter, Private Milton Barrett, who was destined to die in this war, admitted how he "had as soon fought by the side of a Texan as any for tha ar brave and fought like tigers but tha are like a spiret horse. tha are hard to mandage…thes brave men" from Texas.[43]

Indeed, by this time, the First Texas veterans had killed so many Yankees that Lieutenant William Henry Gaston (the brother of Lieutenant Robert Hugh Gaston), of the Texas Guards (Company H), promised in a letter to his sister, "Tell Ma that we have lots of the best buttons you ever say that we cut off of Yankee coats & will send them" back home as trophies of past victories.[44]

SETTING THE STAGE FOR THE DRAMATIC SHOWDOWN AT ANTIETAM

Meanwhile, one of the war's greatest dramas of extremely high stakes was about to be played out around the little market town of Sharpsburg. Situated just north to the Potomac, the town sat on an elevated plateau of gently rolling ground that dominated the terrain west of the well-cultivated valley of Antietam Creek. This obscure place in the middle of nowhere had suddenly become strategically important by the twisting course of the war's fortunes. On this commanding plateau of only a relatively slight height, this fertile ground was covered in rich croplands and scattered woodlots. Lee had taken good defensive positions west of the Antietam. His troops now faced eastward in preparation for meeting the advance of McClellan's six massive corps. Lee had chosen good defensive positions that were centered on the agricultural community of Sharpsburg, taking advantage of the open ridge on which the Hagerstown Pike ran. Constructed in 1856, this pike led north thirteen miles to Hagerstown and entered Sharpsburg from that direction. However, in aligning his troops across the most favorable high ground terrain that resulted in an arc-shaped line, Lee was forced to protect a wider front, which spanned four miles, spreading his depleted army thin out of tactical and geographic necessity.

In preparation for delivering a powerful blow on Lee's overextended battle lines aligned across the fields of green, McClellan planned to cross the Antietam from east to west in order to muster considerable strength north of town to attack Lee's left down both sides of the Hagerstown Road that led south to Sharpsburg. Lee would shortly need large numbers of additional troops on his vulnerable left to parry the massive Union threat north of Sharpsburg.

Before the arrival of Jackson's troops from Harpers Ferry on September 16, Hood's Division received orders to redeploy to the left of Major General Daniel H. Hill's Division, which occupied Lee's center along the Sunken Road east of the Hagerstown Pike and adjacent to the Middle Bridge, where the Boonsboro Pike crossed the Antietam. Drawn from Longstreet's Command on the right, Hood's veterans prepared to move north of Sharpsburg on the evening of September 15. With a big fight brewing in a region as fertile as the rich Brazos and Colorado River bottomlands of east Texas, Hood's veterans, yet to receive rations despite having not eaten in several days, shouldered their muskets. In strides longer than those of most Confederate soldiers (another distinctive quality to Lee's generally taller western soldiers), the Texans marched through a serene landscape not yet torn by war to bolster Lee's weak left north of town.

Near the white-painted brick Dunker Church—appearing as plain as its pious German worshipers, who advertised their self-imposed austerity of their Anabaptist sect (which began in Schwarzenau, Germany, in the early 1700s) by having no gaudy steeple—the Texans hurriedly aligned on the left of Hood's Division.

Meanwhile, Colonel Evander McIver Law's Brigade of battle-tested Alabama, Mississippi and North Carolina troops formed on the Texas Brigade's left to the north. At this time, the Texas Brigade's right was anchored on the high ground (part of a slight ridge on which the north–south Hagerstown Road ran) of the Dunker Church. This modest house of worship was located just east of the road and about one mile north of Sharpsburg. A lengthy battle line of young men in gray and butternut now faced east, while Southerners hoped to live long enough to see the sunrise.

Meanwhile, the hungry Texans, covered in dust and sweat, placed their Enfield rifles in neat stacks amid the West Woods, just west of the Hagerstown Pike and adjacent to and mostly northwest of the little white-colored church of the German Baptist Brethren. This diminutive church was located just east of the southern end of the West Woods and immediately before (west) the pike. These devout German worshipers had earned the sobriquet "Dunkers" from their common practice of

Located on strategic high ground along the Hagerstown Turnpike north of Sharpsburg, the whitewashed Dunker Church was one of the most prominent landmarks on the Antietam battlefield. Here, the German Baptist Brethren, the "Dunkers," had long worshiped their faith, which was popular among the industrious and modest German settlers in the Sharpsburg, Maryland area. *Author's collection.*

the complete baptismal immersion of members in nearby creeks. The homespun Anabaptist house of worship had long been known locally as the "Dunker" or "Dunkard" Church.

From the West Woods, donned with summer foliage on the pike's other side and south of the church and Law's Brigade, proficient Texas foragers, such as Newton "Newt" Monroe Berryman of Company I (Crockett Southrons), went to work. They slipped beyond the lines to do what they did best, heading north through the darkness on their own. While keeping a lookout for Yankee skirmishers, they hurriedly began to collect ears of corn from a large cornfield that bordered the east side of Hagerstown Turnpike, which ran north–south like Antietam Creek to the east. As the ever-capricious gods of war would have it, this broad field of nearly ripe corn was nestled between luxuriant clover fields on either side (to the north and south) and between the West Woods (on the west) and the East Woods (to the east). The Miller Cornfield was shortly to be consumed by the war's most nightmarish carnage. David's grandfather, of the same name, had been one of the first store owners of Sharpsburg, which had been founded in 1763. At this time, the corn in Miller's sprawling field was "tall and ripe and ready for harvest."[45]

On the north, Lee's left under Major General "Stonewall" Jackson remained vulnerable before the blue legions arrayed against it to the north. Arriving from Harpers Ferry early on September 16, as Lee had hoped, five veteran divisions of Jackson's Command (one division under Major General Ambrose Powell Hill had been left in Harpers Ferry to complete final surrender arrangements) reached the army just in the nick of time. Still worn out from the exhausting seventeen-mile march north through the late summer heat to Sharpsburg, these troops had hurriedly aligned on the left of Hood's Division. They faced east and then extended their battle line westward toward the Potomac River to protect the extreme end of Lee's left, which was located just northwest of Sharpsburg. Jackson then relieved Hood of overall command of Lee's left, which was centered on the strategic high ground (the shallow ridge) of the Dunker Church and the Hagerstown Road.

Besides the normal attrition from the rapid march from Harpers Ferry, the slaughter at Second Manassas (another costly Pyrrhic victory for Lee) near the end of August had significantly culled the top officers from Jackson's command. Consequently, five of Jackson's eight brigades were led by colonels with little experience in commanding units of brigade strength. Even worse, among Jackson's Division commanders, Brigadier General Alexander Robert Lawton was more of a desk man than a combat leader, Brigadier General William Edwin Starke had never commanded a division and Brigadier General John Rumph Jones, a former captain of Virginia's Stonewall Brigade, had still to demonstrate his value on the battlefield. These largely untested Confederate leaders were about to be placed in key combat situations and called on to perform beyond their combat capabilities.[46]

Benefiting from the protective screen of the North Woods, troops of the Army of the Potomac approached Lee's weak left and steadily mustered their strength, after Major General Joseph Hooker's First Corps crossed the Antietam on September 16. McClellan's troops now possessed an all-important advantage over the invaders that had long served the Confederates so well—the key psychological factor of defending home soil, now reversed suddenly.

Meanwhile, the showdown in this remote section of Washington County, covered with well-manicured farmlands (even the woodlots were neat and underbrush cleared by these meticulous German farmers), was gradually taking shape in this landscape drained by the Antietam. Targeting Lee's left-center, located near the Dunker Church, "Fighting Joe" Hooker's powerful I Corps, after having stealthily maneuvered, was now in an ideal position to strike a severe blow. The First Corps prepared to spearhead a mighty offensive effort just east of the pike and south toward Sharpsburg along the high ground of the plateau (or slight ridge) by way of the Hagerstown Pike. Meanwhile, Lee's Army had never been weaker or more vulnerable than this day, after having been reduced to as few as thirty-five thousand men, many of whom were generally in poor shape for a decisive showdown.

Major General Joseph "Fighting Joe" Hooker commanded the First Corps, Army of the Potomac, at Antietam. A Mexican-American War veteran and future commander of the Army of the Potomac, Hooker initiated the battle of Antietam by launching his powerful First Corps from the north to turn the vulnerable Confederate left on the early morning of September 17. The confident West Pointer came close to reaping a decisive success north of Sharpsburg before two brigades of Brigadier General John Bell Hood's Division counterattacked to save the day for the reeling Army of Northern Virginia on Lee's mauled northern flank. *Library of Congress.*

Amid the flowing fields of late summer, this mostly open ridge was the dominant high ground and most prominent natural landmark north of Sharpsburg. Distinguished by the whitewashed Dunker Church southeast of the Miller Cornfield and just west of the Hagerstown Pike, the mostly open plateau of high ground was about to become the key to the struggle north of town on September 17. Hooker's primary target to the south lay straight down the north–south ridge and the main road leading into Sharpsburg from the north: the Dunker Church (the only prominent man-made landmark in the area), which stood just west of the Hagerstown Pike like a white beacon rising up amid bright green woodlands and luxurious fields of plenty.

Not liking what he saw regarding what was developing in tactical terms, young Colonel Porter Edward Alexander lamented the tactical rationale behind Lee's audacious decision to make a desperate last stand against the odds at Sharpsburg: "[T]his, I think, will be pronounced by military critics to be the greatest blunder that Gen. Lee ever made....Lee's inferiority of force was too great to hope to do more than to fight a sort of drawn battle. Hard & incessant marching, & camp diseases aggravated by irregular diet, had greatly reduced his ranks, & I don't think he mustered much if any over 40,000 men [while] McClellan had over 87,000, with more & better guns & ammunition."[47]

Colonel Alexander presented an astute evaluation of the overall situation of a badly weakened army far from home soil. With the Rebel army in absolutely no shape for the war's climactic showdown, all that McClellan had to do, seemingly, was to unleash his overwhelming might with simultaneous advances all along the front to destroy Lee's overextended forces, which had marched too far north for their own safety.

However, McClellan's trademark caution rose to the fore. The handsome young general, known as the "Young Napoleon," already had wasted too much of September 16 in reconnoitering and maneuvering his vast legions in preparation for striking his blow. Ever meticulous, if not a perfectionist, McClellan had issued a seemingly endless stream of orders, changing dispositions and making tactical adjustments. Once again, as during the Peninsula Campaign, McClellan's old caution had emerged, as Lee, who knew his man (a fellow West Pointer) well, had hoped in formulating his plans to stand firm.[48]

Because Hooker's Corps had crossed Antietam Creek undetected, Lee still did not know that the entire First Corps was now massed north of Sharpsburg on his left flank and ready to deliver an overpowering assault. While Longstreet's troops on the right faced east and southeast and the men of General Daniel H. Hill's Division held the center and faced roughly northeast, with Antietam Creek before them providing some protection, the Confederate left, positioned amid the open farmlands, benefited from few natural advantages.

This alarming tactical situation on the north meant that the Confederate left was extremely vulnerable, as it was now positioned at a right angle (in order to stretch nearly to the Potomac) to the center and right of Lee's sprawling battle line. Worst of all, Jackson's position on the army's left flank—stretching nearly three quarters of a mile and too far a distance for the nearly six thousand men of his three divisions—was also weak because it was cut almost in half by the Hagerstown Road north of Sharpsburg, the inviting avenue of the impending Union onslaught that was about descend south through favorable terrain (primarily open fields) for a swift and overpowering advance to exploit the element of surprise.[49]

Consequently, along with other leading officers, the ever-observant Colonel Alexander, the young artillery officer of outstanding promise in Longstreet's Command, feared the worst. He penned how "Common Sense was just shouting [to McClellan], 'Your adversary is back against a river, with no bridge & only one ford, & that the worst one on the whole [Potomac] river. If you whip him now, you destroy him utterly, root & branch & bag & baggage. Not twice in a life does such a chance come to any general. Lee for once has made a mistake, & given you a chance to ruin him if you can break his lines, & such game is worth great risks.'"[50]

Positioned along the slight ridge on the Antietam's west side, Lee's thin line stretched to the breaking point out of tactical necessity, given so few troops available. Bracing for the approaching storm about to be unleashed, Longstreet's Command held the right and center, while Jackson's Command, including Hood's Division, occupied the left. Jackson's three divisions anchored the Confederate left along an overly extended front that offered no significant physical barriers to impede the mighty Union advance south through the broad fields. On the far left, just west of the Hagerstown Road, was positioned Jackson's old division, which was now under General John Rumph Jones. Lee's four-mile line stretched from the Lower, or Rohrbach, Bridge (Lee's right flank on the far south anchored on Antietam Creek) and then eventually to the high ground perch of Nicodemus Hill (the anchor of Lee's left flank near the Potomac River) northwest of Dunker Church and on the west side of the Hagerstown Road.

McClellan was about to catch Lee by surprise because the concentrated formations of Hooker's First Corps were hidden in the protective green screen of the North Woods (east of the turnpike and larger than either the West and East Woods) and in position to strike south to turn Lee's weak left flank. Lee was not aware what had transpired, leaving him at "Little Mac" McClellan's mercy. Under the cover of woodlands (first the East Woods and then the North Woods farther west) and slight depressions of this open ground among the gently rolling hills, the First Corps had conducted a stealthy flank march of seven miles. Hooker's Corps, located the farthest west of any Army of the Potomac units, now stood in a perfect position to inflict massive damage on a scale not yet seen in this war. In the North Woods north of Sharpsburg, thousands of Federals prepared to push south along and parallel to the Hagerstown Pike to strike Lee's vulnerable, overextended left.[51]

The Texas Brigade veterans instinctively realized that a big battle was imminent, looming like a thunderstorm that swept over the central plains of Texas in the spring. The Yankees were steadily advancing south, as revealed by the crackling gunfire of heavy skirmishing to the north. During the early morning hours of September 16, the Texans had come under long-range artillery fire from the north. All the while, the Lone Star State soldiers held their position along the Hagerstown Road in the West Woods, located south of the Dunker Church, which stood just below the southernmost corner of the Miller clover field south of the cornfield. Lieutenant Colonel Work described how the Union shells crashed through the tall trees: "Soon the enemy's artillery opened fire in an effort to locate us and fix our range, but with very slightly damaging effect."[52]

In the cool of this early morning, the fighting spirit among the Texans remained high. As so often is the case with these free-thinking individualists from the western frontier, personal initiative had early risen to the fore among the enlisted ranks. Destined to fall wounded on the following day on September 17, Private Jefferson "Jeff" Bowman of Trinity County's Silver Greys (or the Sumter Light Infantry) felt an overpowering urge to kill Yankees. This young soldier "stole away from the company [M] and secreted himself in the upper story of a building near where the Yankees were crossing the creek and at about one hundred and fifty yards from them [and] He fired about sixty shots at them before they located him and dislodged him. They trained a piece of artillery on the house and when the first shot passed through it Jeff 'skedaddled' back to camp" on the double, wrote Sergeant David H. Hamilton of Company M.[53]

Work looked the other way when it came to such individualistic soldiers when they demonstrated their own initiative—that was one secret to Hood's past successes in delicately handling the Texas Brigade's excessively democratic-minded soldiers to earn their devotion and affection.[54] Such a relatively lax attitude also reflected Work's prewar service as a sergeant in a Mounted Battalion of Texas Volunteers, which had protected settlers during the autumn of 1854. At the war's beginning, Work formed the volunteer company known as the Woodville Rifles, which later became Company F, First Texas. He was very familiar with the unorthodox ways of his Texans, who so often fought on their own hook and seldom did anything by the book.[55]

With brightly colored state and national flags fluttering slightly when a warm breeze stirred, Hooker's extensive array of troops then swung south upon gaining the Hagerstown Road in the late afternoon of September 16. Toward the day's end, the blue juggernaut advanced farther south from the northeast to set the stage for the overpowering offensive effort. As if nothing could stop them, these Union veterans marched with disciplined step toward Jackson's troops. With machine-like precision, thousands of confident Yankees hurriedly deployed in lengthy battle lines for their next clash with the legendary Stonewall Jackson and his troops, including the Virginians of the Stonewall Brigade.

To parry the threat and ascertain the Federals' strength and tactics after Law had first determined that large numbers of blue skirmishers were swarming through the East Woods, Hood's Division surged out of the southern end of the West Woods. After advancing, Hood then aligned his troops in a north–south direction for action along the east side of the Hagerstown Pike just below the Dunker Church. The former Texas Brigade commander and adopted Texan (Hood was Kentucky born like Presidents Davis and Lincoln) ordered his division into position, and his troops quickly aligned in a lengthy formation. In a neat line of battle, Law's Brigade of Alabama, Mississippi and North Carolina soldiers pushed northeast across the clover field of green and into the East Woods northeast of the Miller Cornfield.

The sun of September 16 was dropping on the western horizon, the day's intense heat barely subsiding to bring a slight cool that reminded the ex-farmers in the ranks that the first cold snap of early autumn was perceptively in the air. Colonel Wofford shifted the Texas Brigade by the left flank. Ironically, the Texas Brigade was on the verge of having its finest day with an untried Georgian in command. Then, with clattering gear after turning right from the road and in line of battle, the Texas Brigade's troops swung northward across the wide-open space of the clover field below the Miller Cornfield. They pushed forward beyond, or north of, the dusty Smoketown Road (which ran northeast and entered the north–south Hagerstown Road just below the Dunker Church and now a strategic crossroad) and toward the southeastern corner of the cornfield of farmer David R. Miller. The Texans followed behind the advancing Alabama, Mississippi and North Carolina troops of Law's Brigade. To the left, or west, of Law's deployed brigade, the Texas regiments, after surging north about seven hundred yards, halted on the left of the Smoketown Road. Meanwhile, the brigade of young Colonel Evander McIvor Law—the Fourth Alabama's former colonel, who hailed from Tuskegee, Alabama—of Hood's Division of Longstreet's Command, which held Lee's right, was positioned on the right.

The seasoned troops of Hood's crack division, with Colonel Wofford on the left and Law on the right, were among the relatively few Confederate troops engaged on September 16. To meet the threat posed by the advance of Hooker's foremost units—and while Law's soldiers skirmished under the deepening shadows of the East Woods with the Pennsylvania Bucktails (whom the Texans had faced earlier in the war and now appreciated their mettle) of Brigadier General George Gordon Meade's Division, First Corps, consisting of Pennsylvania Reserves—the Texans quickly formed their battle line. This new line of Lee's premier fighting men now faced east just before the sun set over the forested mountains, tinged with blue in the distance.

As on previous fields of strife in the Old Dominion, Lieutenant Colonel Work aligned his First Texas in the center of the brigade's battle line, which stretched over the ground that must be protected against the inevitable Union onslaught. The First Texas now provided a solid anchor for the Texas Brigade's formation—a post of honor and a high compliment to the First Texas's superior quality. The battle-hardened First Texas men were positioned about midway in the clover field and just below the Miller Cornfield's southern border, which stretched a long distance in an east–west direction.

Meanwhile, spanning north to the First Texas's left stood eight small companies of South Carolina soldiers of Wade Hampton's Legion on the left flank. Barely seventy-five Palmetto State Rebels now stood in the thinned ranks of Hampton's Legion, which had acquired a reputation for combat prowess. Hampton's Legion was commanded by Harvard graduate Lieutenant Colonel Martin W. Gary. This diminutive Palmetto State unit had been formed by Wade Hampton, now Stuart's top lieutenant and a cavalry brigade commander from an old aristocratic planter family of vast wealth, before the Battle of First Manassas.

Meanwhile, the Eighteenth Georgia, led by dark-haired Lieutenant Colonel Solon Z. Ruff, who possessed an education from Georgia Military Institute in Marietta (second in his 1856 class) and German heritage like most of the farmers in the Antietam Valley, now held the left center of the brigade's line. Only in his mid-thirties, Ruff was destined to be killed in battle in late November 1863. To the First Texas's right, the Fifth Texas troops were commanded by Captain Isaac "Ike" Newton Moreland Turner. He had taken charge after Colonel Jerome Bonaparte Robertson, the overachieving son of a Scottish immigrant, had been wounded at Second Manassas. Despite being only twenty-two years of age, Turner could be counted on to hold the right flank. Meanwhile, the Fourth Texas—Hood's old regiment, now commanded by Tennessee-born Lieutenant Colonel Benjamin Franklin Carter, who was the former mayor of Austin, Texas—occupied the right center. Destined for a brigadier general's rank until mortally wounded on bloody July 2, 1863, at Gettysburg, the handsome Carter was another rising star of the Texas Brigade.[56]

With his usual skill, Work had led his crack First Texas since the Battle of Gaines's Mill on bloody June 27, 1862. Here, the regiment's colonel (Alexander "Alex" T. Rainey) had been seriously wounded in the successful assault that smashed through the Union defensive line, providing Work with the opportunity to take regimental command. Work then commanded the First Texas throughout the remainder of the Peninsula Campaign and at Second Manassas.[57]

Meanwhile, barefoot Color Sergeant George A. Branard stood in the center of the First Texas's formation. He held the Lone Star State flag aloft for these confident soldiers to see. Born on the Gulf Coast of east Texas and a former private of the Lone Star Rifles (Company L), which consisted of Galveston men, Branard was only nineteen. However, the stoic color sergeant was already a seasoned veteran. He shared the rare distinction of having been one of the few Texas Brigade soldiers to have been photographed by Private Solomon Thomas "Tom" Blessing, of the same company, with his comrades of the Wigfall Mess of Company L (named after Colonel Louis T. Wigfall) when encamped in the brigade's 1861–62 winter quarters at Dumfries, Virginia.

Branard was now respected throughout the command because of his courage and feisty fighting spirit. With the stillness of the late afternoon of September 16 (literally the calm before the storm), the beautiful silk colors of the Lone Star State flag lay limp in late summer heat and high humidity. Branard's reputation had soared at Eltham's Plantation on the Virginia Peninsula. At that time, the Texas Brigade had received its baptismal fire. Color Sergeant Branard, a member of the First Texas color guard, had volunteered to carry the regimental colors in the first fight. In the low-lying

Tidewater lands of the Eltham's Plantation and acting as the regimental color sergeant, the then corporal Branard "bore the flag so daringly and gallantly as to deserve and receive an appointment as color-bearer" of the First Texas. Thereafter, Branard carried the colors throughout the bloody fighting of the Seven Days outside Richmond and also at Second Manassas.[58]

What young color bearer Branard and his First Texas comrades now saw before them at Antietam was a gently rolling countryside of natural beauty, but the tension in the ranks was high. This excellent farming country and fertile landscape drained by Antietam Creek provided a scenic setting. This bountiful and unspoiled region of southern Washington County was a sight to behold, especially so to the Texas Rebels from the arid prairies of the Central Plain. A middle-class farmer's dream come true, this land was amazingly fertile and productive. As far as the eye could see, the emerald-green landscape was covered with lush crops and pastures. To men from the less agriculturally developed and more heavily forested Deep South, this fertile region of seemingly endless bounty (thanks to the hard work of the industrious German farmers, including devout Dunker Church worshipers) was an agricultural paradise. However, this magnificent landscape was about to be transformed into a living hell, splashed with red on the war's bloodiest day.

The Texas Brigade was now aligned for battle in the large clover patch located just below (south of) the southern edge of David R. Miller's thirty-acre cornfield. The clover field and cornfield, situated just east of the Hagerstown Pike and northeast of the Dunker Church, were framed by patches of woodlots (where German farmers had long secured fuel for cooking fires and allowed hogs to graze for acorns) to the east and west—the East and West Woods, respectively. Familiar to Texas foragers who had earlier gathered tasty ears of roasting corn from it, this expansive cornfield (with tall stalks lined in neat rows) was located both north and east of the West Woods.

Bordering the right, or east, side of this cornfield was the East Woods, now overflowing with bluecoat skirmishers (displaying confidence, which usually meant trouble), extending north–south and paralleling the Hagerstown Turnpike just to the west. Southwest of the cornfield, the West Woods also ran north–south for around 1,500 yards and paralleled the Hagerstown Pike just to the east, spanning a short distance from south of the Dunker Church to the cornfield's northern edge.

Entirely devoid of any outside decoration or any imaginable pretension, in keeping with the worshipers' fundamentalist beliefs that emphasized

The powerful First Corps, under General Hooker, crossed Antietam Creek north of Sharpsburg on the afternoon of September 16 and then eased into an advantageous position adjacent to Lee's weak left flank. *Author's collection.*

excessive Christian piety, Dunker Church stood at the southeastern edge of the West Woods. Besides being located near the crucial crossroads where the Hagerstown and Smoketown Roads met near the northwest corner of the clover field just below the Miller Cornfield, what was significant about the whitewashed Dunker Church was the key location of its high-ground perch atop a commanding plateau. Whichever side gained permanent possession of the strategic plateau that dominated the surrounding terrain would surely win the upcoming dramatic showdown north of Sharpsburg. The Miller Cornfield flowed in an expansive carpet of green that covered the gently rolling ground about a quarter mile northeast of the Dunker Church and almost all the way to the two-story stucco house (built in 1800) of farmer David R. Miller, the son of a War of 1812 colonel, located on a rise opposite the Hagerstown Pike.

Spanning about 350 yards east to west and about 250 yards south to north, the Miller Cornfield stood atop the plateau (like the Dunker Church) of high ground that was also gently rolling rather than sharply rising. Positioned at the plateau's northern end, the Miller House stood just east of the Hagerstown Road. The fact that the Miller Cornfield occupied high ground

The two-story David R. Miller House, a modest, whitewashed structure, was located on high ground just east of the Hagerstown Turnpike and north of the famous David R. Miller Cornfield. *Author's collection.*

was most clearly evident to the naked eye on looking east of the cornfield from the Hagerstown Pike's other side. Here, on the plateau's east side, now covered in tall cornstalks, the land dropped only gradually across gentle terrain, dipping to lower ground that provided good drainage, enhancing the healthy growth of cornstalks under the bright Maryland sunshine.

Because of its position atop the commanding plateau, the Miller Cornfield was, in essence, an elevated natural stage in the Valley of the Antietam for the upcoming confrontation of epic proportions. What could not be seen by the naked eye of the Texans at this time, because the tall cornstalks stood higher than the soldiers' heads, was that the cornfield's southern half was divided in the middle by a slight east–west depression. The Miller Cornfield's highest point was beyond this natural dip in the terrain, which divided the field's southern half and was beyond the field's halfway point to about the middle of the upper, or northern, half of the cornfield. Here, roughly two-thirds of the way to the cornfield's northern edge, stood the highest point of the Miller Cornfield. South of the cornfield, the terrain of the clover field gradually dipped toward the Smoketown Road, which met the Hagerstown Pike just north of Dunker Church, to a slight ravine amid the expansive field of clover south of the cornfield, whose green stalks seemed to glisten under the soft September sunshine.

Between the West and East Woods—woodlots that had been long cleared of underbrush (unlike in the South) by German farmers for their livestock to graze and located about half a mile apart—were the clover fields of the Miller farm, which bordered the cornfield on the south and north. Located about 750 yards north of Dunker Church, the high cornstalks rose above the level clover field almost like a rising wall of green. Seemingly laid out by a surveyor or architect, these two clover fields neatly sandwiched the cornfield. This obscure cornfield of farmer Miller would soon become the vortex of Antietam's storm and the most nightmarish killing ground of the Civil War.

Despite having not eaten anything in three days except for some green corn and a half ration of beef, the Texans were ready for the challenge. With gear clattering as they ran forward, a lengthy line of Fourth Texas skirmishers (Company K, known as the Sandy Point Mounted Rifles) under Captain William H. "Howdy" Martin, who hailed from Athens, Henderson County, Texas, advanced with the swiftness and precision of veterans. In faded gray and yellowish butternut uniforms, the Texans pushed onward on the double into the dark shadows of the East Woods to support Law's busy Alabama skirmishers, who gamely attempted to blunt the Yankees' aggressive probe.

Here, the Texans once again demonstrated their worth in fighting the Army of the Potomac's advance elements on the north amid the darkening woodlands filled with sulfurous smoke. Regiments of seasoned Pennsylvania Reserves now filled the East Woods, after having advanced to determine the Confederates' strength and dispositions. In the eerie half-light of early evening, the Texas skirmishers engaged the crack "Bucktails" of the First Pennsylvania Rifles (the Thirteenth Pennsylvania Reserves) in the East Woods. This sharp clash in unfamiliar woodlands resulted in a hot firefight, with musketry crackling like firecrackers and bringing death to more young men and boys.

Wearing white-tailed deer tails in their blue kepis in jaunty fashion, Pennsylvania marksmen were nearly as efficient in killing opponents as the sharpshooting Texans. Armed with fast-firing breechloaders that now fairly roared, the "Bucktails" were some of the best marksmen in the Union army.

With lengthy lines of Federals converging in echelon on the East Woods against the Texas Rebels after Law's Alabama skirmishers were hurled rearward, Work and his First Texas soldiers were fortunate not to have been ordered into the escalating firefight in this sector—the fate of the Fourth and Fifth Texas soldiers, whose command adjoined Law's left, to the right. Under shell fire, the First Texas soldiers remained in position in the open clover field. Here, they lay low on arms in the fading light of September 16.

Sweating Confederate artillerymen continued to respond at a fast rate to the booming Federal guns that caused so much havoc. The artillery duel roared to new heights of intensity, while the mid-September sun dropped lower on the mountainous horizon to the west. When Law's skirmishers were overpowered and withdrew from the East Woods to escape the confused fighting amid the timber, where visibility was reduced by smoke and near-darkness, the ever-aggressive General Hood seized the initiative. Unable to resist the tempting tactical opportunity to strike a blow (the confident Federals had become too aggressive in pushing Law's skirmishers aside), the native Kentuckian ordered his entire division forward into the fray. With a shout, the Texans instantly leaped to their feet from the clover field, quickly forming a line of battle. They then fixed bayonets, while the metallic clanging of cold steel echoed over their position, sounding a challenge to the Yankees. Knowing the importance of battlefield discipline, the Texas Rebels maintained a neat, tidy alignment when most needed—a sight unseen on a drill or parade ground by these men, who cared nothing for superficial outward appearances that impressed generals and the ladies.

Captain "Ike" Turner, who was the brigade's youngest company commander, and his Fifth Texas, on the brigade's right flank, surged east toward the East Woods with fixed bayonets. Meanwhile, the Fifth Texas under Turner, described as "one of the bravest men in the brigade" and who was destined to be killed in 1863, pushed into the East Woods. In the virgin timber that towered above them after entering the East Woods, the Fifth Texas men relieved the hard-hit Fourth Texas skirmishers, who were falling back under heavy pressure with nearly empty cartridge boxes, after Law's skirmishers had withdrawn and with the Yankee skirmishers advancing. Sensing victory with so many Johnny Rebs withdrawing, the Federals were now in close pursuit.

Now on the Texas Brigade's right center, Work and his First Texas went on the offensive before darkness fell to close the curtain of the fighting on September 16. He ordered a company of skirmishers under the country lawyer Captain Howard Ballenger, who led Company M (Sumpter Light

Infantry), First Texas, into the near darkness of the East Woods now overflowing with Yankees. These veterans of the Sumter Light Infantry from Trinity County surged east to support the busy Fifth and Fourth Texas skirmishers, who rapidly blasted away. In the confused fighting under the ancient trees long spared by the axe, Captain Ballenger fell wounded, and a handful of his men were captured by the surging Twelfth Massachusetts Volunteer Infantry.[59]

The close-range fighting that swirled through the smoke-filled East Woods finally ended after about two hours of combat, as darkness descended to close the brief action among the towering hardwoods. But the skirmishing continued deeper into the darkness, serving notice that a major confrontation was all but inevitable with the next sunrise, September 17.

Despite the combat's intensity, losses on both sides on September 16 were relatively light, thanks to the arrival of darkness. However, the fight for the East Woods brought no tactical gain or advantage to either side—Lee's left was still vulnerable in facing the overpowering might of Hooker's Corps. Once again, a good many more young men from the North and South had died for no gain in the sun-baked farmlands and dark woodlots. Meanwhile, all of Colonel Wofford's regiments, except for the Fourth Texas, retired back to the safety of the sheltering West Woods, with the knowledge that the great death grapple was sure to erupt with the red sunrise of September 17.

With a big fight on the horizon that might determine the life of not only the Army of Northern Virginia but also the Confederacy itself, a top priority of the common soldiers was now to obtain nourishment. These famished Texas men knew that they needed every ounce of their strength for the climactic showdown the following day. As the firing gradually died down with the veil of darkness, two soldiers from each First Texas company, as well as other Lone Star State regiments, were detailed to gather roasting ears from the ocean of tall stalks in the Miller Cornfield. As mentioned, the Miller Cornfield was sandwiched between the Hagerstown Turnpike on the west and the West Woods to the east. This summons was welcome news for the starved First Texas boys. Work described how "the 1st Texas...[had] been without food other than an occasional roasting ear snatched from the stalk as opportunity offered and eaten raw."[60]

Riding to the commander-in-chief's headquarters, General Hood was rightly concerned that his troops aligned along the edge of the East Woods were vulnerable, with a large Federal force immediately in front. He therefore requested Lee to have his division replaced so that his weary men could rest and, most importantly, gain a resupply of ammunition for the following day. Temporarily attached to Jackson's Command, Hood was able to make this request because his division, nominally under "Old Pete" Longstreet, was now acting independently based on Lee's direct orders—the situation that had allowed Lee to send Hood's Division north to reinforce his left. Lee now dispatched Hood to Jackson, his top lieutenant, adhering to protocol in following the proper chain of command as long taught at West Point.

The tall, ruggedly handsome Brigadier General Hood was in President Davis's and Lee's good graces. He awoke Major General Jackson, who was in overall command of Lee's left, from a deep sleep. "Stonewall," the former Virginia Military Institute professor, readily agreed to Hood's request that Hood's Division should be withdrawn south and replaced by the two brigades under Lawton, who now commanded General Richard Stoddert Ewell's old division after the Washington, D.C.-born Ewell's wounding (resulting in his left leg's amputation) at Second Manassas, but only if they would immediately rush to their replacements' aid if threatened by a sudden attack.

Hood agreed to the informal gentleman's agreement at Jackson's headquarters, making a solemn promise that he was to faithfully keep. In this ad hoc way, Jackson gained his much-needed strategic reserve on the left for the upcoming crisis that was now inevitable, because Lee's battle line was stretched so thin. The fact that these gaunt, lanky veterans, especially the Texans, were Lee's best combat troops made them an ideal strategic reserve. Hood's Division was now all that Jackson and the army's left wing possessed as a strategic reserve.

On the warm night of September 16, around 10:00 p.m., the exhausted Texas Brigade soldiers were finally relieved by Lawton's Georgia Brigade. In the haunting darkness that these men realized would be the last night for so many young soldiers, the Texas Rebels then retired southwest through the open fields illuminated by the yellow moonlight. With .577-caliber Enfield rifles on shoulders, the Lone Star State men marched back across the dusty Hagerstown Road after climbing over the high split-rail fences that ran along both sides of the pike. Then, the veteran Texans took shelter in the relative safety of the West Woods, about two hundred yards behind and just southwest of Dunker Church.

In the strange stillness of the West Woods, where eastern whippoorwills sounded their lonesome calls through the night, the men of Colonel

Wofford's Brigade lay down to rest. However, this was a troubled rest for many Texans, almost as if they knew that a dozen hours of combat would consume September 17 with a fury seldom seen. Wofford's Texans and Georgians were now in place along with the brigades of Generals Jubal Anderson Early, a crusty West Pointer known as "Old Jubilee"; William E. Starke; Harry T. Hays; and William B. Taliaferro. The Georgia troops of Lawton's Brigade were positioned below the Miller Cornfield. Meanwhile, Trimble's Alabama, Georgia and North Carolina Brigade was positioned in line on Lawton's right below the Smoketown Road.

Meanwhile, nestled between the road and the West Woods, the Virginia brigades of General Jones and Colonel Andrew Jackson Grigsby, named after America's seventh president of Scotch-Irish descent from South Carolina, were aligned, facing north, from where the Federals were expected to advance at daybreak. From left to right (or west to east), the troops of Jones, Grigsby (facing north), Lawton and Tremble were positioned toward the northeast. The strategic Hagerstown Turnpike ran between Colonel Grisby's right and General Lawton's left before continuing south to enter Sharpsburg from the north.[61]

Here, in the slight shelter of a shallow ravine that ran along the southern and western edges of the West Woods and in the eerie darkness amid the open timber that provided shelter, Texas soldiers began roasting ears taken from leather and cotton haversacks. A slight drizzle, a reminder that autumn's cooler weather was on its way in the days ahead to cut the oppressiveness of the July-like heat, caused campfires to become smokier, because of the wet wood. Water was in short supply on the farmlands during this long summer season of drought, so the light rainfall provided a welcome relief to nature and man. The meager food source this night consisted of ears gathered by foragers from the Miller Cornfield. Corporal Hanks, Company K (Texas Invincibles), First Texas, wrote how "[t]hat night we had roasting ears" from the cornfield, where so many men were destined to fall on September 17.

On this overcast, rainy night amid the pristine landscape of western Maryland, other Texans fell asleep in utter exhaustion, after thinking about their faraway homes and wondering about the welfare of families they might never see again. For many Texas boys, this would be their last night on this earth. Nevertheless, these diehard soldiers were determined to do their duty when called into action on the following day.

One Texan who realized that the end for him was drawing nearer was Major Matthew "Matt" Dale, who was now second in command of the

First Texas. In one of his final letters written home to his Anderson County family in east Texas, Matt revealed his iron determination. The major's beloved Anderson County was located about 150 miles north of Houston and nestled between the Trinity and Neches Rivers—a beautiful place that he firmly believed was worth dying for to save from subjugation. Major Dale predicted to the home folk that he would rather "rest easy beneath the sod" than allow the dream of an independent nation to succumb to an untimely death. Far from home and families, some Texas soldiers prayed to be spared from the fast-approaching storm that could not be stopped or slowed. Like the popular Major Dale, a good many young men and boys from Texas made peace with their Maker, while reading well-worn pocket Bibles by the campfire light and praying for a merciful deliverance that would never come.[62]

AMERICA'S BLOODIEST DAY, SEPTEMBER 17, 1862

September 17 began in western Maryland at 5:53 a.m. when the late summer sun broke over South Mountain to the east and a thick blanket of fog hovered over the sparkling waters of Antietam Creek. The Texans were up early, making their final preparations for the inevitable fighting that was about to erupt. Almost every soldier in the ranks instinctively realized that this would be the most important day of the war to date, but they could hardly realize the high cost in lives about to be paid in full. Sunrise broke through the dampness and fog that hugged the ground after the rainy night that benefited the thirsty crops, especially the dry cornstalks, in the dusty fields scorched by the summer sun and heat.

With the first red streaks of daylight illuminating the sky through a thin layer of lingering clouds, General McClellan, situated at his comfortable headquarters at the large brick home of Philip Pry, of French Huguenot descent, was about to unleash the offensive that both sides had expected for days. As ordered by McClellan, Hooker planned to launch his offensive effort south between Antietam Creek and the town with three veteran divisions to crush Lee's vulnerable left. Hooker now possessed a two-corps wing of five divisions extended across nearly a mile-wide front—a most formidable array calculated to decide the day. Hooker had cleverly ordered the First and Twelfth Corps to spend the rainy night in a concealed position on the Joseph Poffenberger Farm, located just north of the David R. Miller Farm and south of Ground Squirrel Church just west of the Hagerstown Road, from where an overpowering advance launched south could catch Lee's weak left by surprise.

With the warm dawn heralding the promise of another hot day, the Texas Brigade was positioned in reserve in the West Woods behind the Dunker Church, along with the remainder of Hood's Division. Even worse, the Twelfth Corps, under New Englander Major General Joseph King Fenno Mansfield, a West Pointer and Mexican-American War veteran, was now on the west side of Antietam Creek positioned on the left of Hooker's Corps, after a short night march to ease quietly into an advanced position. Like five other generals, General Mansfield would not survive this day in hell.

Therefore, the troops positioned on Lee's left, including the Texas Brigade, were about to get hit exceptionally hard on this early morning in Washington County. Indeed, like Hooker's First Corps, the Twelfth Corps was also in position to strike Lee's left flank, located in the West Woods, from the north. Hooker commanded more than thirty thousand troops of two corps opposite Lee's left in the hopes of destroying Lee's Army with one overpowering blow. Eager to strike, General Hooker, a West Pointer (class of 1837) and Seminole War and Mexican-American War veteran, peered south with his binoculars. He then set his tactical sights on Dunker Church, which was visible because it was located atop the commanding plateau just to the rear of Lee's left flank; the German house of worship was an ideal target on high ground, and his powerful corps could descend on it in overwhelming numbers by attacking down and parallel to the Hagerstown Pike.

Knowing that all hell was about to break out, an increasingly worried Colonel Alexander described the host of tactical disadvantages now confronting what little was left of the Army of Northern Virginia on this day of decision: "Lee's right rested on this creek [Antietam] at Burnside's Brigade [the Lower or Rohrbach Bridge] a mile to the right & front of Sharpsburg, & gradually leaving the creek further & further in its front, it bent back toward a big loop of the Potomac [River to the south and the army's rear while] the line was about three miles long in all."[63]

Meanwhile, more than two dozen twenty-pounder Parrott rifles, poised along the low hills on the Antietam's east side, punished the Confederate left at long range. However, the greatest damage was unleashed from the north, where the First Corps's artillery enfiladed the Confederate left. This heavy Union bombardment indicated to Work's veterans that an assault of considerable strength was shortly forthcoming. The savvy Texas Rebels, in the relative safety of the West Woods behind the Dunker Church, knew what to expect because of the intense shelling and the overall weakness of Lee's defensive line. Roaring from a lengthy row of large-caliber guns, this shell fire disturbed the Texans to raise their ire. Nevertheless, these veterans attempted to hastily cook breakfast of bacon, roasting ears and biscuits after rations had been distributed just before dawn. At the sound of the booming guns, the Texans gathered their rifles and gear for the upcoming contest with the boys in blue.

Corporal Hanks, a member of the Woodville Rifles of Company K, First Texas, described how "[n]ext morning very early we were preparing hastily some rations we had received [while] We were in a skirt...of timber in rear of the old Dunkard [*sic*] Church [but] Before we had finished our breakfast the bombshells commenced coming among us fast and furiously." The smoke of campfires rising lazily through the trees revealed targets to sharp-eyed Union artillerymen. Even more ominous, the brisk firing of the advanced pickets escalated to a crescendo of rapid popping, heralding the powerful Union onslaught from the north. Indeed, it was now only a matter of time before seemingly countless numbers of bluecoats advanced for the kill.[64]

Wondering if he would ever again see the Lone Star State, one homesick Texas Rebel thought of home when the early skirmishing had first began: "[O]n the 17th the battle commenced by starlight on an open field, similar to the prairies of Texas."[65] After hustling into line under the trees of the West Woods while under the shell fire, the Texas Rebels realized that every man would be needed in still another one of their key roles against the odds. Shells from the north and east continued to explode around the Texas Brigade soldiers. Explosions threw up sprays of dirt and rocks over them like a spring shower along the Neches, Brazos, Colorado or Navasota Rivers so far away.

Larger numbers of Union shells cut through the treetops of the West Woods, raining down branches, leaves and bark on the Texas Rebels, who protected their heads as best they could. To seek cover from the increasingly accurate shelling, the Texans were soon ordered to move around a slight hill to a relatively safe area nearby and south of Dunker Church, just behind the army's left flank. Here, these seasoned fighting men lay low under the pounding of shot and shell, hugging the ground and wishing to be unleashed against their tormentors.

In lengthy blue waves that spanned for about half a mile in the early morning light of September 17, now casting a reddish glow over the land, Hooker's dense formations poured out of the North Woods. Then, Hooker's legions continued south with confidence and flags flying in the morning sunshine. Thousands of troops of Hooker's First Corps advanced south parallel to the Hagerstown Road. The First Corps, on the right, and the Twelfth Corps, on the left, surged south through the green fields of summer with the key tactical objective of gaining possession of the strategic high ground around the Dunker Church, situated between the West and East Woods and barely a mile to the south. If so, then the attackers might be able to completely overwhelm Lee's left before General Ambrose Powell Hill's Division arrived from Harpers Ferry to reinforce the thin Southern line holding this vital sector north of Sharpsburg. As fate would have it, the Miller Cornfield lay before the First Corps's sweeping advance that rolled south.

New York–born Brigadier General Abner Doubleday commanded the First Division, First Corps, Army of the Potomac, at Antietam. His four-brigade command included the famed Iron Brigade of hardy westerners, who were known for their combat prowess. The West Pointer led his division with skill until he was knocked off his horse by an exploding shell. Abner Doubleday was *not* the inventor of the game of baseball, as long believed. *Library of Congress.*

As envisioned by McClellan and Hooker, the odds were highly favorable for overwhelming Lee's weak left. Not a Rebel trench or fortified position now stood in the path of the Massachusetts-born "Fighting Joe" Hooker and his powerful First Corps. The divisions of Brigadier Generals Abner Doubleday, a New Yorker and West Point man (class of 1842), and James Brewerton Rickett led the First Corps's advance south, as if nothing in the world could stop it. Not a single natural obstacle in this largely open country of hardworking farmers slowed or impeded the Federal onslaught, which continued to steamroll southward with a will of its own.

On the right of Hooker's Corps, west of the Hagerstown Pike, Brigadier General Abner Doubleday, a Seminole War and Mexican-American War veteran, was ordered to hurl three of

The Philadelphia-born Brigadier General John Gibbon (West Point, class of 1847) commanded the crack Iron Brigade of Wisconsin troops (three regiments) and Indiana troops (one regiment) of Doubleday's Division, First Corps. Raised in North Carolina, and while his brothers fought for the Confederacy, Gibbon and his hard-fighting westerners saw one of their greatest successes on September 17, 1862. He commanded the finest combat brigade of the Army of the Potomac, the Iron Brigade. Known as the "Black Hats," these tough westerners achieved significant tactical gains north of Sharpsburg and fought tenaciously for possession of the David R. Miller Cornfield. *Library of Congress.*

his division's brigades through the North Woods and down the Hagerstown Road to turn Lee's left flank. After having formed in line just south of the whitewashed Miller House, located on high ground before the Miller Cornfield to the south, the elite western brigade, under Brigadier General John Gibbon, surged onward with grim determination. A highly capable West Pointer, Gibbon led the mass formation of troops of Doubleday's Division, which was supported by the advance of two divisions east of the Hagerstown Pike, south toward Sharpsburg. In overwhelming numbers, Doubleday's troops surged south toward the Rebels, who held weak defensive positions south of the Miller Cornfield. To Doubleday's left, with rows of bayonets glistening in the bright September sunshine, the troops of Brigadier General George Gordon Meade's Division, in reserve, advanced in the center but slightly to the rear. A West Pointer (class of 1835) from Pennsylvania and a Seminole War and Mexican-American War veteran, Meade was tactically skilled and tough as nails—the consummate professional, destined to win the Battle of Gettysburg in less than ten months.

Like a blue tidal wave, Meade's troops pushed south through Miller's farmlands lying between the North Woods and the East Woods. Meanwhile, Brigadier General James Brewerton Rickett's Second Division advanced south toward the East Woods on Hooker's left, with one of Meade's Brigades surging before the division in a lengthy skirmish line. To the confident attackers in blue, the whitish church of the pious Baptist Brethren worshipers looked like a light-colored beacon, located at the highest point of the slight ridge of green trees and cultivated fields that surrounded the one-story structure.

Here, in an overextended battle line about three quarters of a mile in length, Jackson's three divisions of ten brigades on the left, consisting of about six thousand men, awaited the overpowering Yankee onslaught. Meanwhile, the Texas Brigade soldiers, along with the remainder of Hood's Division, continued to be held in support behind the Dunker Church and Lee's left flank. With a mixture of fatalism and stoicism, the Texas Rebels now waited for when they would be called up, especially if a crisis situation developed on the north, which now seemed inevitable.

Like an ace in the hole held in the capable hands of Lee, the proven master of the tactical offensive, these elite Texas troops remained quietly in place as a reliable strategic reserve in the manner of the longtime role of Napoleon Bonaparte's Imperial Guard. Lee's crack Texans were now ready on the north and in a good position to strike back and perhaps save the day, if ordered to do so. This overall tactical situation was no accident. The ever-astute Lee had released Hood from arrest over a trivial military matter just so that he could now be positioned at exactly the right place at just the right time with his hard-hitting division. Hood was one of Lee's best and most aggressive division commanders. With his boys ready and itching to strike back, Hood was confident of success. He noted with glee that his Texans were in high spirits and more than ready for their supreme challenge of the bloodiest Wednesday in American history.

Directly in Hooker's path, the first Southern line east of the Hagerstown Pike consisted of Ewell's old division, commanded by Lawton, a Marylander who possessed a Harvard College degree and an impressive West Point background. Also in the first line adjacent to Lawton was Jones's Division. This was Jackson's old division of Virginians, including the Old Dominion soldiers of the Stonewall Brigade. These Virginians now stood in formation on the pike's west side about a quarter mile north of the Dunker Church.

Meanwhile, Starke's Brigade of high-spirited Louisiana soldiers and Taliaferro's Brigade of Alabama and Virginia troops were positioned in support behind the Virginians. On high ground on the far left and west of Colonel Andrew Jackson Grisby's Stonewall Brigade stood the troops of Brigadier General Jubal Early's Virginia Brigade of Lawton's Division. In addition, Jones's four brigades were also poised west of the pike along with the Old Dominion brigade of "Old Jube" Early, a caustic ex-attorney born in Franklin County, Virginia, who fought as hard as he cursed Yankees. Most importantly, the high ground around the Dunker Church—the key to the battleground north of Sharpsburg—had to be held at all costs by the outnumbered Confederates.

The Stonewall Brigade's Virginians had been long highly touted as the elite fighting men of the Army of Northern Virginia by the influential Richmond press, which had long embellished their battlefield feats. However, the Texans knew much better. Facing north, the brigades of Jones and Grisby were positioned to the left, or west, of the turnpike. Meanwhile, Lawton's Division, consisting of Lawton's old Georgia brigade under Colonel Marcellus Douglas, and Isaac Trimble's Alabama, Georgia and North Carolina Brigade under the Virginia Military Institute's Colonel James A. "Old Bull Dog" Walker, from left to right, were aligned to the right of the Hagerstown Pike, facing northeast.

In the middle of the clover field immediately south of the Miller Cornfield, the Georgians stood just to the Hagerstown Turnpike's east, while Walker's Brigade was positioned on their right farther east and astride the Smoketown Road, with their battle line extending into the East Woods. Meanwhile, ready for this emergency situation, Colonel Wofford's Texas Brigade and General Law's Brigade of Hood's Division remained in position as a strategic reserve amid the West Woods to the Hagerstown Road's left behind the Dunker Church. The only other support troops positioned on the north was Tennessee-born General Harry Thompson Hays's hard-fighting Louisiana Brigade of Lawton's Division. Known as the "Louisiana Tigers," these Pelican State soldiers, including many ethnic soldiers, especially Celtic-Gaelic men from a heavily Irish New Orleans, were also positioned in the West Woods.[66]

While the early morning daylight bathed the rolling farmlands drained by the Antietam, the main players of the fast-approaching climactic struggle were now set in place north of Sharpsburg. A light fog continued to hug the creek bottoms and other low-lying areas, while thousands of men in blue and gray were about to meet their Maker. From the north, amid the early light around 6:00 a.m., the full might of Hooker's First Corps steadily converged on the high and open ground around the Dunker Church—its primary objective and target of opportunity to deliver Lee's Army a lethal blow if this strategic ground were captured. Supported by nearly a dozen batteries, all three of Hooker's divisions—under West Pointers Doubleday, Meade and Ricketts, from right to left—surged south through the rising clouds of dust from the parched fields of a drought-plagued summer. More than ten thousand First Corps Federals pushed forward like a blue avalanche toward Jackson's thin lines.

On the right, Doubleday's Third Division surged down both sides of the Hagerstown pike, while Meade's Division pushed forward farther to the east in the assault's center. Meanwhile, Rickett's Second Division advanced south through the broad fields and pastures farther east of the road on the left and then into the cover of the East Woods. Along nearly a half-mile front, the three powerful divisions of Hooker's First Corps rolled onward, from west to east, and down the dusty Hagerstown Turnpike. With brightly colored battle flags hanging limp in the early morning heat felt by the sweating common soldiers, the blue formations pushed confidently past the Miller farmhouse, garden and orchard while moving relentlessly onward with determined resolve for their next clash with comparable young men.

On the Union left, after pouring out of the East Woods like a locust plague descending on the grain fields lining the Nile River in ancient Egypt, more than one thousand men of Brigadier General Abram Duryea's Brigade led the relentless advance of Rickett's Division. Duryea's Brigade was the first Federal unit of this size to surge headlong into the high-standing stalks of the Miller Cornfield, after chasing the foremost Georgia Rebels rearward through the rows of corn. Moving south in an expansive blue wave, Duryea's three New York and one Pennsylvania regiments pushed through the dense maze of cornstalks with a will of their own.

Lying down in the clover field and waiting patiently until the Yankees emerged from the cornfield's southern edge just after 6:00 a.m., Colonel Douglas's Georgians of Lawton's old brigade had their percussion muskets cocked. All of a sudden, hundreds of veteran Peach State Rebels stood and opened fire as one. A fiery explosion of gunfire erupted into the faces of Duryea's soldiers, who wavered in the hail of lead. The Rebels blunted the relentless onslaught of the four regiments of Duryea's Brigade of Pennsylvania and New York troops as they surged from the cornfield's greenery with Springfield rifles at right shoulder shift.

Demonstrating a resilient toughness after receiving the murderous close-range volley, Duryea's hard-hit soldiers retired a short distance north to a spilt-rail fence that offered meager protection at the cornfield's southern edge. Here, displaying discipline despite the punishment, the three New York regiments and one Pennsylvania regiment realigned. Then, they defiantly stood their ground, ignoring their escalating losses. These tough Yankees returned fire with spirit from the rail fence that bordered the cornfield, blasting away at the Georgians at a distance of only 250 yards. Nothing existed between the two lengthy lines of antagonists but open ground, guaranteeing even higher losses for both sides.

Despite the mutual exchange of musketry, neither side seemed inclined to give an inch. Instead, opposing formations methodically traded death in the open clover field with the unleashing of a series of rolling volleys that shrouded the northern part of the clover field and the cornfield's southern end in a white cloud. All the while, additional young soldiers fell in clumps amid the drifting battle smoke that hung close to the ground on this windless morning. Fighting without cover in the open, as if these men in blue and gray were contemptuous of death, the lethal musketry reaped a grim harvest. Additional bodies of soldiers from opposite sides of the Mason-Dixon line piled ever higher in the dueling exchanges of gunfire that destroyed more young lives along with naïve hopes for easy victory. Clearly, for what they believed was right, these veteran killers on both sides knew how to destroy their fellow man without mercy or remorse.

To the Georgians' right, meanwhile, the fast-firing men under "Old Bull Dog" Walker, now leading Trimble's Brigade of Alabama, Georgia and North Carolina troops, held firm under the onslaught of Meade's Pennsylvania Reserves. Now serving under a hot-tempered Celtic warrior who had once challenged Jackson to a duel back in their Virginia Military Institute days in Lexington, Walker's soldiers repulsed the Yankees in the contest, which was rapidly developing into a full-blown battle north of Sharpsburg. Meanwhile, Duryea's troops continued to fight with dogged determination from the slight cover of the rail fence along the cornfield's southern edge, until punished by flank fire from three regiments of Walker's Rebels of Trimble's old brigade. Only then were these steadfast New York troops of Duryea, a wealthy New York merchant with a New York State militia background, finally hurled back through the high cornstalks, retiring north and leaving their dead behind in sickening clumps. In the hellish exchanges of musketry, Duryea lost more than three hundred men from the Empire and the Keystone States under the glare of the summer sun. However, the surreal horror that was the struggle for the Miller Cornfield was only just beginning.

While Duryea's hard-hit men fell back through the rows of corn to escape the sweeping musketry and flank fires, General George Lucas Hartstuff's Brigade of Massachusetts, New York and Pennsylvania soldiers, in support of Duryea, surged into the cornfield with the same confidence that had only recently propelled Duryea's men forward. Soon to be cut down, Hartstuff was a grizzled Seminole War veteran who was every inch a fighter. Rickett's troops were determined to renew the contest to secure the Miller Cornfield.

With steady pressure mounting, Southern casualties escalating and Walker's troops retiring under the relentless pounding, Douglas and his Georgia soldiers of Lawton's old brigade found themselves in serious trouble. Douglas, therefore, requested assistance from Hays's Louisiana Brigade, now positioned in support to Douglas's rear. By 6:45 a.m., Colonel Douglas had been killed, going down with his command and adding to the growing casualty list that seemed without end. Despite its best defense, the colonel's Georgia brigade was smashed by the Federal onslaught, with half of its members killed, wounded or captured. In record time, Douglas's Brigade lost more than five hundred men in the nightmarish slugfest.

Then, at the last moment, with Douglas's Georgia troops about to break and answering Lawton's appeals for urgent assistance, five regiments of some 550 Louisiana Rebels of the brigade of New Orleans attorney Harry Thompson Hays, of "Old Bald Head" Ewell's Division, surged some three hundred yards northeast from their support position in the clover field behind Lawton. With a desire to turn back the blue onslaught at any cost, the legendary Louisiana Tigers, who possessed a well-deserved reputation for ferocity, marched past Douglas's reeling Georgia soldiers.

With colorful Pelican flags of blue waving through the stagnant battle smoke, the Louisiana Rebels pushed forward with confidence through the clover field and toward the Miller Cornfield's southern edge. Providing a timely reinforcement for Trimble's Virginians, who were now relieved by the advancing Louisianans on Lawton's right flank, these troops advanced to exploit the gaping hole in the mangled line created by the collapse of Duryea's Brigade—a gory space now littered with dead, dying and wounded New Yorkers and Pennsylvania boys.

Known as the South's most prolific "Yankee slayers" and Union solider "grave diggers," the battle-hardened warriors (a large percentage were Irish) of the Fifth and the "Irish Tigers" of the Sixth, Seventh, Eighth and Fourteenth Louisiana Infantry charged into the cornfield along with some of Douglas's rallied Georgians. They smashed into Hartsuff's Brigade after it had surged out of the cornfield. General Hartsuff, while leading by example in inspiring his troops, fell with serious wounds. Amid the tumult, Colonel Richard Coulter took command of Hartsuff's reeling brigade, which was being cut to pieces. Combined with artillery support that raked the Federal line with a vengeance, the Louisiana Rebels, with assistance from Douglas's rallied Georgia troops, drove the Yankees back through the green stalks of corn.

After chasing the Federals into the smoke-filled maze of the Miller Cornfield, the yelling Louisiana Irish (the majority), Germans, Poles, Creoles, Scots, Jews and other ethnic soldiers (now bound together by Southern nationalism and esprit de corps) charged into the cornfield with bayonets sparkling in the September sunlight. However, these victors were unable to savor their success. After gamely standing their ground, Hartstuff's rallied troops, now under Colonel Coulter's steady leadership, counterattacked with fixed bayonets through the cornfield. Blasted at point-blank range by newly deployed Federal artillery and musketry crashing before them, the Tigers, who wore brass buttons distinguished by the state seal of a mother pelican feeding its brood of young hatchlings (the Pelican State emblem), were caught in a deadly converging fire that swept the cornfield without mercy.

Out of necessity under the severe pounding, the Louisiana men withdrew through the body-littered cornfield to reach the open clover field. Then the battered Louisiana Rebels and the rallied Georgians fell back to a position just south of the Dunker Church to regroup. Here, mostly amid the grim ground of the Miller Cornfield, the Louisiana Tigers suffered devastating losses. The lone Louisiana brigade, under General Hays, of Scotch-Irish descent and a graduate of St. Mary's College (a Catholic school) in Baltimore, suffered more than 60 percent casualties in record time. General Hays was sickened by the carnage, which saw 325 Louisiana Tigers lost in only a quarter of an hour.[67]

From a position in reserve at the north edge of the West Woods, Starke's Louisiana Brigade of Jackson's Division (ordered up with Hays's Louisiana Brigade) rushed into action around 6:45 a.m. When Winder's and Jones's mauled Virginia brigades fell back, these Louisiana troops, including Taliaferro's Alabama and Virginia Brigade, which was in support behind Jones's and Grigsby's Virginians, replaced those shattered units after they retired, advancing first north and then east to the Hagerstown Road. Not long after taking command when General Jones fell, General Starke, the handsome senior brigadier of Jackson's old division, led an attack in an attempt to drive the stubborn Yankees from the field. Starke was a fighter on and off the battlefield, having recently clashed with his superior General Jackson. A native Virginian and a former cotton broker of New Orleans and Mobile, the dashing General Starke, dark-haired and dapper, was soon shot off his horse, hit with three bullets about 150 yards west of the Hagerstown Pike.[68]

Meanwhile, the savage fighting around the cornfield raged to new levels of intensity. For the second time, General Hartstuff's soldiers fought gamely, firing from the relative shelter of the high-rail fence bordering the cornfield's southern edge, where their counterattack finally lost steam due to heavy losses. Meanwhile, the Confederates, who stood before Hartstuff's men, fought in the clover field's openness, presented easy targets and suffered accordingly.

To the east, the last of Rickett's Brigades, New York and Pennsylvania troops under Colonel Peter Lyle, surged forward from the northeast past battered Union forces, pouring out of the East Woods and into the body-covered clover field with silken battle flags flying through the drifting smoke. Even by this time, the carnage had already reached unparalleled proportions in the cornfield and clover field, which had been transformed into gory scenes of mangled bodies and broken dreams. The nightmare that was Antietam sickened even hardened veterans, who had never before seen an epic slaughter on such an unimaginable scale.[69]

THE IRON BRIGADE UNLEASHED

With the desperate offensive effort of Rickett's Division, Hooker's left wing, thwarted to the east and the fighting in the East Woods and the cornfield's eastern half degenerating in a bloody stalemate, it was now the Iron Brigade's turn. The Iron Brigade prepared to launch its offensive effort down the Hagerstown Road in a bid to gain possession of the body-strewn Miller Cornfield, after playing its part in repulsing the howling Louisiana Tigers. Now these western veterans (the best combat troops of the Army of the Potomac) of Hooker's right wing were determined to carry the day at all costs.

With confidence high after their recent successes against Lee's seasoned troops, the rawboned Iron Brigade soldiers marched in disciplined step south in a lengthy line astride the turnpike. These westerners in blue pushed south through the western half of the clover field before the miserable cornfield filled with suffocating clouds of smoke. The four western regiments of the Iron Brigade, consisting of more than one thousand mostly farm boys, were about to deliver a powerful blow. For added muscle, the hard-fighting troops from Wisconsin and Indiana were backed up by the New York Brigade of Colonel Walter Phelps Jr. and the New York Brigade of Brigadier General Marsena R. Patrick, both of General Doubleday's First Division.

Also providing close support for the Iron Brigade's counterattack were the booming guns of Company B, Fourth United States Artillery. These highly effective Company B guns had already provided timely service in supporting the Iron Brigade this warm morning. Ironically, after advancing through the exposed ground of the open clover field just north of the Miller Cornfield, the Iron Brigade, leading the advance of Doubleday's Division south on the Hagerstown Road's east side, entered into the forest of high cornstalks to gain some slight cover. As these westerners soon discovered, there was no shelter from the storm.

East of the embattled Hagerstown Turnpike, leading the way through the cornfield's western half, were companies of the crack Sixth Wisconsin Volunteer and, to its left, the Second Wisconsin Volunteer Infantry. The Sixth Wisconsin had initially spearheaded the Iron Brigade's advance south because this was one of the Iron Brigade's best regiments. Behind these two fine western regiments in support marched the Iron Brigade's remainder, the Seventh Wisconsin Volunteer Infantry and Nineteenth Indiana Volunteer Infantry. Following the Iron Brigade into the cornstalks was Phelps's Brigade of New York troops.

On this day of destiny, the Iron Brigade was led by capable leaders, especially North Carolina–born General John Gibbon. He was a Southerner who remained true to the Union, unlike most of his fellow Tar Heels, who now served in Lee's Army in disproportionate numbers. The irony of a hard-fighting Southern officer now leading the Union army's best combat unit was a fact lost on the Texas Rebels. Gibbon was a hard-nosed West Pointer who had three brothers fighting for the Confederacy. Now leading his brigade in the forefront of Hooker's First Division, Gibbon had been mostly responsible for forging his command's elite qualities. Much like the Texas Brigade, these westerners were their army's shock troops.

One of the most capable Iron Brigade officers, Major Rufus R. Dawes, felt confidence from the inspiring sight of Gibbon's Brigade during its relentless advance. Along the cornfield's southern edge behind the rail fence, the veteran Georgians under Colonel Douglas were now ready to receive the Iron Brigade's attack, regaining this advanced position after having pushed aside Hartsuff's defenders.

Waiting silently with leveled muskets, these men in gray and butternut prepared to unleash a first volley on the advancing Iron Brigade soldiers at close range, when the Sixth Wisconsin reached a high point of the cornfield after leaving the slight depression that divided the field's southern half. Meanwhile, the cannons of Captain William Thomas Poague's Virginia battery (the Rockbridge Artillery) were unlimbered in the clover field to support the infantrymen before them. They had already dueled with the fast-firing guns of Company B, Fourth United States Artillery. In the war's beginning, this Old Dominion battery had consisted of four bronze six-pounders (ironically cast in Boston, Massachusetts, in 1848 for Mexican-

American War service), which had been christened in honor of the four Apostles Matthew, Mark, Luke and John.

Near the narrow Hagerstown Pike and the Dunker Church, Poague's Virginia cannons (two ten-pounder Parrotts and one twelve-pounder Napoleon) of this fine battery unleashed a torrent of shells into the cornfield now swarming with large numbers of advancing Yankees. Explosions sprayed dirt and raised dust clouds throughout the embattled cornfield that had become the eye of the storm, blowing up clumps of men and harvest alike. But all the while, with firm step from months of intense drill, the Iron Brigade troops kept moving through the explosions and swinging relentlessly onward with fixed bayonets.

Wearing their trademark high-crowned black hats of the Iron Brigade and only thirty yards distant and almost to the cornfield's southern edge, Douglas's Georgians, of a full brigade, suddenly stood up and unleashed a murderous volley. Seasoned westerners from the evergreen forests, meadows and blue lakes of Wisconsin went down in bunches. In defiance, the brave men of the so-called Black Hat Brigade nevertheless stood their ground. These western boys then returned fire with spirit, delivering severe punishment. As indicated recently in overrunning well-defended Rebel positions on the commanding heights of South Mountain, these westerners took pride in their distinctive uniforms and in representing the western people.[70]

At this crucial moment, these Iron Brigade men believed that this "was the day [September 17] and they [were] the men, who were to decide the destinies of the nation."[71] Ironically, the Texas soldiers felt much the same about their own role on this Wednesday in hell, ensuring a climactic meeting between two elite fighting machines on the war's bloodiest day. Meanwhile, the Sixth Wisconsin's right companies were hit especially hard along the Hagerstown Pike and in the cornfield's western edge by an enfilade fire unleashed by Rebels from the cover of the West Woods. Streaming from the west, this deadly musketry poured from the Virginians of Stonewall Jackson's old division, including the Stonewall Brigade. On Jackson's left, the blistering fire of Jones's old Virginia Brigade inflicted severe damage among the Sixth Wisconsin's five right companies. From the West Woods, these Confederates stood up from behind the cover of a slight rise and "a low Virginia fence rail" to deliver death on the lengthy waves of Black Hat men from Wisconsin when they advanced closer to the southern edge of the Miller Cornfield. The Iron Brigade had just met the Stonewall Brigade for the first time on a day of decision that survivors never forgot.[72]

To protect the Iron Brigade's vulnerable right flank and confront the much-celebrated Virginia Rebels (worn down from their grueling seventeen-mile march from Harpers Ferry) of the "Old Stonewall" Brigade in the West Woods, General Gibbon had earlier made a wise decision, especially before advancing into the suffocating depths of the Miller Cornfield. He had fully realized that he needed to secure the right flank of not only the Iron Brigade but also, more importantly, the southward advance of Hooker's First Corps. As if anticipating tactical developments to come with prophetic vision, he had ordered the Seventh Wisconsin and the Nineteenth Indiana, in support behind the two (Second and Sixth) Wisconsin regiments, on a flank march west through the open ground of the Miller barnyard and across the Hagerstown Road and to its west side—a desperate effort to outflank their fast-firing tormentors.

Additionally, to bolster the Wisconsin soldiers' offensive effort in this crucial sector during the first phase of the Battle of Antietam, Doubleday also sent forward Patrick's New York brigade, which advanced into the cornstalks behind Colonel Phelps's Brigade, to reinforce the two Iron Brigade regiments west of the road and into the West Woods. However, only two of General Patrick's regiments crossed the little dusty road, with the other Empire State regiments reassigned elsewhere.

With this added muscle and the battered right flank now finally secure, the Iron Brigade units unleashed a concentrated musketry to severely punish Jones's Virginia Brigade. Swept by the withering fire, these foremost Old Dominion troops began to fall back toward the West Woods. With a cheer, the Wisconsin soldiers charged to overpower the remaining defenders along the Virginians' rail fence position that bordered the pike.

Sensing victory, the elated Wisconsin soldiers continued to advance south through the drifting smoke with fixed bayonets and cheers. Spirits were high with this initial success that had left so many Rebels dead and wounded, scattered like fallen autumn leaves across the ground. Major Dawes had early learned his war-fighting trade as the captain of the volunteer company the Lemonweir Minute Men. Meanwhile, the major continued to lead the Sixth Wisconsin forward from the front and with skill.

Here, west of the pike, these two Iron Brigade regiments and Patrick's Twenty-First and Thirty-Fifth New York gained an advanced position to strike south into the West Woods' northern edge to solidify the right flank of Hooker's First Corps. Meanwhile, the remaining two Iron Brigade regiments were responsible for pushing south and overrunning the cornfield on the other side, east of the Hagerstown Road. Consequently, the Iron Brigade was now equally divided, with two regiments advancing on each side of the Hagerstown Pike during the determined bid of the "Black Hats" to secure the strategic high ground around the Dunker Church. With the threat on the right flank no more after the foremost Virginia Rebels of Jones's Brigade had been hurled rearward through the cornfield's southwestern edge, the way was now open for the Iron Brigade to advance deeper into the cornfield and beyond.

More timely assistance was forthcoming for the soldiers of the Sixth Wisconsin, which had been vulnerable because its left flank hung in midair. Now the Sixth Wisconsin was reinforced by Phelps's New York Brigade, which included the green-uniformed marksmen of the Second United States Sharpshooters, for the united offensive effort to overrun the stubborn Confederate position.

In addition, to protect the Federals' advance and knock out the angry Rebel cannons, two guns of Battery B, Fourth United States Artillery, under Lieutenant James Stewart, unlimbered on a grassy knoll before the West Woods. Here, just west of the pike and opposite, or north, of the cornfield's northwest corner, the two Union artillery pieces stood on high ground before the haystacks and the large Miller barn located just west of the pike and near the family's two-story house. Shortly, the four remaining guns unlimbered to the left of the two-gun section, adjacent to and facing the cornfield's northern edge, as if anticipating that the Rebels would soon attack through the vast expanse of corn.

Roaring with authority, the twelve-pounder Napoleons, bronze smoothbores, were part of a battery of well-trained regulars formerly commanded by Colonel Gibbon. Proud of a distinguished lineage and "long arm" prowess, the gunners traced their unit's antecedents to the War of 1812. Symbolically, a close relationship existed between the Battery B, Fourth United States Artillery, and the Iron Brigade, not only because of the strong Gibbon connection, but also because many Iron Brigade members now served as ad hoc artillerymen of this premier long-arm unit. During the Civil War, this crack battery suffered the "greatest aggregate losses" of any Union light battery, including the most casualties of any artillery unit on September 17. Symbolically, despite this battery's superior performances in providing effective support fire, the Iron Brigade was also destined to suffer higher casualties than any other Union brigade during the four years of war.[73]

While the struggle in the East Woods raged, the Federal advance stalled against the firepower of Lawton's Georgia Brigade, now under Colonel John H. Lamar, and the surging tide of Yankees drove Jones's Virginia troops out of the cornfield's southwestern edge and into the West Woods to allow the Iron Brigade, with Phelps's New York Brigade close behind, to continue to rise to the challenge. With a will of its own, the Iron Brigade continued to advance through the cornfield east of the road, with the Sixth and Second Wisconsin, from right to left, surging onward.

Gaining additional ground in taking less punishment than previously, these Federals now pushed through farmer Miller's rows of corn without suffering from the punishing flank fire from the west. Meanwhile, Duryea's beaten New York and Pennsylvania men continued to retire through the westerners' ranks. To close a gaping hole between the East Woods and the Second Wisconsin's right flank left by the withdrawal of Duryea's Brigade during its relentless advance, the Iron Brigade staged a right wheel maneuver through the neat rows of corn.

With the long leaves of the green cornstalks entangling equipment and Springfield rifled muskets, the Iron Brigade soldiers placed weapons on right shoulders, after officers barked, "Right shoulder shift!" Now the Iron Brigade boys, with Phelps's New Yorkers close behind them, pushed farther into the cornfield's smoky depths—this order allowed them to push more easily through the rows that stood higher in this fertile soil than the cornfields last seen in Virginia. With confidence high, these resilient western Yankees were now determined to win the day at any cost.

On and on in pushing through the rising yellow haze of choking dust, the Second and Sixth Wisconsin soldiers marched in disciplined alignment through the cornstalks under a searing September sun. Finally reaching the cornfield's southern edge, the Iron Brigade soldiers quickly scrambled over the split-rail fence recently held by the Georgians. The westerners in blue paid no attention the clumps of Peach State dead and seriously wounded lying either motionless or moaning in pain behind the fence rails splintered by a hail of bullets. Then, with smooth precision, the disciplined westerners realigned ranks with a smart crispness that made the officers proud of their men, as if on the parade ground in their state capital of Madison, the city on the lakes. Before the Badger State soldiers stood the open clover field of farmer Miller—a perfect killing ground where Duryea's New York and Pennsylvania Brigade had been cut to pieces. But now within sight to the south of the surging bluecoats loomed the high ground of the slightly elevated Hagerstown Road Ridge around the Dunker Church, now the key to the battlefield north of Sharpsburg. Consequently, this vital strategic point was the Iron Brigade's main tactical objective on this bloody morning.

Smeared with a grimy mixture of dust and black powder, the westerners in blue knew that the high-ground perch must be taken at all costs. With drums beaten by young musicians to keep the marching feet of hundreds of men in near perfect step, the Second and Sixth Wisconsin troops continued onward into the expansive field of clover just below the cornfield—the eerie place in the open and from which many young westerners would never return.

East of the pike, meanwhile, the Georgia Rebels of Lawton's old brigade of Ewell's Division had been waiting for the Iron Brigade's soldiers to emerge from the sheltering cornstalks. They were fairly lusting for the opportunity to inflict massive damage on the cocky "Black Hats." After having delivered initial punishment on the bluecoat westerners who were adding to their reputations, the Peach State men retired from the fence along the cornfield's southern edge. The surviving Georgia soldiers then hurriedly realigned in new defensive positions throughout the clover field.

All of a sudden, in a repeat of the tactics that had so severely devastated General Duryea's New York and Pennsylvania Brigade only a short time before, a line of Georgians of nearly brigade strength suddenly stood up from their prone positions. To the Yankees' shock, the Peach Staters rose up as one from the clover field of bright green. Then, with the careful aim of veterans, these Deep South soldiers unleashed a murderous volley that tore through the ranks of the Second and Sixth Wisconsin. However, the New Yorkers behind them hurriedly moved forward to fill the gaps in the westerners' decimated line and opened fire.

Gamely holding their ground beside their fallen comrades, the Iron Brigade soldiers likewise returned fire with spirit. Now the fight was on in earnest. Close-range volleys were exchanged across the bloodstained clover field, with both sides delivering death with each fiery explosion of musketry that rippled down the lines. Caught out in the open and without cover, Lawton's Georgia regiments were decimated by the volleys unleashed by the Iron Brigade's soldiers.

Meanwhile, the colorfully uniformed Zouaves of the Fourteenth New York Volunteer Infantry from Brooklyn and Colonel Phelps's Brigade reinforced the hard-hit Sixth Wisconsin. Here, the Badgers continued to fight beside the turnpike after advancing beyond the cornfield's southern edge and into Miller's large clover field. Known as the Fourteenth Brooklyn Zouaves, these New Yorkers were members of a chasseur (or "hunter" in French, which meant light infantry) regiment and wore a modified French chasseur uniform. These New Yorkers had recently fought well at South Mountain. They wore fancy red pantaloons and uniforms inspired by legendary French soldiers who had long fought a brutal war against Islamic tribes in North Africa. Little did these New York Zouaves realize that standing patiently in a strategic reserve position only a short distance to the south were Lee's elite troops—hundreds of veteran Texas Rebels, who had thoroughly destroyed another Zouave regiment at Second Manassas, the Fifth New York Volunteer Infantry. Not realizing the Fifth New York's tragic fate at Texas hands only a few weeks before, the New York Zouaves, known to the Rebels as the "Red Legged Devils," now swung into position to reinforce and fill the gaps of the riddled Sixth Wisconsin.[74]

Meanwhile, the close-range combat quickly escalated to new levels of intensity. Leading the Sixth Wisconsin after the lieutenant colonel was cut down, Major Dawes was horrified by the mounting losses. Punished by the blistering fire, three regiments of Lawton's Georgians, under Colonel Douglas, were soon overpowered by the "Black Hats" of the Iron Brigade on the right and Duryea's New York and Pennsylvania Brigade on the left. Smashed by the musketry from infantry and the exploding shells from the blazing guns of Company B, Fourth United States Artillery, Lawton's troops were hurled rearward. The combined might of the steadfast Wisconsin men of the Iron Brigade and the feisty New York Zouaves fueled the relentless advance through the clover field on the east side of the Hagerstown Pike.

All the while, the Wisconsin and New York attackers gained additional ground and momentum, while surging ever closer to their key strategic objective just to the south: the crucial high ground that anchored Lee's mauled left around the little Dunker Church and the busy Rebel guns booming from the commanding plateau. Soon the bluecoats advanced several hundred yards south of the cornfield, pushing forward with battle flags waving in the smoke-laced air from Confederate shell bursts, while the cries and prayers of wounded men grew louder. It now appeared that the Iron Brigade troops might be the first command to advance sufficiently south to overwhelm the strategic plateau around the Dunker Church (the key to Lee's position on the left) and seal the Army of Northern Virginia's fate.[75]

Now it was Stonewall Jackson's turn to take the offensive in an attempt to turn the tide against the attackers, who just kept coming. From the West Woods to the west, the last two remaining brigades consisting of Virginia troops of Jackson's old Stonewall division, including the Stonewall Brigade, advanced east into the clover field just southwest of the cornfield in support of Lawton's troops. This counterattack was launched to rescue Hays's Louisiana and Lawton's Georgia soldiers, who had retired deeper into the clover field (south of the cornfield) before the massive blue onslaught. Now thrown headlong into the meat grinder that was the vicious struggle for possession of the Miller Cornfield, these Confederate troops quickly aligned along the fence, where a lengthy row of Rebel muskets now rested for a more steady aim, bordering the Hagerstown Pike.

Here, along the pike's west side, the two veteran Virginia Brigades of more than one thousand men opened fire at close range on the New York and Wisconsin troops surging through the clover field across the road, raking their right flank with a scorching musketry. Additional "Black Hat" soldiers of the Iron Brigade and Phelps's New York brigade were cut down, blunting the offensive effort of Doubleday's Division on the right of Hooker's First Corps. However, the savage struggle for the Miller Cornfield had reached levels of intensity that had been unimaginable to these young soldiers only a few hours before on this nightmarish Wednesday morning in Washington County.

Meanwhile, the Rebels along the fence line bordering the road were severely punished from the north by the shot and shell pouring from the guns of Battery B, Fourth United States Artillery. The two cannons in the Miller barnyard raked the Stonewall Brigade on the left flank, enfilading the Virginians—the pride of the Old Dominion—deployed along the pike and toppling clumps of men like ten-pins. Hit with canister (clusters of iron shot that was the infantryman's ultimate nightmare) from the fast-firing field pieces, the Old Dominion soldiers continued to fall to the vicious enfilade fire from Company B's deadly guns. Like so many of Lee's units, the Stonewall Brigade soldiers were of largely Scotch-Irish descent, tracing their ancestry back to north Ireland. But the Stonewall Brigade also included a good many Germans, who were not unlike their fellow Maryland countrymen-farmers, including those who had transformed the Antietam Valley into an agrarian paradise. Most of the Stonewall Brigade men hailed from the Blue Ridge Mountains, the Virginia Tidewater, and the fertile Shenandoah Valley.

Under heavy pressure and raked by successive volleys, the Sixth Wisconsin and the Fourteenth New York troops shifted to face to the left. After taking severe punishment, and to escape even more of the same, they fell back to cornfield's southern edge. Here, the New Yorkers and Wisconsin boys took cover behind the rail fence, which provided inadequate shelter. Instinctively, to escape the leaden storm, wiser survivors lay prone to return fire, reducing visibility to expert Rebel marksmen. Then, the two Iron Brigade regiments that had shifted from the east to the Hagerstown Turnpike's west side and were now located in the West Woods, the Seventh Wisconsin and the Nineteenth Indiana, opened a vicious fire from the north to riddle the rear and the vulnerable left flank of the Rebels, who were exposed along the rail fence bordering the pike. Meanwhile, the Virginians were also hit hard by a frontal fire streaming from the rail fence position held by the Sixth Wisconsin and Fourteenth New York along the cornfield's southern edge, while also being swept with the concentrated artillery fire.

Hit by vicious converging fires from multiple directions, including the merciless blasts of canister erupting from the guns of Company B, Fourth United States Artillery, from the north, this punishment, coming not only from the front but also from the rear and flank, was simply too much for the hard-hit Virginia boys of the Stonewall Brigade. Under the withering fire, the Virginians started to give way, especially after having lost their division commander, General John B. Jones, as well as his successor, to the artillery fire in the leaden tempest that was now raging out of control. Like so many Fourth, Fifth, Twenty-Seventh and Thirty-Third Virginia soldiers, General Jones had been cut down when a shell burst just above the general's head.

Finally, the mauled Stonewall Brigade retired to the West Woods' edge from where the Virginians had come shortly before with confidence and high hopes for success. Then, Colonel Grigsby took charge of the shattered division after General Starke had fallen to the scorching fire unleashed by the Iron Brigade's soldiers, who were skilled in shooting down mounted officers. In a testament to the Iron Brigade's combat prowess and lethality, a good many Virginians raced rearward to escape the slaughter. Like so many of his comrades, one Old Dominion soldier "ran like a deer." In the savage slugfest between two elite units, a Wisconsin lieutenant of the Iron Brigade proudly described the decisive outcome: "Our brigade whipped Jackson's famous Stonewall Brigade…in a fair and square fight."[76]

The Virginians' stunning defeat and the Stonewall Brigade's collapse spelled ill tidings for Starke's Louisiana Brigade, which had counterattacked out of the West Woods to reinforce Grisby's and Jones's Virginia Brigades. After initially having advanced north and then aligning to face east to avoid decimation from a close-range fire sweeping over its right flank, as well as to meet the Iron Brigade's threat to the east, Starke's Louisiana Rebels held their ground along the sturdy fence line bordering the west side of the turnpike. Here, starting around 6:45 a.m., these Pelican State soldiers, including good fighting men from the swamps and bayous of Cajun country, made a determined stand along the Hagerstown Pike.

About five hundred yards north of Dunker Church, the survivors of the First, Second, Ninth, Tenth and Fifteenth Louisiana, along with the attached First Louisiana Battalion, loaded and fired east from behind the solidly constructed rail fences (some six rails high) that ran along the road's western edge. At a range of only about thirty to fifty yards, this close-range flank fire raked the right of the Iron Brigade soldiers now continuing to surge south on the road's other side, or east, through the clover field. The Iron Brigade's exposed right was hit by the Pelican State soldiers' enfilade fire that was especially lethal. However, the Sixth Wisconsin and Second United States Sharpshooters wheeled to the right and then attacked their tormentors in the hope of eliminating this scorching flank fire.

From the clover field south of the Miller Cornfield, the Iron Brigade soldiers, especially the Sixth Wisconsin men, as well as the Second United States Sharpshooters, methodically cut down scores of Louisiana boys. Wearing captured knapsacks and other Union accoutrements, Louisianans fell in sickening piles behind the rail fence along the west side of the Hagerstown Road. The high-rail fence that bordered the road's west side offered little protection from these well-placed volleys. The Sixth Wisconsin's devastating fire, unleashed at close range from the east, riddled the Louisiana men and their Pelican State flags, with lead balls tearing through colorful banners, fence rails and flesh. While loading and firing as fast as possible, the Louisiana Tigers discovered to their horror that their thin cover behind the high-rail fence along the pike was totally inadequate against the Iron Brigade's accurate fire. Consequently, additional Louisiana bodies began to pile up behind the fence. For the first time in this war, the famed Louisiana Tigers, known for their ferocity, were being systematically declawed, but it had taken the Union army's best troops to accomplish this considerable feat.

In addition, the guns of Company B, Fourth United States Artillery, continued to unleash an accurate fire down the turnpike and its environs, especially between a small farm lane and the rail fence running along the road's west side, helping to litter the ground with clumps of Louisiana bodies.

These blazing guns enfiladed the Louisiana brigade's left flank from north to south, causing extensive damage. Also, after surging south through the West Woods, the other Iron Brigade troops, the Nineteenth Indiana and the Seventh Wisconsin, poured a hot fire into the Louisiana Rebels that ravaged their rear and left flank.

The mangled bodies of Louisiana's best and brightest, especially young men and boys from among the Tenth Louisiana Infantry—which left twenty-five dead along the gory rail fence line that had now become one of the terrible killing zones at Antietam—littered the ground around the rail fences bordering the pike. This hard-fighting Louisiana Brigade was a true Confederate foreign legion, including soldiers who had been born in Greece, France, Mexico, Ireland, England, Scotland, Germany and other faraway places.

Like a row of falling dominoes, the sudden collapse and rout of the highly touted Stonewall Brigade led to disaster for the Louisiana Rebels of Starke's Brigade, the Second Louisiana Brigade. One angry Louisiana soldier wrote how the Virginians on the left had "run and left our Brigade alone." To exploit their success, the cheering Iron Brigade soldiers surged ahead into the ground vacated by the reeling Stonewall Brigade to outflank the Louisiana Rebels. After defending the fence line along the pike from about 6:45 a.m. to 7:00 a.m., the Louisiana soldiers of Starke's decimated brigade finally withdrew south toward the Dunker Church. The battered survivors retired to the relative safety of the West Woods along with Taliaferro's shattered brigade after fifteen minutes of the most nightmarish slaughter ever experienced by these Louisiana Rebels.

Later, an elated victor of the Second United States Sharpshooters took possession of the fallen silk flag of the First Louisiana Infantry after the brave color bearer had been killed at the rail fence. Along with the Louisiana troops, Lawton's Georgians, who had rallied when the Pelican State soldiers counterattacked, were also driven from the field. Now with the Hagerstown Road sector cleared of almost all Rebel defenders and two of Stonewall Jackson's Divisions (Lawton's and Jones's decimated commands) crushed by the Union juggernaut, the best tactical opportunity now (at about 7:00 a.m.) existed for completely turning Lee's left flank and then systematically destroying the Army of Northern Virginia.

Here, in the body-strewn fields north of Sharpsburg, Lee's mauled left had been all but destroyed by this time. The best units of the Army of Northern Virginia had been mauled and swept from the field by the steamrolling blue tide that was immune to Confederate valor. With businesslike efficiency, the great onslaught of bluecoat attackers had "tor[n] apart the Stonewall Division almost effortlessly" in a remarkable display of combat prowess.[77]

Reinforced by fresh troops with full cartridge boxes, the Iron Brigade now once again took the offensive with so many Rebels streaming rearward, advancing down both sides of the pike in triumph. East of the Iron Brigade, meanwhile, Duryea's Brigade, after losing more than three hundred men, was replaced by Phelps's New York Brigade, solidifying the Iron Brigade's left to add protection and fueling momentum for the attack's continuation south toward the all-important high ground around the Dunker Church. Meanwhile, the elated "Black Hat" men of the Seventh Wisconsin and Nineteenth Indiana, reinforced by the New Yorkers of Patrick's Brigade, continued to advance south across the open ground west of the pike, driving Jackson's troops before them and scattering additional Southern troops. On the east side of the turnpike and sweeping the last obstinate Rebels rearward like a giant broom, the Second and Sixth Wisconsin led the steamrolling attack, along with the Fourteenth New York and lethal marksmen of the Second United States Sharpshooters.

In the collapse, Grigsby's and Jones's troops were now in full flight, hoping to escape the Union juggernaut that was brushing aside everything before it. The rapidly advancing Iron Brigade troops were now only about two hundred yards from the strategic high ground topped by the little German church, the vital objective that would bring the Union the war's most important victory.[78]

At this time, seemingly nothing could stop the relentless onslaught of thousands of victorious Yankees, who were spearheaded by the crack troops of the Iron Brigade. Incredibly, even two of the Confederacy's most famous units, the Stonewall Brigade and the Louisiana Tigers, had been badly mauled and hurled aside—an unprecedented development in the history of this war. The bulk of Hooker's First Corps had fallen on Jackson's two lonely divisions under Generals Lawton and Jones, and they had been thoroughly vanquished. Thanks to the hard-hitting blows delivered by Doubleday's First Division, First Corps, and especially the hard-fighting westerners of the Iron Brigade, General McClellan was now presented with a golden tactical opportunity to reap the most decisive success of the war. Stonewall Jackson's battered left and center was in a state of complete collapse by this time.

All across the front along Lee's left, Jackson's defeated Rebels continued to fall back in large numbers, with a wide gap torn in their line by the "Black Hats" of the Iron Brigade and other relentless attackers. Presenting a hellish scene, hundreds of Jackson's men were now lying dead and wounded across the field. With the vicious fighting consuming and spitting out whole Rebel brigades and divisions, Lawton frantically requested support before it was too late, as the vicious fighting increased the already staggering casualty rate.

After Lawton's and Jones's Divisions were hurled back by Hooker's overpowering onslaught, consequently, the call finally went out to General Hood before it was too late. An excited aide-de-camp from Lawton, who was now wounded and out of action, requested the much-needed support from Hood, who had earlier promised Lee to reinforce Lawton with his crack division if he suddenly found himself in trouble. And now Lawton and other battle-dazed commanders on Lee's collapsed left were indeed in very serious trouble, facing their greatest crisis.

As Lee had fully anticipated, the thirty-one-year-old Hood was eager to confront the surging Yankee tide. This young division commander was determined to make good on his promise to Bobby Lee. The army's elite fighting men were already "mad as hornets" because the Yankees had interrupted their breakfast—still another reason to unleash "one of the most legendary attacks of the war." As fate would have it at this time and place, the Texas Brigade was now presented the supreme challenge of saving Lee's Army before its left was completely turned and unparalleled disaster resulted.[79]

With the sudden order to prepare to advance from the West Woods behind the Dunker Church, the Texans immediately fixed bayonets in the early morning light. They prepared for their supreme test, knowing that the day's greatest crisis was now at hand. However, Color Sergeant George A. Branard did not take the colors of the First Texas out of the case as usual. Recently appointed Color Sergeant David B. Bronaugh, a former merchant and originally a member of Company A (Marion Rifles), unfurled the regimental colors. A bachelor who was not worried about leaving a widow and orphans behind to mourn his loss, the never-say-die Bronaugh was a worthy replacement for Branard. A former saloonkeeper from the gulf port of Galveston, Corporal John Hanson of Company L (Lone Star Rifles) prepared to carry the prized regimental banner at the forefront. Twenty years old, he had been promoted to corporal only in April 1862. Like the Virginia-born Bronaugh, Hanson was destined to be cut down on this awful Wednesday morning, with wounds to both legs and his arm.

Not only during the push north during the Second Manassas Campaign but also in the march to a rendezvous with destiny at Antietam, Branard had trudged barefoot mile after mile like many of his comrades. In total, the Texas soldiers had marched about 250 miles to reach the pristine lands drained by Antietam Creek. The hard, mechanized roads of Maryland had wreaked havoc on the color sergeant's bare feet. Branard's feet were in such bad condition (cut and bloody) that Lieutenant Colonel Work had ordered him to remain behind at the field hospital. Color Sergeant Branard was essentially disabled by this time. At least eight (and perhaps as many as thirteen) First Texas color bearers were about to be killed and wounded in Antietam's raging storm. Branard's bloody feet might well have saved his life, sparing him from an unkind fate.[80]

In the West Woods behind the Dunker Church, some Texas soldiers silently said prayers that they had learned long ago in rough-hewn log cabin chapels on the frontier wilderness, making sure that well-worn pocket Bibles were placed next to their breasts for spiritual and physical protection. Other men threw away playing cards with the certainty of hard fighting imminent. In the words of Corporal Hanks regarding the Texans' mood on the eve of once again meeting the boys in blue: "We would make vows that if we were spared [in battle then] we would be more Christian.…The boys would throw away their old greasy packs of cards…not wishing to be killed with them in their possession."[81]

On this terrible field of strife north of the Potomac, where Confederate dreams were to have come true, Corporal Hanks never forgot the dramatic moment when "[t]he command rings out loud and clear, 'Load and cap your pieces, men. Hold them well up.' The jingle of the hundreds of iron ramrods up and down the line denotes that something horrible is soon to take place. Besides every old soldier knows from experience what is in store for him."[82]

In a hurry, all extra gear, especially cumbersome blanket rolls wrapped around shoulders, was stripped off by men who now benefitted from the shelter of the trees of the West Woods. This excess weight, sure to have impeded the swiftness of the upcoming attack, was laid in piles by Texans making last-minute preparations for undertaking their greatest challenge. The First Texas men were eager to confront the victorious Federals, who seemingly could not be stopped this morning, because they had a lofty reputation to uphold. Here and now, to these men, this was not a disastrous situation but a rare opportunity—the Texans now knew that they had been called on in an unprecedented situation to literally save the day for Lee and the Army of Northern Virginia.

Consequently, these Lone Star State veterans realized that they needed to go into action with firm resolve and with as little weight as possible, as when battling Indians, especially the Comanches, who had long raided isolated frontier settlements of Texas. During this great showdown to determine that fate of America, the Texans' challenge was to somehow restore Lee's virtually nonexistent left, as the Army of Northern Virginia's life was now threatened as never before.

Some young frontiersmen and yeomen farmers stripped off gray and butternut jackets with brass Texas buttons, distinguished by a Lone Star design, and prepared to go into battle in homespun cotton shirts that had been made by mothers or wives. From the lessons of the frontier experience as hunters and farmers, these Texans, including some Texas Revolution veterans, realized that the high 70 percent humidity not long after 7:00 a.m., when the glowing red sun lay just above South Mountain on the eastern horizon, meant another scorching summer day. Fortunately for the Army of Northern Virginia, the morale and esprit de corps in the Texas Brigade's ranks could not have been higher. Just before embarking on their most important charge of the war, perhaps some Texas boys sang or hummed the brigade's unofficial anthem and popular Lone Star State song "The Yellow Rose of Texas."

Then, with a proper discipline and order seldom demonstrated by them on the parade ground before high-ranking officers, including even General Lee, the Texas Rebels advanced in a nearly perfect line. On the double, they pushed east through the dark shadows of the West Woods to gain the strategic Hagerstown Pike. With a red sun rising higher into a clear sky of still another Indian Summer day, the ragged Texans then turned north up the turnpike on the double with a clanging of gear and long-stride gait.

Like a flood raging over the broad cotton fields of the lower Brazos just before it entered the Gulf of Mexico in a rainy April, the Texans then shifted right off the road to pour through the gap (through which Law's Alabama, North Carolina, and Mississippi troops had just passed) in the high-rail fence in front, or just north, of the Dunker Church. At this point, east of the Hagerstown Pike, the badly wounded General Lawton was borne rearward on a litter, as if offering a grim warning to the Lone Star State men about the Texas Brigade's tragic fate in the upcoming showdown in the Miller Cornfield.

Once they had moved beyond the rail fence, which presented only a momentary obstacle to slow the advance east, Colonel Wofford then hurriedly formed his veteran brigade of Texas, Georgia and South Carolina soldiers in a lengthy battle line in the open clover fields across from the Dunker Church and just north of the Smoketown Road. Here, Lieutenant Colonel Work quickly aligned his troops of the First Texas (the brigade's finest combat unit) in the Texas Brigade's center.

For the first time in the war, the Texas Rebels were about to meet a good many troops who were every bit as tough and hard-fighting as themselves—the Iron Brigade—a guarantee for the most nightmarish clash of arms on America's bloodiest day. This crack Union brigade had earned its complimentary sobriquet with its combat prowess, and it was well-deserved. As a strange fate and destiny would have it, the greatest crisis in the Army of Northern Virginia's lifetime set the stage for one of the most important confrontations of the Civil War: the Texas Brigade versus the Iron Brigade.

With fixed bayonets, meanwhile, the Iron Brigade soldiers continued to surge rapidly south less than two hundred yards from their vital objective: the high ground of the Dunker Church. As Hood had carefully molded the Texas Brigade into an elite fighting machine for just such a challenge, so these western men were also forged into a hard-hitting command by the old regular General John Gibbon. Made formidable by high-quality leadership, intense training, West Point–like discipline, and a superior esprit de corps, the Iron Brigade was Gibbon's pride and joy. Now north of Sharpsburg, he was in the process of having one of his finest days.

This hard-fighting command had been known simply as the "Black Hat Brigade" before overrunning the tenacious defenders of Turner's Gap at South Mountain only three days before. Here, the men had been bestowed with their prized Iron Brigade sobriquet by General "Fighting Joe" Hooker. These tough fighting men consisted of the "best blood of Wisconsin and Indiana," just like the Texans represented the best and brightest of the Lone Star State. The Sixth Wisconsin contained companies like the Prairie du Chein Volunteers, the Sauk County Riflemen, the La Crosse Light Guards, the Buffalo County Rifles, the Grant County Grays and the Beloit Star Rifles. One Sixth Wisconsin company (H) consisted of Germans and another of Irish (D) soldiers, whose members were known for the Celtic-Gaelic spunkiness, sense of humor amid adversity, and fighting spirit in crisis situations.

Much like the Texans, these rugged westerners in blue were self-reliant and resourceful. To more refined easterners unfamiliar with distinctive western cultural and ways, the men of the Iron Brigade were described as "rough, vulgar blackguards." However, such rough-hewn qualities of these crack westerners were exactly what were needed to deliver a fatal blow to the reeling Army of Northern Virginia. Like their .58-caliber Springfield rifled muskets, the Iron Brigade soldiers embraced their distinctive regional identity with pride. This distinctiveness challenged these hardy fighting men from the Old Northwest to continue to demonstrate their sterling western qualities by outfighting their eastern comrades in blue—just like the Texans were now equally determined to outfight Virginians (especially the famed Stonewall Brigade, which consisted of easterners in their western eyes) and everyone else on either side for that matter. Ironically, like the Texans, the Iron Brigade's men were determined to demonstrate their valor not only to the rest of the army but also to the people from their faraway homeland.

The Iron Brigade's ranks included many young men and boys of Scandinavian and Norwegian descent, representing the West's cultural and ethnic diversity. More than 40 percent of the Iron Brigade consisted of Irish, Scandinavian, German and English soldiers. These ethnic soldiers carried the old language, value systems and cultural folkways of their ancient homelands now toward Dunker Church. Many Norwegians in blue were motivated by their own distinct cultural heritage of "the honorable name of Norsemen," fighting as fiercely as the legendary Vikings, whose raids had long terrorized Europe's western coast, including Ireland. These Norse, German and Irish soldiers were about to meet the equally determined Anglo-Celtic soldiers, of mostly Scotch-Irish ancestry, from the Texas frontier, bayou country and prairies in a dramatic showdown, when everything was at stake.[83]

Clearly, the Texas Brigade men faced an unprecedented challenge on this day of destiny. After all, the Iron Brigade had already gotten the best of the famed Stonewall Brigade that morning, which was no small accomplishment. On this bloodiest Wednesday in American history, Gibbon's westerners were most responsible for having mauled the veteran units of the collapsed Confederate left. Although the recent clash at Brawner's Farm had been the Iron Brigade's first battle in which it had lost more than seven hundred men in the murderous slugfest, these men had demonstrated a remarkable resiliency in having whipped the famous Stonewall Brigade.

One stunned Stonewall Brigade soldier described the embarrassing defeat: "The old Stonewall Brigade suffered....Oh, how we suffered" in the vicious fighting north of Sharpsburg. However, this bloody meeting between the Iron Brigade and the Stonewall Brigade had been less important than the upcoming showdown between the Iron Brigade and Texas Brigade, because much more was now at stake.[84]

In a climactic confrontation in which America held its breath, the fate of Lee's left and the entire battle was about to be largely decided by one of the two best combat brigades of their respective armies—the Texas Brigade or the Iron Brigade—during the key turning point of the most decisive engagement of the eastern theater to date. A strange destiny had seemingly brought these young men and boys more than one thousand miles from the westernmost part of the South to face fellow westerners from the Northwest in an obscure thirty-acre cornfield of a humble farmer named Miller on the war's bloodiest day.

Chapter 3

Saving the Day at Antietam

Quite simply, the overall tactical situation could not have been more critical on Lee's left, where a wide gap had been ripped into the Confederate line. Now thousands of Union troops were pouring through it with victory cheers by the time the Texas Brigade arrived on the field east of the Hagerstown Turnpike. Brigadier General John Bell Hood, mounted on his favorite war horse, surveyed the most disturbing crisis situation that he had ever seen, while the wounded General Lawton was carried rearward. Lee's hardest-hitting division commander described when the Texas Brigade's fast-moving troops reached Lawton's body-strewn sector below the Miller Cornfield: "The only Confederate troops, left on that part of the field, were some forty men who had rallied round the gallant H[ar]ry Hays [but his band of Louisiana Tiger] soldiers had expended all of their ammunition" in firing at too many advancing Yankees to count.[85]

But this tactical situation was actually even graver than explained by Hood. Commanding what little was left of Lee's collapsed left, Jackson was stunned by the unbelievable amount of destruction that had been so swiftly administered on Lee's northern flank, which had been shattered beyond all repair: "More than half of the brigades of Lawton and Hays were either killed or wounded, and more than a third to Trimble's, and all the regimental commanders in those brigades, except two, were killed or wounded. Thinned in the ranks, and exhausted of their ammunition, Jackson's Division and the brigades of Lawton, Trimble and Hays retired to the rear, and Hood...again took position from which he had been before relieved."[86]

Indeed, at this time, the Confederate left was virtually nonexistent, and the day apparently had already been lost to the Army of Northern Virginia. In a dramatic Union breakthrough of Lee's left, the massed strength of Hooker's First Corps now seemed primed to achieve its principal objective of overrunning the all-important high ground around the Dunker Church. Rapidly advancing Union troops were now less than two hundred yards from this key strategic objective. If successful, then the Federals would completely roll up Lee's left flank and march south down the Hagerstown Pike along the slight ridge that led into Sharpsburg's northern end to gain the Confederate army's rear, ensuring the ever-vulnerable army's systematic destruction just north of the Potomac. Like his men, General Hooker knew precisely what was at stake this morning, because this ever-escalating battle would "decide the fate of the Republic."[87]

Indeed, by this time, Stonewall "Jackson's entire line [on the left] between the turnpike and Smoketown Road in the pasture" was simply no more—two divisions had been destroyed. In record time, successive Confederate lines had been thoroughly shattered on both sides of the road, collapsing like a deflated balloon. On Lee's left, consequently, there was no organized front after thousands of Rebels were killed, wounded, captured or simply swept off the field by "Fighting Joe" Hooker's First Corps. On the shattered left, which had only recently anchored Lee's entire battle line north of Sharpsburg, a full two-thirds of a brigade, under Colonel Grigsby—who had been the Stonewall Brigade's commander at the day's beginning and now led what little remained of the mauled division—was either killed, wounded, captured or missing.

A large percentage of Lawton's and Hays's troops simply had been swept away or slaughtered by this time. Having never before met their match on any battlefield, Hays and his Louisiana Tigers had been forced to retire to escape certain annihilation. Lawton's Georgia Brigade had simply melted away under the relentless pounding. More than a third of Trimble's North Carolina, Alabama and Georgia Brigade were killed or wounded, and this shattered Old Dominion unit withdrew to escape destruction.

Ensuring an even greater crisis situation beyond the high attrition in the enlisted ranks, the top Confederate leadership on Lee's left also had been cut to pieces. General Lawton and Colonel Walker, the latter of whom commanded Trimble's Alabama, Georgia and North Carolina Brigade and was known for his hot Celtic temper, were wounded, and

Colonel Douglas, who commanded Lawton's Georgia Brigade, was killed. As mentioned, General Jones had been stunned by the concussion of an exploding shell. Brunswick County, Virginia–born General Starke, a former stagecoach operator who had once served on Lee's staff, had been shot off his horse when hit by three bullets. He suffered the fate of his son, who had been recently killed in battle, completing the tragedy of one Virginia family.

Quite simply, never before in the Army of Northern Virginia's history had so many high-ranking officers been knocked out of action than on Lee's decimated left. And now thousands of surviving Rebels were streaming rearward down both sides of the Hagerstown Turnpike during an unprecedented disaster. The end seemed very near and inevitable for Lee's Army, with its back to the Potomac River. The river now blocked the army's escape route back to Virginia at this crucial moment in the fast-diminishing life of what had been the Confederacy's most successful army.

To the right, or south, the thin lines of General Daniel H. Hill's overextended division in the center could provide no timely support or reinforcements to what little remained of the army's mauled left. All the while, the battered survivors of Lawton's, Hays's and Trimble's Brigades steadily retired from the field of carnage, after suffering unprecedented losses. Against the overpowering odds and in total disbelief about how quickly his command of experienced troops had been virtually annihilated, General Jackson had seen his prized command smashed to pieces right before his eyes. Stonewall Jackson was appalled by the slaughter.

Jackson's once magnificent command was either destroyed or fast disappearing from the gory field before the raging blue tide that proved unstoppable. It now appeared that the inglorious end of Lee's Army and its overly ambitious invasion of the North had come on this bloody Wednesday morning. Decisive victory was now at long last in the grasp of McClellan, who now seemed all but destined for the White House as the new Democratic president in the future. With fewer than two thousand men of his small division of only two brigades now ready for action, only one Southern commander was left in an advanced position on the field north of Sharpsburg to make the desperate attempt to turn the tide of battle before it was too late. As never before, "Hood was needed to save Lee's left."[88]

Indeed, the extent of the crisis on Lee's left at this time could hardly have been greater: "In a time amazingly brief, the enemy had cut a gap on either side of the Hagerstown road. Every Confederate Brigade that had occupied the ground from [Brigadier General Jubal] Early's right to D.H. Hill's left had been swept aside [and now] No organized force of more than a few score men remained to confront the enemy, [who were] still pressing on, now were close to the Dunker Church" and decisive victory.[89] One Union soldier emphasized how for the first time in this war "'Stonewall Jackson' has found his match."[90]

Confronted with a chilling prospect, General Hood explained the no-win tactical situation that he now faced: "Not far distant in our front were drawn up, in close array, heavy columns of Federal infantry; not less than two corps [including the First Corps and eventually the advance elements of the Twelfth Corps] were in sight to oppose my small command, numbering, approximately, two thousand effectives."[91]

As mentioned, after pouring out of the West Woods and passing through a gap in the fence along the pike at the Dunker Church and pushing into the open fields on the Hagerstown Pike's east, Hood's veterans braced for the fast-approaching blue tide. However, and almost incredibly under the circumstances, Hood still felt confident despite the seemingly unwinnable situation that now stared his diminutive command squarely in the face. Here, at this crucial moment, Hood rose to the challenge in splendid fashion. The native Kentuckian wrote how he felt encouraged "with the trusty Law on my right, in the edge of the wood, and the gallant Colonel Wofford in command of the Texas Brigade on the left, near the pike." In the sprawling clover field lying just below, or south, of the Miller Cornfield, the Fifth Texas now stood next to Law's left, with the Fourth Texas, the First Texas, the Eighteenth Georgia and the Hampton Legion extended to the left and toward the dusty pike, respectively.[92]

From the beginning, in gaining their advanced position before the massive Union onslaught steamrolling through the fields of late summer, the Texans were astounded by what they saw around them on this hellish battlefield: the bodies of hundreds of Lawton's Georgians and men from other defeated Confederate units lying in sickening clumps, while the vanquished survivors streamed rearward in a wild flight that no one could stop. There was no Confederate battle line before them, like the Texans had expected to see. Meanwhile, the rows of Federal artillery, possessing the advantage of being more powerful and longer range than the Confederate artillery, pounded Hood's Division during Antietam's "artillery hell," as the battlefield's openness ensured a lethal accuracy.

Positioned in the clover field, Private James M. Polk, Company I (Navarro Rifles), Fourth Texas, who had survived a wound during the Texans' assault at Gaines's Mill, described the intense cannonade: "The air was full of shot and shell and we were in an open field, with no protection and it seemed impossible for a rat to live in such a place [and] the dead and dying were in every direction" on the open ground. Enfilade fire streaming west from rifled Union artillery (unmatched by the smoothbore Confederate guns) was directed at the high ground east of the Antietam to punish the vulnerable right flank of Hood's Division.

From west to east, Hood's battle line of gray and butternut now stretched from the Hagerstown Turnpike, through the clover field south of the cornfield and to the East Woods, where his right flank was anchored—a thin formation of two brigades facing an advancing torrent of victorious bluecoats rapidly descending from the north. Lawton's Georgia; Trimble's Alabama, Georgia and North Carolina; and Hays's Louisiana Brigades of Tigers had been swept from the field. Smashed by Hooker's repeated blows, these seasoned troops had been destroyed or cast aside. To the astonishment of the Texas veterans, what little was left of these decimated units continued to retire, moving off the field in defeat after the merciless pounding. With fixed bayonets, the Lone Star State men now faced the raging flood of bluecoat attackers largely on their own.

Quite unlike in any previous engagement, the Southern officer corps—so effective in having orchestrated past successes on Virginia soil—in this sector was now practically nonexistent after the thorough decimation of so many units. The glaring absence of decimated Confederate leadership now placed the Texas Brigade's common soldiers in a desperate position to compensate for these grievous losses and fill the void on the left, when the Army of Northern Virginia faced its greatest crisis.

Clearly, Stonewall Jackson had suffered his most crushing defeat, and it had left him astounded. He now correctly feared for the Army of Northern Virginia's very existence. In Jackson's words, recording the extent of the unprecedented disaster on the collapsed Confederate left, "More than half of the brigades of Lawton and Hays were either killed or wounded, and more than a third of Trimble's [now] were killed or wounded." Indeed, more than one thousand of Lawton's, Hay's and Trimble's men had been killed or wounded. "Every Confederate brigade from Early's right to Harvey Hill's left ha[d] seen combat and been smashed," leading to the greatest crisis faced by General Lee on any battlefield.[93]

Indeed, the sheer magnitude of the emergency situation could not have been greater by this time, after Hooker's First Corps had "struck furiously [to leave] A great gap [that had been] was torn in the Confederate flank between Early's brigade, supporting the cavalry on the extreme left, and D.H. Hill's line on the centre [while the victors were] streaming down the Hagerstown road and through the West Wood, close to the dominating ground of the Dunker Church....[T]his was a threat of immediate disaster."[94] Hood was staggered by this shocking realization, which seem to herald the army's demise. He estimated that his small division now faced "the overwhelming odds of over ten to one against us" in one of the war's most one-sided confrontations.[95]

Veterans like Captain Samuel A. Willson, now commanding Company F (Woodville Rifles, which had been organized by Work), First Texas, were astounded by the tremendous odds now arrayed against the Texans. Willson had been born at the small community of St. Augustine, Texas, in the year the Texas Revolution erupted (early October 1835) to alter the destinies of three republics: Texas, Mexico and the United States. Admitted to the bar in 1852, and thanks to a special legislative act that allowed him to practice law before reaching the age of twenty-one, Captain Willson, a former district attorney who had represented the Texas Secession Convention in 1861, saw little, if any, chances for success at this time.[96]

In such a crisis situation, history-minded Texans in the ranks thought back to the spirited defense of the Alamo. Drawing moral strength from the historical example of the "Cradle of Texas Liberty," they recalled how a relative handful of Texians (along with some Tejanos, fighting men recently from the United States and Irish immigrants) were overwhelmed in the early morning of March 6, 1836, by General Antonio López de Santa Anna's *soldados*. Hood's Texas soldiers had been raised on stories about the Alamo's South Carolina–born commander, Lieutenant Colonel William Barret Travis, who had gone down fighting on the north wall. From the faraway Lone Star State, the young men and boys (mostly of Anglo-Celtic descent like most of the Alamo's defenders) now aligned in the clover field below the Miller Cornfield must have wondered if the Texas Brigade was about to meet a comparable tragic fate of annihilation against such formidable odds.

Almost as daunting as the great odds that the Texans faced in confronting the onslaught of Hooker's First Corps was the importance of the overall tactical situation in which they now found themselves. The severe crisis that confronted Hood's Division (Wofford's Texas Brigade and Law's Brigade) was now the turning point of this epic battle, when everything was at stake—the destinies of not only two armies but also two republics. Whichever side gained permanent control of the crucial high ground of Antietam's suddenly strategic plateau, on which the Hagerstown Pike ran north–south around the little Dunker Church, would win the war's most important battle to date.

To exploit their already significant tactical gains, the victorious units of Hooker's First Corps continued to push relentlessly south down both sides of the Hagerstown Road, with colorful United States and regimental banners leading the way toward Hood's diminutive division aligned across the clover field of green. While their bayonets sparkled in the September sunshine, thousands of victorious Federals swung across the fields and south on both sides of the pike with the determination to overrun the high ground to ensure the Army of Northern Virginia's early death. If "Little Mac" McClellan's troops could secure the elevated perch of the commanding plateau at the Dunker Church, then the seemingly endless blue legions would win the day.

Then, with so many front-line Rebel units smashed and cleared away from both sides of the road as far as the eye could see, the way was now wide open for the Union juggernaut to proceed south only a short distance down the Hagerstown Pike to capture Sharpsburg and cut the road (by which Hill's Division of troops now advanced from Harpers Ferry in a race to reach the battlefield in time) leading south across the Potomac and to Virginia. The capture of Sharpsburg would guarantee that Lee's Army would be cut off from an escape route south and back across the Potomac—a fatal combination that all but guaranteed the Army of Northern Virginia's destruction.

With decisive victory in sight, the elite Iron Brigade regiments pushed rapidly south along both sides of the Hagerstown Pike toward the high ground around the Dunker Church, long before the possible arrival of reinforcements from Lee's center to bolster the collapsed left. Lying before the Federal advance were the shattered remains of Confederate units and piles of dead and wounded Rebels: a sight that fueled the elation of the victorious Yankees. The golden road to Richmond was about to be laid bare once the Yankees captured the high ground around the Dunker Church and then Sharpsburg to gain Lee's rear to deliver a death stroke.

Indeed, with the day's supreme crisis at hand on this nightmarish morning, only one force now stood between the war's most decisive Union success and the complete turning of Lee's left flank: the army's last remaining strategic reserves positioned on Lee's collapsed left. This band of veteran troops consisted only of two undersized brigades of Hood's Division. From the beginning, Lee had made his audacious decision to take a risky defensive stand against the odds in the hope of exploiting any available tactical weakness by launching a counterattack that might reap a decisive victory to reverse the war's course and gain foreign recognition from both England and France, while also bestowing strength to the North's peace party.

Quite simply, because he had wisely kept his ace in the hole (the elite Texas Brigade) in his last possible hand to play, this was now Lee's final opportunity to decisively alter the war's fortunes. The placement of a strategic reserve—now at this advanced point in the clover field just south of the cornfield—and the careful choice of troops to act as Lee's strategic reserve were two of the best tactical decisions made at Antietam. Indeed, if any troops could save the day, it was the army's best fighters, the veterans of the Texas Brigade. In consequence, Lee had earlier ordered the Texas Brigade and Hood's Division north from Major General Longstreet's First Corps, which held Lee's center and right, to reinforce his left as a strategic reserve in timely fashion.

Combined with his tactical brilliance, the concept of a strategic reserve had been one reason for Napoleon Bonaparte's conquest of one European monarchy after another to create an empire second only to the Roman Empire. Napoleon explained how often "[t]he fate of a battle is the result of a single instant [when] the smallest reserve accomplishes victory"—this instant had now come at Antietam. By employing his strategic reserve at the right time and place, the native Corsican had often reaped success because of the superior performance of his elite Imperial Guard ("Old Guard") during key battlefield situations to save the day.

For Southern fortunes, the threadbare Texas soldiers of Lee's "Grenadier Guard," or "Old Guard," were now in the exactly right place at the right time to emulate the legendary role of Napoleon's elite "Old Guard." At this time, the Texans could have readily identified with the Napoleonic slogan that the Old Guard dies but never surrenders. Most importantly, these Lone Star State soldiers (ironically, who appeared to be the antithesis of Napoleon's splendidly uniformed Imperial Guard) had been saved by General Lee for just such an urgent tactical role of supreme importance: to reverse the tide and save the day at a key political moment in American history, just when the British government was beginning to seriously consider intervention in America's fratricidal war, after Lee crossed the Potomac River with grand visions for success.

Ironically, although Lee's finest combat troops were now in position at exactly the right place just below the Miller Cornfield at exactly the right time, the Texans were so few in number as to be hardly classified as a strategic reserve proper. Private James M. Polk, Fourth Texas, explained how the odds had to be at least four to one. However, closer to the truth, General Hood was convinced that he faced odds of more than ten to one. Indeed, other Texas Brigade units were likewise decimated by this time. Unfortunately for the South Carolina soldiers, the Hampton Legion contained only seventy-five men.

At this crucial moment in the face of the onslaught of Hooker's First Corps and almost by any measure, these young Texas soldiers hardly appeared capable of reversing the tide. Twenty-three-year-old Captain George T. Todd, a Virginia-born lawyer from Jefferson, Texas, now led the men of the Marion Rifles of Company A (Henderson Rifles), First Texas. Educated at the Hampton Academy at Hampton, Virginia, near the southern end of the Virginia Peninsula, and at the University of Virginia, he wrote how at this time "we were nearly barefooted and worn out with marching and skirmishing." In addition, the Texans were famished, dust-covered and disease-ridden to an unprecedented degree after the lengthy march north. They now looked more like emaciated men in need of an assignment in the rear or even immediate hospital care than the Confederacy's finest combat troops, who possessed a reputation of rising to any battlefield challenge.

All the while, these Texans knew that Hooker's victorious troops were "equipped with everything [they] could wish," lamented Corporal Orlando Thacker Hanks, of the Texas Invincible of Company K (Texas Invincibles), First Texas. As Hood's crack soldiers were Lee's last remaining reserves on a morning of unprecedented disaster, they would somehow have to do the impossible by attempting to snatch victory from the jaws of defeat, like what General Sam Houston and his ad hoc force of Texians and United States volunteers had accomplished against Santa Anna's advance force with a daring afternoon attack that caught the generalissimo by surprise and won decisive victory at San Jacinto on April 21, 1836.[97]

The First Texas soldiers were confident that they could accomplish what all other Rebel troops had been unable to achieve this morning against the odds. In a letter to their parents, officer-brothers Robert "Billy" Hugh Gaston and William Henry Gaston, well-educated Smith County, Texas siblings in Company H (Texas Guards), First Texas, revealed the determination that was now reflected throughout the ranks: "I don't think you all ought to be at all dispirited because we have [gone] off [to war]. For I think that it will be a great deal better for us to toil through a long war or even to die on the battlefield than to stay at home [and] not contend for their rights."[98]

By this time, not long after 7:00 a.m., this mid-September morning in western Maryland was growing not only hotter but also deadlier by the minute, "[f]or the Federals the day was almost won." With a blue wedge driven deeper down both sides of the Hagerstown Road and with large numbers of the advancing Yankees "within yards of the Dunker church and the vital high ground," the challenge could not have been greater or the stakes higher for the Texas Brigade than at this critical moment. One Texas Brigade member was awed by the unnerving sight before him: "[I]t seemed that the whole world was in arms against us. A grander sight I never witnessed. Their new, bright flags were waving in every direction [and] They had [seemingly all] massed in our front."[99]

Now was the crucial moment for the Texas Brigade to unleash one of the most desperate offensive efforts of the war in a long-shot bid to plug the gaping hole in Lee's collapsed line. To stem the surging blue tide, Stonewall Jackson's only hope was now to unleash his last reserves—fewer than two thousand troops of Hood's small division. Hood's two brigades somehow how to repel three strong divisions of the advancing First Corps and the lead elements of the Twelfth Corps, in support, at any cost.

Ironically, the Texans had been ordered "to the front, only to find that there was no front" on Lee's collapsed left, because it had been so thoroughly smashed by repeated sledgehammer blows. The fewer than two thousand soldiers of Hood's Division represented the usual strength of an Army of Northern Virginia brigade. To cover such a wide front of open ground in this vital sector, the battle line of Hood's Division was exceedingly thin, stretching hundreds of yards across the clover field from the body-strewn Hagerstown Turnpike to the East Woods.

Even the final deployment of Hood's troops to move into an excellent final position for the opportunity to strike back had cost precious time. As noted, after having surged out of the West Woods and raced east in a column of fours past the Dunker Church atop the plateau, Law's troops (followed by the Texas Brigade) had then poured through a gap in the fence, a full six rails high, to reach the Smoketown Road, which spanned northeast to the southern edge of the East Woods. After marching up the road and then turning left into the clover field to deploy for battle, Law aligned his Alabama, Mississippi and North Carolina men in the pasture on the right (east) side of the Smoketown Road. These hasty deployments were made before the lengthy formations of the advancing troops of not only the Iron Brigade but also Colonels Phelps's, Coulter's and Lyle's Brigades—an unnerving sight with so few Rebels left standing firm on the field, now covered with dead and wounded Confederates, in this vital sector.

As mentioned, the Texas Brigade, on the other (west) side of the Smoketown Road but east of the Hagerstown Pike, also had to accomplish a good deal just to have moved into a suitable position to strike back. After pouring out of the West Woods behind the onrushing troops of Law's Brigade, the Texans had surged past the Dunker Church on the double. In serving in an honored position with the Texas Brigade's ranks, Lieutenant Colonel Work's First Texas held the center of the brigade's line. On Work's right stood the Fourth and Fifth Texas, respectively, from west to east across the clover field.

In this crucial situation, the eight small regiments and a single South Carolina legion of Hood's small division were at long last ready and about to attack, with Law's Brigade of Alabama, Mississippi and North Carolina troops on the right and the Texas Brigade on the left. These veteran regiments, four of Law's Brigade and the three Texas and one Georgia regiments, along with Hampton's South Carolina Legion, were all that remained of the right of Lee's collapsed left wing by this time.

The shocking sight that now presented itself before the First Texas soldiers was enough to take their breath away. Thousands of Federals surged south through the fields of summer, sensing total victory if they gained the high ground. Before the Texas Brigade's thinned ranks steadily advanced the troops of Doubleday's Division and the brigades of Colonel Phelps, as well as Generals Marsena Patrick and Gibbon, the old regular. Passing the bodies of hundreds of dead and wounded Rebels, these elated victors in blue now believed that the day was won.

So many regimental and United States flags were clumped together above the dense Union formations that the Texans knew that they were confronting great odds. Nevertheless, they were determined to do their best in a desperate bid to reverse the fortunes of war. However, the Texas Rebels could not be unleashed until the defeated throng of Rebels of what little was left of Lawton's shattered brigades cleared the front and departed the clover field. After the beaten Southerners streamed south and past the poised Texas Brigade ranks, it was finally time to launch the desperate bid turn the tide. General Hood made a typically bold decision to immediately attack in this seemingly no-win situation.

To the average Texas soldier, this situation seemed not unlike that at San Jacinto, when General Houston, mounted on his war horse Saracen, led his Texians forward in a headlong attack to catch an overconfident Santa Anna, who had not lost a battle on Texas soil, when it appeared that the dream of an independent Texas Republic already had been crushed. Symbolically, when on the verge of winning back Texas for Mexico, Santa Anna had long rejoiced in his nickname of the "Napoleon of the West." Now General McClellan, in his mid-thirties, was seemingly at long last about to verify his own misplaced moniker, the "Young Napoleon," after his failures during the Peninsula Campaign. On another warm afternoon of bright sunshine in April 1836, when the overall tactical situation was another case of "conquer or die," barely 850 of Houston's men had decisively turned the tide. And now on this bloody morning at Antietam, when the victorious Union formations stretched from west of the Hagerstown Road to the East Woods, a comparable number of Texas Rebels under arms were about to attack in another desperate bid to save the life of another infant republic.

With a wild Texas yell born of the faraway frontier and fixed steel bayonets reflecting the early morning sunlight, the Texans surged north from the clover field northeast of the Dunker Church. The Texas Rebels attacked with only the faint hope of restoring the collapsed Confederate left. They charged impossible odds with enthusiasm to meet the onslaught of thousands of Federals. General Hood never forgot how despite "the overwhelming odds [now] against us," his troops audaciously attacked the surging blue legions. With their beautiful Lone Star State flag leading the way north, Work encouraged his yelling First Texas soldiers, on the brigade's center, toward the sun-drenched cornfield in Antietam's most audacious offensive effort to save the day.

But to the Texas Rebels, despite the odds arrayed against them, this was the tactical opportunity to not only equal but also outperform their Texas Revolutionary heroes. For the Texas Brigade, the reversal of the day's fortunes called for first defeating the Iron Brigade. At this time, the Iron

Brigade's attack had already reached an advanced point of less than 200 yards from the Dunker Church, standing like white beacon on the edge of the West Woods. Still spearheading the First Corps's mighty assault, the Iron Brigade was now the foremost attacking unit, advancing only about 220 yards north of the Texas Brigade's left and slightly northwest of the First Texas. As if nothing in the world could stop them, the Iron Brigade soldiers continued to charge down the east side of the Hagerstown Road south of the cornfield.

All the while, the Iron Brigade attackers of the Sixth and Second Wisconsin, intoxicated by the "hysterical excitement" of success, blasted away at the advancing Texans. An awed Major Dawes, leading the Sixth Wisconsin, recalled the dramatic moment when the Texas Rebels attacked with the kind of spirit witnessed at the Alamo and San Jacinto: "We push on over the open fields halfway of the little church [but now] A long and steady line of Rebel Gray, unbroken by the fugitives who fly before us, comes sweeping down through the woods around the church" and charging north through the clover field.[100]

Now unleashed in Lee's last bid to save the day, the Texans continued to move swiftly onward on the double with fixed bayonets. They fired by files on the run, delivering punishment of their own. Meanwhile, the lithe and lean Texas Rebels ignored the carnage all around them, surging past the clumps of dead and wounded men from Lawton's and Jones's shattered divisions. To save the Army of Northern Virginia before it was too late, the cheering Texas Rebels pushed north through the exploding shells of Company B, Fourth United States Artillery. One of the army's best batteries, these disciplined regulars of Battery B unleashed an accurate fire that inflicted damage on the counterattacking Confederates. By any measure, these artillery regulars were tough and determined gunners, especially Sergeant Joseph Herzog, an expert artilleryman of German descent. To end his intense suffering when shot in the lower bowels, the Teutonic sergeant pulled out a revolver and put a bullet through his head.

Meanwhile, to the Texans' right, Law's Alabama, Mississippi and North Carolina troops advanced northeast, with the surging Texas Brigade to their left. With Hampton's South Carolina soldiers on the brigade's left pushing north and parallel to the pike, the Eighteenth Georgia on the left center, the First Texas in the center, the Fourth Texas on the right center and the Fifth Texas on the right, Wofford's Brigade surged onward with battle flag flying and the determination to reverse the day's fortunes.

But in their enthusiasm to strike a blow, the onrushing First Texas troops shortly became slightly out of alignment and veered too far eastward, passing to the left rear of Law's Brigade, which exchanged fire with Hartsuff's Massachusetts, New York and Pennsylvania men. Ironically, for the same reason, the same alignment problem had plagued the First Texas during its Second Manassas attack. Fortunately, this new dilemma was solved by the tactically astute Lieutenant Colonel Work, who made a swift tactical readjustment while on the move.

However, another tactical problem for Hood's counterattack suddenly developed that proved even more serious. While engaged in a close-range firefight with the "Black Hat" men of the Iron Brigade on the open ground south of the cornfield, Colonel Wofford ascertained that his two units on the left (the Hampton Legion and the Eighteenth Georgia, from west to east, or left to right) were now in danger of being outflanked on the left by Union troops positioned at the Hagerstown Road. This tactical situation compromised the potential success of Hood's desperate counterattack. After ascertaining the disadvantageous tactical situation, Hood took immediate action, ordering his troops to undertake a left oblique movement in order to advance farther west and along the Hagerstown Turnpike to counter this escalating threat. The advancing Georgia and South Carolina troops completed this difficult maneuver under fire without halting or losing their momentum: a fine testament to their superior soldierly qualities.[101]

According to Lieutenant Colonel Work, the Texans, Georgians and South Carolinians had advanced north on the double across the clover field only 150 to 200 yards when it was "discovered that the left flank of the brigade was exposed to attack."[102] The Texas Brigade troops were at risk of being outflanked and driven from the field if the advancing Federals could fully exploit their tactical advantage. But thanks to Hood's timely adjustments, the Georgians' and South Carolinians' swift change of front and the slashing attack of the Texas Brigade's left, the two Iron Brigade regiments east of the pike were greeted with a blistering fire that dropped many westerners in blue, while others continued to advance south below the cornfield.

Despite this tactical success, a more serious dilemma remained to be solved before Hood's counterattack had a true opportunity to turn the tide of battle. In tactical terms boding ill for success, the Texas Brigade was now split in two during its fast-moving advance. At this time, the South Carolina legion, Fourth Texas and the Georgia regiment on the left charged in a different direction than the First Texas (in the brigade's center), which surged straight ahead. With these two regiments on the left changing front and attacking farther west, the First Texas was advancing in the center and directly north toward the cornfield—the counterattack's original direction. In addition, attacking units on the Texas Brigade's right (on the left of what remained of Lawton's Georgia brigade) suddenly found themselves about to overlap the Georgians' left, after the First Texas's two sister regiments on the right advanced to gain Lawton's left rear.

To correct these tactical problems, which sapped the counterattack's strength and momentum, Colonel Wofford rode rapidly east to Work and his First Texas. Major William Henry Sellers, Hood's able adjutant and a Texas Revolutionary War veteran, was likewise on the scene in a desperate attempt to rectify the vexing situation. Major Sellers labored to sort out the tactical confusion to the First Texas's right before the Fifth Texas could overlap the left of Lawton's Brigade from behind. On the Texas Brigade's right, the troops of the Fourth Texas, which included companies like the Mustang Grays (Company F) and the Guadalupe Rangers (Company D), were ordered to lie down in the field, while the Fifth Texas was sent toward the East Woods to Law's right.

Knowing that a crisis was now at hand, Wofford ordered the First Texas to move rapidly by the left flank, going to the rescue. Not merely done to support the South Carolina soldiers of Hampton's Legion to the left, this adroit tactical maneuver was also a timely effort to maintain proper alignment during the attack in the face of the Iron Brigade's onslaught, as well as a plug for the ever-widening gap between the right of the Eighteenth Georgia and the First Texas's left.[103]

Work explained how "I was ordered to move by the left flank, following a corresponding move of the Eighteenth Georgia and Hampton's Legion upon my left."[104] Work's veterans of the "Ragged First" shifted smartly to the left with seemingly effortless ease, failing to slow their momentum. To bolster his left, Hood also ordered the Fourth Texas troops to double-quick from the First Texas's right to the left, or west.

All in all, this was a most timely tactical adjustment, as pressure from the Iron Brigade's right on the Texas Brigade's left flank at the Hagerstown Road had caused the First Texas to shift toward the left to meet a new threat. With gear clattering and a determination to succeed, Work continued to lead his soldiers, panting and sucking for air in the heat, west on the double. After his seasoned command, consisting of young soldiers in the prime of life, raced west to the left for about one hundred yards, Work directed his regiment to quickly realign its ranks. Here, in the body-covered clover field, the First Texas soldiers formed in two neat lines on the Eighteenth Georgia's right.

With probably no more than two hundred soldiers in the ranks after additional men were cut down by the hot fire of the Iron Brigade's soldiers, the thin First Texas battle line now only spanned a length of about 160 feet, from west to east and perpendicular to the Hagerstown Pike to the left, or west. Understanding the value of every minute in a key battlefield situation and with tactical problems in alignment finally corrected, Work then ordered the First Texas forward to attack in conjunction with the brigade's remainder. With a Texas yell that contained elements of the Rebel Yell combined with the Comanche war cry from the Southwest frontier more than one thousand miles away, Work's veterans sprang forward with fixed bayonets. The Texans again surged straight north toward the lengthy formations of the Iron Brigade, whose members continued to blast away as rapidly as possible. The flowing silk of the Lone Star State flag led the way before Work's onrushing ranks—an inspiring sight that had emboldened the Texans.[105]

Meanwhile, the four Iron Brigade regiments continued to push down both sides of the pike. East of the Hagerstown Road, the Badgers of the Sixth and Second Wisconsin attacked south through the clover field located below the cornfield, spearheading the assault of Doubleday's Division. These hard-fighting men basked in their Iron Brigade name, generated from General Hooker's compliment after overrunning General Daniel Harvey Hill's defensive position at Turner's Gap at South Mountain on September 14.

However, glory was now something that was out of date on the bloody morning of September 17. What was happening this morning was a surreal level of carnage and bloodletting heretofore unseen in the war. Even the loftiest reputation of the most revered unit, such as the Stonewall Brigade, could be quickly ruined during this escalating conflict that was resulting in an unparalleled amount of death and carnage.

Almost symbolically, the Iron Brigade was about to clash head-on with the Texas Brigade in a dramatic showdown when the stakes could not have been higher. The swirling contest north of Sharpsburg was boiling down to a bloody meeting between the elite troops of both armies to determine of their respective armies would prevail. That much-touted "Iron" nickname for the westerners in blue was about to be severely dented by the Texans' slashing counterattack, which packed the most punishing blow ever received by the Iron Brigade.

Without a moment to lose, the Texas Rebels unleashed another volley while surging north through the drifting smoke. This accurate volley, erupting from a previously unknown strategic reserve of veteran Texas Rebels, who had recently emerged from the West Woods, stunned the Iron Brigade soldiers. The Yankees were staggered by the close-range volley from the Texans' .577-caliber Enfield rifles. Some of the finest Iron Brigade officers (always the special target of Lone Star State marksmen) fell in the din.

Then, without halting to either reload or reform, Work's attackers, assisted by Hampton's South Carolina Legion, Fourth Texas and the Eighteenth Georgia, smashed into the Iron Brigade's Second and Sixth Wisconsin with a vengeance. The swiftly counterattacking Rebels hurled back the blue wedge that had been pushed deep down the Hagerstown Pike. Red-stained bodies of Badger State soldiers lay thick on the open ground, after having been cut down by the Texans' murderous fire.

With piercing yells, the Texans blunted the Sixth Wisconsin surge south just east of the Hagerstown Road and the Second Wisconsin, which advanced to the road's right, or east. Sensing a key tactical opportunity to turn the tide, the cheering Texans continued onward without halting, while firing on the run. With the Lone Star State flag waving out in front of the onrushing ranks to inspire everyone onward, the First Texas soldiers continued to surge north toward the cornfield and through the clover field. Thanks to their success in gaining so much ground thus far, the attacking Texas Brigade secured timely support on the left, where the Pelican State Tigers of Starke's Louisiana brigade, as well as veterans from other units, took heart at the sight of Hood's slashing counterattack. These Louisianans had gamely rallied to advance north on the turnpike's west side. Most importantly, the Texas Brigade's counterattack was not only gaining additional momentum in the sweeping charge northward, but also electrifying additional numbers of Southerners to rally and undertake the offensive with them.

The fire delivered by the First and Fourth Texans, Georgians, and South Carolina troops was devastating to the Iron Brigade attackers, who were reinforced by the Zouaves (or "Red Legs") of the Fourteenth Brooklyn Regiment, blunting their southward advance. Seemingly, every shot fired by the Texans found a bluecoat target. The tall black hats made the Iron Brigade's westerners seem taller than other Yankees, providing more visible targets to sharpshooting Texans.

Consequently, the close-range volleys from Hood's troops "staggered Hooker's advance" of the mighty First Corps for the first time that day. Westerners of the Union army's elite brigade fell in rows across the green clover, finding a final resting place far from home. Meanwhile, some Iron Brigade survivors fled north and into the cornfield's relative safety to escape the Texans' blistering fire. But a good many young westerners found tragic ends to their own dreams of decisive victory in a hail of Texas bullets. Four brave color bearers—always special targets fairly lusted after by Texans—of the Sixth Wisconsin were cut down in quick succession. Some of the most effective First Texas marksmen were former members of the regiment's special sharpshooter detachment, which had acted independently under Captain "Ike" Turner since the Peninsula Campaign.

The Texas Rebels' fire staggered the most deeply penetrating Union attack of the day. In relatively short order, the Texas Brigade stopped the assault of troops of Brigadier General Abner Doubleday's First Division (mostly New Yorkers of ten regiments, but also including the Iron Brigade), Hooker's Corps. Commanding the Sixth Wisconsin and carrying the Sixth's colors, Major Dawes was appalled by the slaughter. For the first time, these iron men had met their match in the unleashed Texan Rebels, who were going for broke this morning. All in all, this was a bloody lesson at the Texans' hands that these westerners never forgot.[106]

Continuing to unleash their shrill war whoop at the invigorating sight of the Iron Brigade soldiers turning tail and heading for the relative safety of the high stalks of the Miller Cornfield, Work's First Texas—along with the newly rejuvenated Georgia, Fourth Texas and South Carolina troops (thanks to the Texas Brigade's counterattack)—continued to surge toward the cornfield in pursuit. The Lone Star State attackers rushed ahead with their usual abandon, as if chasing white-tailed deer along the brownish-hued bayous and cane brakes in east Texas.

Sensing the reversing of the tide and the winning of an astounding success, the Texas Rebels loaded and fired as fast as they could while advancing briskly over the open ground. With the bluecoats on the run, these Lone Star State men realized that they could not halt to catch their breath, which risked losing the hard-earned momentum. Exploiting the initiative and hard-won tactical advantage, Work's men now knew that killing as many Yankees as possible meant saving the day. Such Darwinian realizations fueled the Texas Rebels ever onward with the determination to do or die.

Difficulty experienced by the Texans in aiming at targets in the thick clouds of smoke hugging the ground on this windless morning saved the lives of some Iron Brigade soldiers during their wild dash to reach the cornfield's cover. Lamenting how the reduced visibility negated the overall effectiveness of their legendary marksmanship, one Texas soldier described how "the smoke was so dense that the enemy could scarcely be seen to return his fire." In return, numbers of Iron Brigade soldiers gamely halted their flight north toward the green cornstalks to turn around and blast away at the fast-approaching Rebels.

While leading the way before the First Texas attackers, Color Sergeant John Hanson went down seriously wounded while carrying the colors and imploring everyone onward. But another color guard member, Private James M. Day, born in 1833, immediately picked up the fallen banner. Recently reduced from the rank of corporal for a relatively minor infraction, the young private, a member of Company M (Sumter Light Infantry, also known as the Silver Greys) from Trinity County, waved the colors to encourage the Texans onward.[107]

The Texas, South Carolina and Georgia soldiers, now functioning in harmony like a well-oiled machine and driven onward by the sweet scent of victory in the air, unleashed another concentrated volley. At close range, this next explosion of gunfire dropped additional Yankees, who never again saw their homes and families. More good fighting men of the Iron Brigade and Colonel Phelps's New York brigade went down in the clover field to rise no more. One horrified Iron Brigade soldier described the slaughter: "We got into a hornet's nest [and were] nearly cut to pieces."[108]

Clearly, the Texas Brigade troops were now in the process of doing the impossible, snatching an amazing victory from the jaws of defeat. Meanwhile, additional Federals turned and fled toward the cornfield to escape the Texans' hot fire. This was the first time in the Iron Brigade's history that these men had ever showed their backs to the enemy—a shocking development that seemed to mock their unit's hard-won sobriquet. Perhaps some bluecoats had heard of the cutting down of hundreds of ill-fated Fifth New York Zouaves at Second Manassas by these same Texas Rebels, or perhaps they even recognized the Texans' Lone Star State flag. If so, they might have realized that they now faced the most lethal killers in Lee's Army.

Leading the way in this remarkable reversal of the tide, Lieutenant Colonel Work encouraged his First Texas soldiers onward across the clover field and through the drifting smoke. Incredibly, "in ten minutes the fortune of the day seemed to have changed," wrote a stunned New Yorker, who never forgot how quickly the battle had been turned by the hard-charging Texans. Moisture in the air from the previous night combined with the firing of thousands of muskets to create thick clouds of white smoke that blanketed this hard-fought sector. Hugging the ground and obscuring the grotesque piles of bodies, a sulfurous haze hung limp on this early summery morning which was the last of so many men in blue and gray.

Meanwhile, additional Iron Brigade soldiers from Wisconsin and Indiana were systematically cut down by the deadly Texas marksmanship. When peering through the smoke in taking aim at targets at close range, the Lone Star State men demonstrated their superiority over the Iron Brigade in this respect.

Ironically, the Marion County men of Company D (Star Rifles), First Texas, had first marched off to war in the same type of black-felt Hardee hats (but in gray uniforms instead of blue) now worn by the boys of the so-called Black Hat Brigade. In the war's beginning, seven Oliver soldiers of Company D, First Texas, had adorned tall black hats that were little different than those now worn by the Iron Brigade men. Of these brothers and relatives of Company D, William Oliver was mortally wounded, and Henry Oliver died of disease.

Meanwhile, with the pursuing Texas Rebels close behind, the beaten Iron Brigade soldiers now on the run hardly seemed like elite troops compared to their fellow westerners in gray and butternut. While charging toward the sprawling field of high cornstalks, the First Texas soldiers continued to unleash their high-pitched war cry, piercing the air and unnerving some Yankees. They steadily pushed up the gradually sloping ground of the commanding plateau while biting off paper cartridges, loading and firing on the run. It seemed like a replay of the Texans' amazing success at Second Manassas all over again, when they had smashed through the Fifth New York Zouaves and killed so many of them. The Texans continued to keep up the momentum without halting to rest or realigning their ranks because of their determination to exploit the tactical advantage to the fullest with their opponents on the run. The Texas Brigade Rebels were intent not just on simply achieving a battlefield success but also on utterly destroying the enemy in a merciless style of warfare that characterized the harshness of the Texas border warfare with Mexico and Indian fighting that had spanned generations.

As never before, the Iron Brigade troops from Wisconsin and Indiana were pushed beyond the breaking point. Not even the repeated defensive stands of the surviving Iron Brigade's soldiers were enough to stop the relentless attackers. Meanwhile, these Yankees from the Midwest continued to occasionally stop in the field of clover, turning to fire back into the Texans' faces. However, such last-ditch resistance only caused more Federals to be killed by the onrushing Georgians, South Carolina men and First Texans, who concentrated their fire on those "black-hatted fellows," especially Second and Sixth Wisconsin officers and brave color bearers.

No contingent of Iron Brigade soldiers—not even the splendid fighting men of the Wisconsin Rifles (Company K) or Portage City Guards (Company G), of the Second Wisconsin, or the Montgomery Guards (Company D) or Buffalo County Rifles (Company H), of the Sixth Wisconsin—could stand firm against the Texans. Larger numbers of Hoosiers and Badgers were hit by the Texans' scorching fire, dropping like brightly colored leaves on a windy autumn day along the Sabine River.

A good many black hats, the sight of which had once spread fear among Southern troops, now lay scattered and stained with red beside their dead and wounded owners. This first meeting between the Texas Brigade and the Iron Brigade soldiers was an especially lethal one. In a rarity of this war—the bloody meeting of the three best combat brigades in the eastern theater (the Iron Brigade, the Stonewall Brigade and the Texas Brigade) in the same sector north of Sharpsburg—the threadbare Texans had accomplished more in tactical and destructive terms than their better-known elite counterparts, the Stonewall and Iron Brigades.

Unlike the Texas Rebels, other Confederates had feared the very sight of the Iron Brigade troops, knowing that those high-crowned hats meant the hardest fighting ahead. Meanwhile, the charging Texans were fueled to greater exertions to crush the Iron Brigade to demonstrate not only that they were the eastern theater's elite troops but also that they were worthy inheritors of the distinguished legacies of the Texas Revolution—dual motivations that fueled combat prowess on the morning of September 17. Had the Texans understood that the better-known Stonewall Brigade—long promoted by the three Richmond newspapers, especially the influential *Richmond Whig*, and made legendary by Stonewall Jackson's achievements—had already been defeated, this realization would have provided them with a powerful motivation to excel. After all, here was the golden opportunity to outshine the much-touted Virginians of the renowned Stonewall Brigade, which had been severely beaten by Hooker's Corps. And in thrashing the Iron Brigade, the Texans had performed in the splendid manner that almost everyone, including Stonewall Jackson, had expected of the men of the now-vanquished Stonewall Brigade. At last, the Texans' success in turning the tide demonstrated their combat superiority to the Stonewall and the Iron Brigades—no small accomplishment.

Most of all, by decimating the finest combat unit of the Army of the Potomac, outfighting the Stonewall Brigade, and saving the day on this morning, the Texans were now at center stage for winning what might be a decisive success for the Confederacy. In fact, this was now the long-awaited opportunity for the Lone Star State men to outperform even the Texian heroics at the Alamo and San Jacinto.

Meanwhile, Lieutenant Colonel Work continued to lead his screaming First Texas soldiers onward on the bloodiest morning of the Civil War. He described how the Texas Rebels pushed the Federals rearward and followed them north and ever-closer to the Miller Cornfield. The Lone Star State flag of the First Texas, now carried by Private John Hanson, flapped overhead. As on previous battlefields, the oversized banner of bright red, white and blue, distinguished by the large white star (which had first symbolized the Republic of Texas, established on March 2, 1836), served as an inspirational beacon to the onrushing soldiers. Waving through the palls of smoke, this colorful banner encouraged the Texas Rebels onward into the vortex of hell. One soldier was impressed by the First Texas men, who steadily advanced "in a rapid and gallant manner, pressing the enemy" for a considerable distance.[109]

But perhaps the best description of exactly what the Texas Brigade had accomplished was revealed by a young South Carolina private of Hampton's Legion. He wrote how "like a hurricane we swept over the land" of farmer Miller, driving the Yankees rearward. But most important, "the fortunes of the day" had changed, thanks to the Texas Brigade's sweeping attack that hurled back everything before it.[110]

At the First Texas's head and leading the way, Lieutenant Colonel Work understood the supreme importance of what the Texas Brigade was now accomplishing in pushing the Federals farther rearward: the reversing of the battle's course. Even more significant tactical gains were now possible, because the Texas Brigade had been unleashed. If Hood's Division successfully restored Lee's left and attacked farther north sufficiently to push all of the deep bulge of the Federal penetration back, then perhaps even the right flank of Hooker's First Corps might be turned and decisive victory might be won—if everything went right.[111]

Because Great Britain and France were looking for an opportunity to intervene if Lee won a decisive victory on Northern soil and bestow official recognition on the Confederacy ever since the Army of Northern Virginia's sparkling victory at Second Manassas, there now was more at stake than ever before. Prime Minister Lord Palmerston, England's head of state, had outlined the growing possibilities for official intervention on September 14, only three days before the climactic showdown at Antietam.

Most importantly for the Confederacy, if Southern victory were won at Antietam, England almost certainly would then officially recognize the infant Southern republic; then France would follow suit. The much-anticipated political scenario would lead to a negotiated peace and a successful Southern experiment in rebellion—if Lee could secure a decisive victory at Antietam, especially if the Army of the Potomac was destroyed. Clearly, much was at stake for America's future regarding the success or failure of Hood's fierce counterattack, because this was the decisive battle now waged in the most decisive theater of war in perhaps the most decisive year of the conflict: the high tide of Confederate offensive operations on multiple fronts, including the western theater, and fortunes.

At such a key moment, Lieutenant Colonel Work might have wondered at the strange destiny that had so abruptly interrupted his routine life as a Tyler County lawyer and brought him all the way from the Lone Star State to the eye of Antietam's storm. Now he and his First Texas were playing a leading role during the war's most decisive battle to date, and he would become famous across the Confederacy if the Texas Brigade and Hood's Division achieved a decisive victory.

Like Work, Major Matt Dale, from Palestine in Anderson County, was in the forefront of the slashing attack toward the Miller Cornfield. He encouraged the First Texas's right wing forward through the thick haze drifting over the battlefield. Behind Work and Dale, who made a highly effective leadership team this Wednesday morning, more than two hundred screaming First Texas attackers continued to swarm north with flags waving overhead. Although the First Texas primarily fought the Second Wisconsin in front, Work's soldiers also severely punished the Sixth Wisconsin's left with their scorching fire—a bloody showdown between premier fighting men from the Confederacy's most southwestern region and veteran bluecoats. The Texans' onslaught and scorching fire were too hot for a good many reeling Wisconsin soldiers, who were now in a full flight that astounded Major Dawes.

Nothing could stop the Texans' attack at Gaines's Mill and Second Manassas, and now this desperate offensive effort against the odds was no different. Meanwhile, confidence among the Texas Rebels continued to grow ever higher, when the extent of their success became more apparent. With the counterattack beginning to reach a crescendo, the onrushing Lone Star State soldiers continued to hurriedly load and fire their .577-caliber Enfield rifles at the foremost Iron Brigade targets, who were now too close to miss. The Texans' accurate fire cut down additional young men in blue, including drummer boys and color bearers, who dropped regimental and United States flags, as well as western officers, who displayed courage in attempting to rally their troops under such a blistering musketry.

The Texans' rapid firing of Enfield rifled muskets without halting was so hectic that black powder burned lips and choked throats of elated Texas soldiers, who reloaded on the run. Work's men now eyed the green wall of cornstalks that stood just ahead, peering through the sulfurous smoke that left an acidic taste in their mouths. Scattered groups of retreating Iron Brigade soldiers continued to retreat into the sea of tall stalks that were tasseled on top and promised shelter from the leaden storm.

With dense clouds of smoke often obscuring targets even when so close to their quarry, the Texans began to fire blindly into the forest of cornstalks, knowing that they were quite likely to hit Iron Brigade soldiers. But plenty of Iron Brigade targets still remained at the northern end of the clover field just south of the cornfield, and the westerners in blue continued to suffer severely in the open for their stubbornness and fighting spirit. The clover field before the Miller Cornfield was now covered with a thick carpet of bluecoat bodies, a grim testament to the Texans' marksmanship.

In the frontier tradition of no-quarter warfare, the Texas Rebels now seemed intent on shooting down every Iron Brigade soldier without pity before they could disappear from view into the cornfield's depths—the most effective form of frontier fighting based on harsh Darwinian realities—almost as if these Lone Star State frontiersmen were still battling Comanches. All the while, Work's lethal soldiers loaded and fired more rapidly, knowing that every Yankee who they shot down before they escaped into the corn would not have to be faced later.

Like the one-sided Texian victory at San Jacinto, the Texas Brigade's assault against the odds had seemingly reversed the tide of the Confederacy's most important battle. Ironically, at that time, the enemy of the charging Texians also had worn fancy uniforms of blue, when Santa Anna's confident army of *soldados* (mostly Indian and mixed-raced fighting men) had invaded Texas to trap the Alamo garrison—a fact not lost to the history-conscious Texas Brigade soldiers during this desperate counterattack, which continued to gain momentum just like Houston's frontal attack on that hot afternoon at San Jacinto. And if decisive victory could be won this morning by the hard-charging Texans, then Antietam might well rank with the legendary Battle of San Jacinto before day's end.

Propelled farther north by such motivations, the Texas Brigade soldiers raced onward, fueled by adrenaline and the sense that they were in the process of making history. The Texans continued to charge north, ever closer to the Miller Cornfield, which now seemed larger than any seen in the Lone Star State. All the while, the Texas Rebels continued to scream their distinctive war cries. Surviving Iron Brigade soldiers had never heard such Comanche-like yells before. Advancing steadily northward, the Lone Star State attackers leaped over dead and wounded Iron Brigade soldiers. This brutal fight had become all about survival and killing as many opponents as possible. While demonstrating a trademark overeagerness to shoot down additional bluecoats, some onrushing Texas soldiers slipped on blood splashed on the clover and tripped over fallen Yankees during the rapid pursuit.

Of all the Texas Brigade attackers, the First Texas was perhaps the most vulnerable in terms of assaulting across more unfavorable terrain than its sister regiments. In the sympathetic words of a Fourth Texas soldier: "The [killing] ground in front of the 1st [Texas] rose gradually" toward the Miller Cornfield, the eye of the storm.[112] Major Dawes, Sixth Wisconsin, described the rout of the Iron Brigade soldiers: "Back to the corn, and back through the corn, the headlong flight continues."[113]

At this time, the Texans charged across a generally level green clover field that gradually rose toward the cornfield and presented no obstacles besides dead and wounded Federals. Feeling that they now possessed the long-awaited opportunity to shape a nation's destiny in this late summer of decision, the Texas soldiers neared the cornfield's southern edge.[114] Retiring north through the rows of corn with the dwindling band of survivors of his hard-hit command, Dawes described how the mature corn "stalks [were] standing thick and high."[115]

Despite the odds, the Texans' charge was successful in smashing through all resistance before the cornfield's southern edge and as far as the eye could see. In systematic fashion, these attackers crushed not only the Iron Brigade but also the New Yorkers of Colonel Phelps's Brigade. Seemingly nothing could stop the Texans with their fighting blood up and with the Yankees on the run. Most importantly, by this time "[t]he entire I Corps started to bend like a twig [and now] the entire shebang snapped!" Thanks to the hard-hitting counterattack of Hood's crack division, the seemingly unstoppable Union effort to advance beyond the cornfield and capture the strategic high ground around the small church was completely thwarted. However, thanks to what Hood's Division had accomplished against the odds, the determined Federal bid to achieve decisive victory north of Sharpsburg was now over. Clearly, it had been a very close call and narrow brush with disaster for the Army of Northern Virginia. Chaplain Nicholas Davis, the primary spiritual leader of the Fourth Texas, described how the First Texas "made a desperate charge, and forced overwhelming numbers of the enemy to retire in confusion before them [and as in the past, the irrepressible] Major Dale [was the] first in the charge, and seemed lost to all sense of danger." Experienced leaders like Major Dale continued to encourage the Texas soldiers onward to accomplish what conventional wisdom and the military textbooks had said was impossible.[116]

By this time, the din of the escalating battle was deafening. Even the morning sun almost seemed to refuse to shine through the dense shroud of smoke covering the field and rising slowly on this hot morning. A veteran member of the Texas Invincibles, Corporal Hanks, Company K, First Texas, described how "the smoke at times was very heavy on the field," after the discharges of thousands of muskets. Another Texas Brigade soldier, appalled by the seemingly endless number of fallen men around him, wrote how "officers and men fought with the rifle, and the dead and wounded lay in heaps [while the mid-September] sun was obscured by the smoke that hung over us, and partly hid the horrible sight from view."[117]

As the result of the rapid advance, the bitter fighting and the pall of smoke, the overall original alignment of Hood's counterattacking division was altered. Now the Texas Brigade, Hood's left wing and the Fourth Texas veered to the left toward the cornfield's western edge and toward the Hagerstown Pike. Meanwhile, the right wing of Hood's Division, Law's Brigade, surged toward the cornfield's eastern edge and the East Woods, where the Fifth Texas soldiers now advanced with resolve and fixed bayonets. Therefore, the First Texas was now separated more widely from the Fourth Texas to the west, or left, and the Fifth Texas to the east, or right. Now on their own but still unstoppable, the First Texas attackers continued to surge directly toward the middle of the cornfield. Hood's small division, fortunately, received support from Lawton's last brigade—seven Virginia regiments under hard-bitten General "Old Jube" Early, a crusty West Pointer of ability—which attacked west of the Hagerstown Road through the West Woods.

Finally, after charging north hundreds of yards and through Miller's clover field, the Texas Brigade soldiers, drenched in sweat and covered with dust, finally reached the southern edge of the cornfield. The Texans were already breathing heavily in the morning's rising heat after their long sprint north while battling the Iron Brigade and then during their vigorous pursuit. Exhausted but with adrenaline pumping through young bodies, these powder-stained Lone Star State veterans did not halt to catch their breath, because they instinctively realized that victory called for continuing onward on the double. These Texas veterans knew better than to allow a golden opportunity to slip away, forfeiting hard-won gains and the momentum.

CHARGING INTO THE HELLISH CORNFIELD

Ignoring the fact that the Fourth and Fifth Texas were separated on either side of the First Texas and well beyond mutual supporting distance, what was most exhilarating to Work's men was that the Texas Brigade had the "Black Hat" boys of the Iron Brigade on the run. Without an officer bellowing an order to do so, the Texas Rebels surged straight into the tall cornstalks, maintaining the initiative.

After crossing over the rail fence that ran along the cornfield's southern edge without slowing or pausing to catch their breath, the onrushing First Texans entered the Miller Cornfield with such force that "the corn blades rose like a whirlwind." The lengthy line of Texas soldiers made the forest of tall cornstalks rustle loudly as they poured through the rows of mature plants like a herd of white-tailed deer leaping through a cane brake thicket along an east Texas bayou. Intoxicated by the thrill of victory, the Georgia, South Carolina and First Texas soldiers surged deeper into the corn, pursuing the Wisconsin Yankees of the Iron Brigade and the New Yorkers of Colonel Phelps's Brigade. Most of all, these men were chasing the dream of decisive victory on Maryland soil to save their beleaguered nation.

Meanwhile, on the Texas Brigade's far left, near the pike, the South Carolina Rebels of Hampton's Legion gained the cornfield's southwestern edge. To the right of the South Carolina Rebels of the Hampton Legion, the Eighteenth Georgia attackers poured into the cornstalks to the South Carolinians' right. However, the attack of Hampton's South Carolina Legion and the Eighteenth Georgia almost immediately lost steam upon entering the cornfield when the attackers were stunned by blasts of canister from the guns of Company B, Fourth United States Artillery, and musketry pouring from the west side of the pike. Rallied Federals of Colonel Phelps's Brigade and the Iron Brigade unleashed a murderous fire that raked the Texas Brigade's left flank. Colonel Wofford wrote how he now saw "Hampton's Legion and Eighteenth Georgia [now] moving slowly forward," while the bodies fell faster in the corn. In desperation, Wofford attempted to get these units moving forward again, but the punishment, especially from the regulars of the United States Artillery, was too intense on both the front and left flank of the Georgia and South Carolina soldiers.

After having surged into the cornfield's left center, meanwhile, the First Texas troops were not slowed by musketry, cannon fire or the Iron Brigade's best efforts, unlike the vexing situation on the Texas Brigade's left. Without halting to reform or align ranks, and at a time when he could no longer be seen by the vast majority of his followers because of the height of the cornstalks, Lieutenant Colonel Work led his First Texas troops deeper into the expanse of green, which had become the primary bone of contention at Antietam.

The Virginia Military Institute discipline instilled into the Harrison County boys by Captain Frederick S. Bass of Marshall, Harrison County, now rose to the fore, surging through the ranks of the Marshall Guards, Company E, First Texas. These veterans poured through the sea of corn with Rebel Yells, continuing to go for broke. All the while, these mostly yeoman farmers noticed the fine quality of the high-standing corn, thanks to the rich soil and ample rainfall of Washington County. The stalks stood taller than those in the cornfields of Texas, and the large ears of corn were nearly ready for harvest that would come earlier this year because of the drought.

Meanwhile, during the relentless charge north, the attackers' feet kicked up a large cloud of dust that rose over the neat rows of corn that spanned north across level ground. Among the green stalks, the charging Texans suddenly ran up against still another line of Yankee infantrymen. This unexpected resistance (due to low visibility) came from rallied troops of the

At right is a tintype of a young Confederate private of the western theater, perhaps from Texas. He is holding a six-shot pepperbox pistol across his chest. *Author's collection.*

Iron Brigade's Second and Sixth Wisconsin, perhaps the best regiments, and the equally resilient soldiers of Colonel Phelps's New York brigade.

During one of the most legendary attacks of the Civil War, Work described that his soldiers kept charging, loading and firing during the surge through the dark-colored stalks. To the left of Work's First Texas, meanwhile, the Fourth Texas pushed through the cornfield's southeastern edge, while to the right of Hood's old regiment (Fourth Texas), the Fifth Texas surged into the East Woods.[118] Once in the broad expanse of corn and finally out of the open clover field, the onrushing Texans instantly felt less vulnerable, but this was only an illusion. Indeed, this momentary sense of security shortly proved deceptive to the Rebels who had penetrated into its expanse.

Indeed, for the Lone Star State attackers, the ugly reality of the Miller Cornfield was quite different than initially imagined. Ironically, the Texans in the cornfield initially felt that they were somewhat sheltered from the leaden storm, compared to the open clover field, where so many men had been cut down. But in fact, they might as well have been advancing across a freshly plowed field, because the hail of lead was not slowed, despite the thickness of the standing corn. This was especially the case when the advancing Texas Rebels suddenly found themselves practically atop hidden groups of defenders, which were encountered at close range before they could be seen.

The Texans now no longer spied the pockets of bluecoats standing firm amid the rows of corn, until it was too late. The attackers were greeted by explosions of close-range fire. A stream of bullets cut through the rows of stalks and young men who never saw their homes again. The projectiles made the green leaves rustle and fly to pieces. For the Texans, this was still another grim aspect of the cornfield's particular hell: bullets came from multiple directions from unseen opponents to cut down more Texas boys who fell to rise no more.

Rallied Iron Brigade soldiers of the Second and Sixth Wisconsin and members of Colonel Phelps's New York Brigade, including the Second United States Sharpshooters, had made a determined defensive stand about sixty yards north of the fence along the cornfield's southern edge and along a slight depression located about halfway amid the cornfield's southern half. However, the relentless Texans continued to apply heavy pressure, firing with accuracy despite their exertions of their long run in the suffocating heat and humidity of late summer. But a combined point-blank volley from the First Texas and the fire of the Georgia, Fourth Texas and South Carolina attackers of the diminutive Hampton Legion (on the far left and barely of company strength) to the left eliminated this defensive stand of a large number of Yankees who had made their defiant last stand amid the corn. This intense musketry forced the defenders to flee farther north and deeper into the cornfield.

Despite the yelling Texans surging farther into the cornfield, the western soldiers in black hats continued to display feisty qualities and resiliency. These westerners steadily turned to fire on their pursuers while they retired deeper into the cornfield, sending bullets ripping through the Texans' surging ranks. The Federals knew that the Texas Rebels were close and coming hard, because of the sight of the rising cloud of dust just to the south, the noise of treading feet, the crunching sound trampled cornstalks, the closeness of Rebel Yells, and the brief glimpses of sunlight occasionally flashing off Texas bayonets and .577-caliber Enfield rifled-musket barrels. All the while, therefore, Union soldiers continued to simply fire into the mass of cornstalks to an average man's height, even though relatively little could be seen.

It was one thing for the Texans to receive a volley on a conventional battlefield; it was quite another for the advancing line to be swept by frontal and enfilade fires from an unseen enemy at close range. Clearly, the attackers endured a living nightmare that was the Miller Cornfield this morning. A stream of bullets zipped through the rows of corn and inflicted more destruction among the Texans, sounding like angry bees buzzing around heads. These projectiles clipped off the nearly ripe ears of corn, which fell in clumps in an unplanned harvest of sorts. These were unnerving sights and sounds for the Texans, who could now tell exactly how frighteningly close bullets whizzed by them, in the cornfield. The possibility of death or maiming was omnipresent. However, the Lone Star State men bested their fears, continuing onward with distinctive war cries that echoed over the cornfield.

Despite taking severe punishment from the Iron Brigade's soldiers, the First Texas, now on its own (in the brigade's center) while pushing steadily north through the cornfield's center, continued to sweep through the corn. With a momentum all its own, the command advanced ever deeper in the seemingly endless cornfield. Great clouds of dust were kicked up by the advancing Texans to reveal their exact locations to Union artillerymen. With fixed bayonets and flags flying, the First Texas soldiers poured rapidly through the cornstalks, loading and firing during this primeval struggle for survival. Most importantly, the attacking First Texas men continued to succeed in "driving them before me," wrote Work, all along the line, despite the increasing casualties.[119]

The swirling combat at close range between the Second and Sixth Wisconsin soldiers and Colonel Phelps's New Yorkers and the Texans took on a life of its own. The increasingly vicious struggle for the cornfield seemed to take full control of the soldiers' hearts and souls in an almost hypnotic fashion as the combat raged unabated to reach new levels of intensity.

Lieutenant Colonel Work and his now fewer than two hundred First Texas soldiers had unknowingly entered into the most challenging of combat conditions and situations. By this time, the entire Lone Star State regiment had seemingly vanished into the cornstalks. To Southern soldiers still in the clover field to the south, who had first viewed Colonel Wofford's attackers entering the cornfield's southern edge on the run, it seemed as if the entire Texas Brigade had simply disappeared. Confederate soldiers who listened to the roar of rolling peals of musketry and watched the initial triumphant surge into the cornfield must have wondered if the Texas Rebels would ever return from the Miller Cornfield. After all, the First Texas, still surging forward in the Texas Brigade's center, had seemingly been swallowed whole by the maze of corn.

In this strange environment so unlike any previous battlefield, the Eighteenth Georgia soldiers to the First Texas's left early lost sight of Work's men surging onward at such a brisk pace in charging straight through the heart of the forest of tall cornstalks. In turn, by this time, Work and his veterans, after entering the cornfield, could no longer see any support on either side of them, after the Fifth Texas had veered northeast toward the North Woods and the Fourth Texas had headed northwest toward the Hagerstown Road, after Hood ordered the Fourth Texas to bolster the left.

For all practical purposes, the swirling cauldron of the cornfield had consumed the small-sized First Texas. This grim field of nearly ripe corn was now almost like some unearthly black hole of death. During the fighting that raged with such intensity through the Miller Cornfield, only the battle flags of the First Texas and its sister regiments could be seen by the foremost Federals. Yankee soldiers only saw the brightly colored banners—so threatening but still strangely beautiful at the same time—jolting up and down above the green cornstalks. For the First Texas Rebels, meanwhile, it seemed as if the Eighteenth Georgia, somewhere to its left in the cornfield, had simply vanished as well. The men of the regiments of Wofford's Texas Brigade could not see the flags of other Texas Brigade units during an offensive effort that was in disarray.

Catching groups of antagonists by surprise, Work's attackers continued to smash into pockets of stubborn Yankees from what little was left of a strong battle line that had once stretched across the cornfield. Amid the cornstalks, young men in blue and gray quite suddenly met face to face, and reflexes now determined who lived and died. What resulted was vicious hand-to-hand combat in the smoky confusion, while the noise of battle grew into a deafening roar. Lone Star State soldiers, who looked more like scarecrows in their ragged, nondescript dress, continued to run headlong to additional Yankees, which resulted in "often locking bayonets," wrote one Texan.

Benefitting from their frontier background, the Texas Rebels held a decided advantage in this kind of savage close-quarter fighting, while battling on their own hook. Texans swung musket butts like clubs, knocking down startled bluecoats unable to parry the blow. In this most vicious combat, Texas and Iron Brigade soldiers crossed bayonets, jabbing and stabbing with cold steel between the rows of corn. Again and again, small bands of First Texas Rebels and Second and Sixth Wisconsin Yankees and Empire State Yankees blundered into each another so suddenly that antagonists had no time to take stock of the situation. Swirling out of control, the close combat was now simply a case of every man for himself. For the astute Texans, especially the Indian fighters from the plains, this was much like western frontier fighting, where tactical flexibility, adaptability and individual initiative were necessary for simple survival. With the thick clouds of dust rising up between the green stalks, an eerie haze hung heavily over the parched cornfield, creating a nightmare as bloody as it was surreal.

Another feature of Texas frontier warfare dominated the savagery of the cornfield combat. With only limited visibility and at close range, the deadly six-shooters of Texas officers proved invaluable in the maze of the cornfield. Work's surviving officers fired Navy and Colt revolvers at bluecoats so close that they could have knocked them down with a rock. Unleashing a high rate of fire, they quickly emptied their barrels. These Lone Star State officers possessed a decided advantage over Yankees armed only with their .58-caliber Springfield rifles, which were time-consuming to reload and fire. After all six rounds were expended from revolvers, some Texas officers crossed swords with Union officers in the hellish cornfield, where only the strong and most experienced and those with the quickest reflexes survived. After grappling hand-to-hand amid the corn, westerners in blue and gray died side by side hundreds of miles from their homes. When Texas officers were cut down, powder-stained privates took the initiative to lead the charge and maintain the momentum.

Amid the summery heat, deafening noise and confusion of close-quarter fighting, the invigorating sight of the red regimental battle flag with the St. Andrews Cross and especially the Lone Star State flag continued to inspire the Texans onward. These prized banners were carried by courageous color bearers at the forefront, where bullets cut through the silk and left the flags in shreds. Sewn by ladies for their boys and presented to them in a sacred ceremony, the regimental battle flag literally represented the heart and soul of the regiment. These banners were now stained with the blood of fallen color bearers.

With visibility at a minimum amid the sea of tall stalks, drifting layers of smoke and rising dust, all that Work's attackers had to do to make Confederate dreams come true was follow their flags and continue charging farther north. After victory was reaped in western Maryland on this day of decision, then the great dream of marching into Pennsylvania would become a bright reality. These beloved red and Long Star State banners led the way through the cornstalks and ever north toward where Work's attackers hoped to achieve the decisive victory to forever alter the war's course. The invigorating sight of the cherished Lone Star flag was especially inspirational to the fast-firing soldiers, who realized that the fate of America was about to be determined.

With so much at stake on this bloody morning in Washington County, few First Texas soldiers faltered in their supreme challenge. However, horrified by the extent of the savage nature of the fighting, some Lone Star State men were less than heroic. Having had their fill of killing on such a massive scale, some half-stunned soldiers remained behind hoping to survive, allowing their comrades to advance without them. They now hid in the corn or played dead to escape almost certain death. By this time, the hellish cornfield was "plowed with bursting shells and made slippery with blood," wrote one astounded Yankee.[120]

Meanwhile, artillery fire from the bronze guns of Company B, Fourth United States Artillery, continued to punish the attacking Texans without mercy. By this time, Union artillerymen had even intensified their fire, unleashing shotgun blasts of canister that tore through the cornstalks and attackers' bodies. Captain George T. Todd, formerly the sergeant major of Work's regiment, led the veterans of the Marion Rifles (or the Star Rifles) from Cass and Marion Counties, Company A, First Texas, in the "charge through the cornfield, under heavy fire." However, "before getting through the field [the young captain and former attorney leading Company A] was placed 'hors de combat,' by a shell or shrapnel crushing his foot." The fast-working regulars of this United States artillery unit dropped additional men from the Texas Brigade's ranks. Only by later defying the orders of an amputation-prone Confederate surgeon at a field hospital was Captain Todd able to save his foot and perhaps his life as well.[121]

However, almost every soldier in Work's ranks kept up with the fast-moving regiment during its wild charge through the body-strewn cornfield. The field's dry and loose dirt allowed even the barefoot First Texas men to easily keep pace with the steamrolling advance northward—a boon because every single First Texas soldier was needed in the already thin ranks. With opposing soldiers only able to see a few yards in any direction among the cornstalks, sudden encounters between the pursing Texans and bands of Iron Brigade soldiers continued to be frequent. The helpfully uniformed Iron Brigade soldiers—in dark frock coats, light-blue trousers, white leggings and Hardee hats—were shocked upon first seeing their Texas opponents at close range amid the cornstalks.

The Second and Sixth Wisconsin soldiers were also astonished by the sight presented by Work's soldiers of the "Ragged First," which was rather remarkable considering the overall poor condition of Lee's Army in general. At this time, these First Texas veterans (dirty, barefoot and dressed like vagabonds) looked not unlike paupers from slums of the Badger State's larger cities. However, these Lone Star State soldiers also appeared especially ferocious, with flowing long hair and busy beards (a traditional western frontier look) that almost gave them an appearance more like eighteenth-century pirates than traditional soldiers of conventional warfare. Tall and lean, these crack fighting men appeared like hungry wolves from the central prairies of Texas, utilizing a combination of hatred and predatory skills to kill every Yankee in sight. All the while, the high-pitched war cries of the Texans continued to echo over the smoke-laced cornfield to unnerve additional Federals, who may have thought that they were facing Indians from the Texas plains.

The close-range fighting in the Miller Cornfield spiraled to new levels of intensity, and the First Texas's attack through the cornfield took on a life of its own from those attacking units on either side of Work's regiment, with the Fourth Texas continuing to veer to the northwest and the Fifth Texas to the northeast. The combined effect of the hand-to-hand combat, the Iron Brigade's stubborn resistance, and the more rapid pursuit of the First Texas soldiers led to greater fragmentation of the Texas Brigade's assault into three parts. Meanwhile, the First Texas continued to surge north through the very heart of the cornfield, driving a deeper wedge north in its unstoppable advance. Lieutenant Colonel Work lost his grip on the First Texas, because it was impossible to maintain control in this situation in which the Texans were going for broke.

Indeed, the Texas soldiers were already well known to become uncontrollable when unleashed on the offensive, desiring to fight on their own terms while pressing an enemy who they knew could not be allowed time to rally. Most of all, the dark-bearded lieutenant colonel, who spoke with a slow Texas drawl of the western frontier, lost control because this was only the inevitable cost that had to be paid as his onrushing men tasted victory after smashing through the Iron Brigade. As written in his battle report, Lieutenant Colonel Work admitted that when his boys had their fighting blood up, "it became impossible to restrain the men"—a slashing charge that could not be slowed by Work, the Iron Brigade or any other Yankee troops.[122]

All the while, the Second and Sixth Wisconsin Yankees continued to offer resistance during their retreat north through and then entirely out of the cornfield. Already, the first few Yankees, half-stunned by the savagery of the close-range combat, had emerged from the sun-drenched expanse of corn at the field's northern edge. Large numbers of battle-dazed Union soldiers were now beaten troops after having suffered severe punishment at the Texans' hands. The first worn-down survivors emerged from the smoky cauldron of the cornfield and then realigned their ranks in preparation for facing the Texas attackers once they poured out of the field from the south. Meanwhile, back in the cornfield, the vicious combat continued to swirl. Desperate to somehow slow the rampaging Texas Rebels, the Federals continued to frantically bite off cartridges, loading and firing at attackers. Work described how the First Texas men were "pressing the enemy close" during the wild running fight through the dusty cornfield.[123]

Rippling through the standing corn, the accuracy of the First Texans' fire was evident from the fact that not a single Sixth Wisconsin color bearer escaped the slaughter. Every color guard member was either killed or wounded by the Texans, who shot them down as fast as they could pick up the fallen Badger State flag.[124] It seemed that nothing in the world—not even the hard-fighting Iron Brigade or the regulars of Company B, Fourth United States Artillery—could stop Work's steamrolling regiment. Racing past the bodies of fallen Yankees, the powder-streaked Texans were only encouraged by the gory sight of so many fallen bluecoats. The running fight no doubt reminded the Texas Rebels of the Mexicans' rout from Houston's uncontrollable charge at San Jacinto, when their forefathers had vanquished hundreds of *soldados* after smashing through their initial defensive line that protected their tented encampment. But Hood's attackers were not now facing Mexicans from the Matamoros, Toluca and Guerrero Battalions on the gulf coastal plain, but facing fellow Americans in a Maryland cornfield. Revealing the horrors of the fratricidal conflict without any hint of racial factors in play (as during the Texas Revolution), the Texans were now shooting down young men and boys, who looked more like themselves, from Wisconsin, Indiana and New York with abandon, eliminating some of the North's finest fighting men.

Sensing a decisive victory in the making, Work's men continued to exploit the tactical gains after shooting down additional Iron Brigade defenders. Utilizing the knowledge of frontier warfare and combat savvy that had been sharpened on Virginia's gory battlefields, these Texas veterans knew that not a moment could be wasted to give the reeling opponent time to regroup. Most of all, they realized that this was a key combat situation in which "[o]ne, two, even three may fall…but on [the Texans] go conscious of but one thing and that is to conquer or die," in the words of Corporal William David Henderson Pritchard, Company I (Crockett Southrons), First Texas.

A young Confederate private of the western theater. A standard-issue musket is on his shoulder. *Author's collection.*

Born in 1844 and an ex–farm laborer, Corporal Pritchard was destined to be cut down in this penetrating assault, like so many of his comrades.[125]

Indeed, the Texas Rebels fully realized that everything was now at stake to fulfill Lee's overall strategic goal of launching the great counterstrike that might bring a decisive victory and then propel his victorious army into the Keystone State, where Philadelphia was ripe for the taking.[126] Meanwhile, the uncontrollable Texans continued to rush north, yelling like banshees. Here, in the sweltering cornfield, while bullets made the air sing, the charging Texas Rebels felt like they had entered an uncharted region of hell.

The extent of the Texans' remarkable success against the odds was evident by the large numbers of Federals fleeing and lying dead and wounded, scattered in sickening clumps throughout the cornfield. To Work's consternation, but in a repeat of its offensive successes at Gaines's Mill and Second Manassas, the First Texas was now not only going for broke but also going its own way. All the while, the men of Work's regiment were engaged in unorthodox fighting without support on either side in attacking straight north through the cornfield's midsection.

Elated by their success in smashing through every Union force that they had encountered, the hard-charging Lone Star State men continued to far outdistance the brigade's advancing line on both sides. But with the

Fourth and Fifth Texas (from left to right) lingering behind and veering in more northeastward and northwestward directions, respectively, the First Texas troops advanced not only on their own but also farther north than the brigade's remainder: the necessary tactical requirement to exploit the tactical advantage to the fullest.

Representing a budge in the center, this inverted "V" formation of the Texas Brigade's advancing line—instead of a standard linear formation as taught at West Point—meant that the First Texas received the brunt of frontal and flank fires that cut viciously through its ranks. At this time, the First Texas was leading the counterattack of not only Wofford's Brigade but also Hood's Division—a tactical situation that caused even greater vulnerability, higher losses and more potential danger for the First Texas than any other divisional unit. A price had to be paid for the regiment's outstanding success in gaining so much ground, pushing aside all opposition and continuing to charge northward. Paradoxically, because of the depth of Work's penetration, the regiment's overall disadvantageous tactical situation became evident to the men when their ranks were raked by hot fire from multiple directions. Work realized the ugly new reality that his regiment was now largely on its own, as in "pressing the enemy [both so rapidly and so] close [that] We had advanced in considerable distance ahead of both the right and left wings of the brigade."[127]

Rising to the tactical challenge, Lieutenant Colonel Work took immediate action to deal with this disastrous situation. He dispatched Captain John R. Woodward, who commanded the regiment's left wing, to the left in an attempt to reach the Eighteenth Georgia. Here, somewhere amid the blinding sea of cornstalks, he hoped to find Colonel Wofford, the brigade's leader and the Georgia regiment's former commander. If he reached the Georgians in time without getting hit, which seemed like almost an impossibility, then the former commander of the Anderson County soldiers of Company G (Reagan Guards) would request that the Eighteenth Georgia rapidly advance north so that the regiment's right could align with the First Texas's vulnerable left, which now hung in midair and suffered accordingly from a damaging flank fire.

Work's order to send an urgent message to Colonel Wofford requesting the Eighteenth Georgia's commander hurry his regiment up to take position on First Texas's left was timely. This personal initiative revealed exactly why Work was a highly effective commander, especially in such fluid battlefield circumstances. Caught in a tactical dilemma that forced him to act on his own, the resourceful lieutenant colonel took the initiative at the right time—much like his men (including noncommissioned officers, and even privates in some cases, who had taken charge, after so many officers were cut down), who had demonstrated flexibility in the assault.

Indeed, unlike some other Confederate regimental leaders, the tactically astute Work quickly adjusted to the ever-changing battlefield situation. Worried that Captain Woodward might have been killed or wounded before delivering his urgent message and determined to secure support that was now so desperately needed on both sides of the rampaging First Texas, Lieutenant Colonel Work then dispatched Private Amos G. Hanks, Company F (Woodville Rifles), on the same crucial mission. To gain support that was located somewhere rearward on either side of the First Texas amid the ocean of cornstalks, Private Hanks of the Woodville Rifles raced to the left, or west, in an attempt to locate Colonel Wofford and the Eighteenth Georgia in the cornfield's southwestern edge. Private Hanks, Company F, First Texas, however, was shortly shot down. He lost a leg for his solo attempt to secure much-needed assistance before it was too late to save the First Texas, whose tactical dilemma grew more serious with each passing minute. Then, an increasingly desperate Work dispatched Private Charles Hicks from the Woodville Rifles of Tyler County (Company F) on the same urgent mission. But he was killed somewhere in the tangled maze of corn, never reaching Colonel Wofford or the Georgians, who continued to charge away from the First Texas to increase the distance between Work's left and the Texas Brigade's remainder to the west—a potentially disastrous tactical development.[128]

Ironically, this disadvantageous tactical situation in which the First Texas's troops suddenly found themselves resulted from the extent of their amazing battlefield success. All the while, the First Texas troops gamely forged ahead with abandon, despite the lack of support on either side. This elite regiment still spearheaded the brigade's assault, charging through the cornfield's center and exploiting tactical opportunities—a Texas blitzkrieg when most needed on this day of decision. As the foremost Texas Brigade regiment penetrating farther north than any other regiment of Wofford's Brigade and without support on either side, this tactical situation guaranteed that Work's soldiers would continue to lead the way north well beyond any other Confederate troops at this time. As on previous battlefields, the First Texas's common soldiers had taken the initiative to exploit what was already an amazing success to the fullest and reap even greater gains by not halting.

A Rebel soldier holding his musket across his chest in a traditional photographic pose of Civil War soldiers on both sides. *Author's collection.*

In this sense, therefore, the bloody struggle in the cornfield evolved into very much a private soldiers' war. The mostly middle-class soldiers (fewer working-class men than any other Texas Brigade regiment) of the First Texas continued to perform beyond expectations. These common soldiers relied on their instincts well-honed skills to maximize their success as much as possible. With the New York and Wisconsin Yankees on the run, the First Texas veterans realized that their gains had to be additionally exploited to reverse the tide at Antietam. This crucial situation meant that the attack could not be slowed or halted under any circumstances. Consequently, the superior élan of the troops propelled Work's command farther north than any other unit of either the Texas Brigade or Hood's Division, outfighting and surpassing every other Confederate regiment.

Less concerned about the First Texas's increasing vulnerability than exploiting the tactical gains of the day's successful Confederate attack, Work saw the potential for even greater opportunities for success. Consequently, the Texas Rebels continued to push onward like men possessed, knowing that time was running out. Basking in the extensive gains achieved by his command, the lieutenant colonel now understood that his crack regiment was on the threshold of significantly influencing the outcome of not only the battle but also perhaps even the war itself.

Sensing as much, the great-great-grandfather of Texas governor Rick Perry, Sergeant David H. Hamilton, Company M (Sumter Light Infantry), wrote how in this sweeping "charge we drove the Yanks back one half mile in our front" as far as the eye could see. But one final obstacle now stood before the Texans, and it had to be overwhelmed by additional hard fighting. Along the lengthy rail fence bordering the cornfield's north side, the most stalwart men of the Second and Sixth Wisconsin and the New York soldiers of Colonel Phelps's Brigade made one last defensive stand. Here they continued to fight back in the hope of still retaining possession of the body-strewn cornfield on which so much depended.

At the height of their success, the First Texas attackers were about to run headlong into what was essentially a tactical ambush. With charging First Texas soldiers only thirty yards distant and continuing to trample down clumps of cornstalks as they came on, the fence line was now crowded with Yankee soldiers with newly loaded muskets. From this rail fence, a lengthy sheet of fire suddenly exploded in the Texans' faces. Texas attackers dropped along the cornfield's northern edge. The momentum, nevertheless, of the Texans' charge could not be broken so easily, even by this murderous fire.

Despite suffering under the stinging punishment, the Texans continued to charge without halting to exchange volleys, as was customarily the case. At the point of cold steel, Work's men then pushed the Wisconsin soldiers from the fence line after another savage flurry of close-range fighting, including with clubbed muskets. The battered survivors of the Second and Sixth Wisconsin fled farther north, retiring a good distance toward the higher ground around the Miller House (which could be seen in the distance on a rise), after having taken another beating by the Lone Star State men. At long last, after some of the day's hardest fighting, the Miller Cornfield was now all Confederate after Work's soldiers drove the remains of the final two defending Iron Brigade regiments from their defensive position.

By this time, at about 7:30 a.m. on this scorching morning, Hood's soldiers, especially the First Texas, had accomplished the impossible. Against the odds and the enemy's finest troops, all of whom had fought with great valor and determination, the Texans had cleared the cornfield to reverse the tide of battle at a time when a decisive defeat for the Army of Northern Virginia had seemed inevitable to almost everyone. Most importantly, by this time, the advance elements of Hooker's Corps were reeling from the Texans' counterattack, which had swept everything before it like a giant broom. Astounded by what had been accomplished, General Hood could hardly believe that his two hard-fighting brigades had turned the tide. And no Texas Brigade regiment had played a more important role than the First Texas, which led the attack of not only the Texas Brigade but also Hood's Division.

Almost incredibly, Lieutenant Colonel Work and his First Texas soldiers had smashed through three lines of the army's finest infantry, one before the cornfield, another in the heart of the cornfield and still another at the cornfield's northern end in a good defensive position at the rail fence: all achieved while defeating perhaps the two finest regiments of the best combat brigade of the Army of the Potomac, the Iron Brigade.[129]

In the words of a Fourth Texas soldier who sang the First Texas's well-deserved praises: "The 1st Texas had advanced some distance beyond the remainder of the brigade toward the north side of the cornfield, breaking two lines [actually three] of the enemy."[130] Therefore, one astute Federal soldier understood the extent of the crisis and what was at stake: "It was a critical moment; unless that advance is checked, all is lost."[131]

Most of all, Work realized that a golden tactical opportunity still existed to capitalize on the extensive gains already won by his regiment's success in charging north for such a long distance. If only large numbers of reinforcements, especially on each flank, could be received to assist the First Texas in timely fashion, then Work's soldiers could then resume their assault north to achieve even more tactical gains that might lead to decisive success.[132]

However, considerable danger still existed for the First Texas because of unexpected developments that did not bode well for Work and his men. Indeed, the First Texas continued to hold the most advanced position of any Texas Brigade unit, after having attacked farther north than any other command. As mentioned, Work's regiment had advanced more rapidly than other Texas Brigade units after having gained more ground and vanquished more opponents than any other Confederate troops this Wednesday morning.

But the astounding tactical success achieved by this single Lone Star State regiment left the hard-fighting command in an increasingly serious tactical dilemma: both the right and left flank of the First Texas continued to hang in midair without support of any kind on the east or west. Hence, the First Texas's exposed advanced position was increasingly vulnerable on a day when such weaknesses usually resulted in disaster. The farther that the First Texas had charged north on its own, the farther it had outdistanced support on either side, which veered both northwest (Fourth Texas) and northeast (Fifth Texas). And now these other regiments were nowhere in sight of Work's men, who felt a sense of aloneness. Quite simply, the success of the First Texas now left it terribly vulnerable and in more potential danger than ever before.

Despite having played less significant roles in driving the Federals out of the cornfield, the attackers on the left, Hampton's South Carolina Legion and the Eighteenth Georgia, had not only not kept up with the First Texas's northward advance but had also been unable to achieve comparable tactical gains. Although fighting tenaciously in the cornfield's southwest edge and in the turnpike sector, these regiments had been unable to achieve successes compared to Work's First Texas, which had outfought their comrades.

In part, this potentially disastrous tactical situation developed because on the left across the pike in the West Woods, the Nineteenth Indiana, on the Iron Brigade's far right, and the Seventh Wisconsin had shifted fronts from south to east to enfilade the left flank of the advancing South Carolina, Fourth Texas and Georgia units. This vicious flank fire had thwarted the best offensive efforts of the Hampton Legion and the Eighteenth Georgia, despite the Georgians' repeated attempts to capture the United States battery, whose mission was to protect the Iron Brigade.

Unlike the First Texas, which had gained the cornfield's northern edge, neither the Georgia nor South Carolina regiments had advanced as far north or through the cornfield's middle like Work's command, which had nevertheless spearheaded the thrust north on its own. In fact, the South Carolinians of the Hampton Legion were under heavy fire and pinned down for some time in the cornfield's southwest corner near the Hagerstown Turnpike, far to the First Texas's left rear—a hot firefight that threatened to end the offensive effort on the First Texas's left flank and jeopardize Lieutenant Colonel Work's success in having so deeply penetrated so far north and through the cornfield's entire length from south to north.

In addition, the Georgia Rebels had advanced only a few yards deeper, or north, into the cornfield than the South Carolina troops until blasts of canister from the guns of Company B, Fourth United States Artillery, and the enfilade fire of musketry streaming from troops on the turnpike's other side (west) ended all chances that they would advance sufficiently far north to align with the First Texas's left. Not even the reinforcing Fourth Texas, after attacking west and farther away from the First Texas, could turn the tide in this key sector along the turnpike just south of the Miller Cornfield. While the Georgians, like their Fourth Texas and South Carolina comrades, faced west and fought in the cornfield's southwest corner after having been hurled rearward, Hampton's Legion was positioned farther south just below the cornfield's southwestern edge and the Fourth Texas was located even farther south, on the legion's left. Of course, while fighting through the cornfield, these sharp setbacks, which thoroughly sabotaged the best offensive efforts on First Texas's left, had been entirely unseen by Work in the brigade's center. After all, as mentioned, Work's men had gained the most ground of any of Wofford's units in attacking straight north through cornfield's center, especially after reaching the cornfield's northern edge.

The bulk of the Texas Brigade's attack on the left (southwest of the First Texas) was stalled by the concentrated fire of Iron Brigade soldiers and advanced elements of Phelps's mostly New York troops. After turning to face east, the Nineteenth Indiana, which protected the Iron Brigade's right flank, unleashed a blistering enfilade fire that raked Wofford's left flank. The Texas Brigade's left was also raked by canister from the guns of Company B, Fourth United States Artillery, which was now manned by a good many former Iron Brigade infantrymen after replacing fallen gunners. Nevertheless, despite and enfiladed left flank, the First Texas had continued forward through the cornfield with a momentum of its own, gaining more ground until reaching the fence along its northern border.[133]

Tactically, the situation on the First Texas's right was equally dismal regarding the possibility of achieving greater gains in the near future. As with the two Texas Brigade regiments to Work's left-rear that created a north–south vertical gap between the First Texas and those units, a wide gap had also opened on the regiment's right, but more so in horizontal terms with the brigade's right. This east–west gap was opened wide because Law's left (now on the First Texas's right due to the repositioning by Hood of the Fourth and Fifth Texas to the extreme left and right, respectively, on each flank of the division) surged farther to the right, or east, in pushing Colonel Coulter's Massachusetts, New York and Pennsylvania Brigade through the cornfield. By this time, the Fifth Texas was battling the Yankees beside the troops of Law's right-most units far to the east in the East Woods, while the Fourth Texas supported the Eighteenth Georgia and Hampton's Legion after retiring deeper into the cornfield's southwest corner.

While the First Texas was far ahead in an advanced position along the cornfield's northern edge, the troops of its left (Fourth Texas, Hampton Legion and the Eighteenth Georgia, left to right) had remained stationary and clumped together in the cornfield's southwestern corner and south of it along the Hagerstown Turnpike. And far to the east or right of the First Texas, the left units of Law's Brigade (two Mississippi regiments and the "Bloody Sixth" North Carolina regiment) advanced sufficiently north to reach the cornfield's northeastern corner.

Because of the breakdown of the brigade's and the division's offensive efforts, the First Texas had been in its lonely advanced position for some time. Indeed, as mentioned, the attack of Hood's Division had broken into three segments: on the left, the defensive stand of the Eighteenth Georgia, Hampton's Legion and the Fourth Texas in the cornfield's southwest corner and farther south along the Hagerstown Turnpike; the push of Law's left, three regiments, through the cornfield's southeastern half and the attack of the two of Law's regiments, as well as the Fifth Texas, on the right into the East Woods; and the fierce counterattack of the First Texas.

As an unkind fate would have it, the First Texas was left the most vulnerable by not only the brigade's but also the division's fragmentation. Work and his men were now isolated far before and northeast of Hood's far left, as well as far to the west of the left of Law's Alabama, North Carolina and Mississippi Brigade—a badly exposed position and an extremely dangerous tactical situation for a small Texas regiment now low on manpower and ammunition, without support on either side. Indeed, this was a surefire tactical recipe for the regiment's annihilation in an advanced and exposed position on its own, if the Union offensive effort became renewed in strength.[134]

Without knowing exactly what had transpired around them regarding the tactical developments on both flanks other than no fellow Texas Brigade members could be seen on either side of them, the First Texas soldiers still felt that they were on the verge of success. In part, this grim reality that the regiment was facing was evident by the sight of so many men, including First Texas color bearers, cut down. Horrified by the cruel decimation of these courageous and dedicated men, one Texas soldier described how "just as fast as one man would pick it up, he would be shot down."[135]

Not knowing the ugly irony of how the extent of their tactical success only placed them in far greater danger on the war's bloodiest day, the First Texas soldiers had advanced so far north that they were now totally exposed. The First Texas was already at least 150 yards north in advance of the South Carolina and Georgia troops, who remained at the cornfield's southwestern edge and farther south along the pike, after Work's soldiers had gained the other side, or northern side, of the Miller Cornfield in their spirited counterattack.

Most importantly, a good opportunity still existed for achieving even greater success for Work and his elated men. Confidence continued to increase among Work's sweat-covered men, who were blackened with powder stains from having ripped open so many paper cartridges with their teeth in firing rounds. The Texas Rebels were now thankful that they finally had left the nightmarish cornfield and its surreal combat behind them. Knowing fully what was at stake this hot morning in western Maryland, a frustrated Work sensed the winning of decisive victory. In his own words, he realized how if only the Eighteenth Georgia and Hampton's Legion "would have supported me promptly and effectively upon my left, and that portion of the enemy's force in our front would have been routed, the tide of battle, there turned, and the day been ours."[136]

According to Lieutenant Colonel Work—who continued to be unaware of the exact situation on either flank amid the suffocating smoke, lack of communication and high rows of corn—additional tactical gains still could be won if the assault of the entire Texas Brigade continued northward. However, he did not realize that the units to his left had been repulsed by rifle volleys and canister from the guns of the Company B, Fourth United States Artillery, and would not regain the initiative precisely when most needed to achieve greater gains.

At least in the minds of never-say-die First Texas soldiers who followed their veterans' instincts, their tactical success in already having taken possession of the Miller Cornfield presented an even greater opportunity. The First Texas soldiers—including resilient fighting men from the Lone Star Rifles (Company L), the Reagan Guards (Company G) and the Crockett Southrons (Company I)—were now poised on the threshold of far greater success, if they could only be supported (from the rear and on both sides) in timely fashion for one last united offensive effort to break through the Federals now formed before them north beyond the cornfield.

Consequently, the fighting spirit among Work's boys remained high despite the heavy losses in the hellish cornfield. But more importantly, the fighting blood of the First Texas men was up as during their successful charges at Gaines's Mill and Second Manassas. Most of all, therefore, they were eager to continue charging farther north as far as they could go, before the reeling Federals regrouped. After all, they had defeated the Iron Brigade's Second and Sixth Wisconsin and elements of Colonel Phelps's Empire State Brigade that also included the Second United States Sharpshooters. Even now, the survivors of the two reeling Wisconsin regiments were retreating toward the rise around the Miller House after having taken a beating.

A grim testimony to the First Texas's deadly marksmanship was seen in the fact that the Sixth Wisconsin, now limping rearward in defeat, had suffered the highest losses of any Iron Brigade unit on this nightmarish morning. This fine western regiment had lost nearly half of its strength in the sun-baked cornfield, where so many men and dreams and died. And now, after catching their breath and reloading their overheated Enfield rifled muskets,

A Confederate private with a revolver displayed over his chest to impress the folks back home. *Author's collection.*

the victorious First Texas soldiers were determined to accomplish much more on this day of decision.[137]

Most importantly, by this time, the hard-fighting troops of Hood's Division, especially the First Texas, had succeeded in reversing "the fortunes of the day" with their successful counterattack. In disbelief, a reporter of the *New York Tribune* stated, "In ten minutes the fortune of the day seemed to have changed"—a remarkable tactical result that was due primarily to the success of the Texas Brigade, whose devastating attack had been spearheaded by the First Texas soldiers.

But that impressive tactical success was also leading to serious consequences for the First Texas, which was now more vulnerable than ever before. In response to the Texans' sweeping charge, a panicked Hooker had responded by ordering forward his final reserves of two Pennsylvania brigades from General Meade's Division—the Second and Third Brigades—and calling for support from Brigadier General Joseph K.F. Mansfield's Twelfth Corps.[138]

Chapter 4

Tenacious Last Stand at the Cornfield's Northern Edge

The First Texas soldiers had smashed through not only the finest troops of the Iron Brigade, especially the Second and Sixth Wisconsin, but also elements of Colonel Phelps's Brigade of mostly New Yorkers to reach the embattled northern edge of the Miller Cornfield, after "a remarkable display of bravery."[139]

Fortunately, the tactical dilemma of the First Texas having pushed so far ahead by at least 150 yards of the Texas Brigade's remainder—and hence its enhanced vulnerability at this advanced point—was not perceived by the Federals, until Work's elated soldiers had finally emerged from the cornfield's northern edge and then continued their attack even farther north. Continuing to lead the way as throughout the morning, Work and the First Texas color bearers encouraged everyone onward from the rail fence line in the hope achieving the decisive success to reverse the war's course. In pushing farther north beyond the cornfield and toward the buildings (to the northwest) of the Miller farm located just east of the Hagerstown Road and on the rise that dominated the horizon to the northwest, the First Texas continued onward to spearheaded not only the Texas Brigade's assault, but also the overall offensive effort of Hood's Division.[140]

In the open clover field north of the Miller Cornfield, large numbers of fresh Federal troops and a section of guns of Company B, Fourth United States Artillery, under Lieutenant James Stewart, who had positioned his guns near the Hagerstown Road, loomed ominously in good defensive positions to present a formidable challenge to the onrushing Texas Rebels.

This sight failed to slow Work's men, who were now going for broke. However, the open ground before the charging Texans was a natural killing field that promised to become a final resting place for many attackers.

Significantly, these Union troops were no longer the defeated men of General Doubleday's Division but rather veterans of two brigades of Pennsylvania Reserves of the Third Division, Hooker's First Corps, commanded by the highly capable Brigadier General George Gordon Meade. In transforming the state's militia into a new fighting force to meet the emergencies at the war's beginning, Pennsylvania governor Andrew Curtin had created the Pennsylvania Reserve Corps. The troops of the Eleventh Pennsylvania Reserves were now aligned in solid defensive positions. The Eleventh Pennsylvania Reserves were poised behind a rail fence along the northern border of the north clover field, awaiting the First Texas's arrival.

While two Union guns of this excellent regular battery, under Lieutenant Stewart, continued firing west of the turnpike before the Miller barn, the other four guns were aligned on the same side of the Hagerstown Road, facing and firing southeast toward the cornfield. In addition, the four guns of Captain Dunbar R. Ransom's Battery, Battery C, Fifth United States Artillery, First Corps, was also about to take a good defensive position on higher ground almost directly east of the Miller House and directly before the attacking First Texas. Born in Fayetteville, North Carolina, but raised in Vermont and having attended West Point, Captain Ransom possessed artillery skills that were destined to cost the First Texas additional lives. And on the Nineteenth Indiana's left, the Seventh Wisconsin faced east to unleash an enfilade fire into the Texans' exposed left flank, now vulnerable because Work's troops had advanced north well beyond the cornfield.

As if this were not enough, the greatest challenge now lay before Work's onrushing soldiers, who had already accomplished far more than anyone had expected of these men: a formidable mass of fresh infantry, with full cartridge boxes, stood their ground in support of the fast-firing artillery. These Yankees included rallied troops of the Iron Brigade, including Second and Sixth Wisconsin, and Colonel Phelps's Brigade, which had been just been driven out of the corn and then from the split-rail fence along the cornfield's northern edge. After seeing how many Yankees had found new cover behind the rail and rock fence on the north side of the clover field, a shocked Work realized that additional hard fighting lay ahead.

These fresh Federal troops bolstered those soldiers, especially the rallied Second and Sixth Wisconsin men. When first ascertaining that Doubleday's units were being hurled back by Hood's counterattack, the ever-competent Meade, who was riding his favorite horse, Baldy, had wisely ordered Lieutenant Colonel Robert Anderson's and Colonel Albert L. Magilton's Pennsylvania Brigades (Third Brigade and Second Brigade, respectively, of Meade's Third Division), Pennsylvania Reserves, forward.

Focused on hurling back Hood's attackers at any cost, the Pennsylvania-born Meade, the consummate professional despite a hot temper and lack of patience, also had been responsible for the placement of Ransom's four field pieces in a commanding firing position on high ground directly before the First Texas. Defending home soil, these highly motivated troops of the Pennsylvania Reserves had taken defensive positions along a lengthy rail fence, bolstered by a low rock wall located well beyond the cornfield's northern edge at the northern border of Miller's clover field. A most timely reinforcement, these troops were Hooker's last reserves, the Pennsylvania boys, who had been ordered up to stem Hood's counterattack that seemingly could not be stopped.

Looming ominously in overpowering strength before the First Texas stood the troops of Anderson's Division, General Meade's Third Brigade. The dense line of blue-clad troops consisted of the Eleventh Pennsylvania Reserve Regiment, with the Eighth Pennsylvania Reserve Regiment (just below, or south, the Miller House and whose right flank lay on the Hagerstown Road) to its right and the Twelfth Pennsylvania Reserve Regiment to its left. The Eleventh and Twelfth Pennsylvania Reserves of the Third Brigade, under Colonel Thomas F. Gallagher, were part of Meade's Third Division, First Corps, just like the Eighth Pennsylvania Reserves, Second Brigade, of the same division. The Eleventh Pennsylvania Reserve Regiment consisted of hardy fighting men—especially a large number of Scotch-Irish (the same predominant demographic as the First Texas men) from seven counties (Armstrong, Jefferson, Butler, Fayette, Westmoreland, Indiana and Cambria) in western Pennsylvania just west of the Allegheny Mountains. Here, busily preparing to greet the First Texas attack, the Pennsylvania soldiers of the "Bloody Eleventh" now "lay waiting on the ground, their rifle barrels resting on the lower fence rails" and the low stone wall on the clover field's northern edge, which Work described as "a tumbled-down rock fence."[141]

Lieutenant Colonel Work wrote how after "[p]ursing the Federals through [the cornfield] to near the farther (North) side [of it,] a Federal battery [Captain Ransom's Battery C, Fifth United States Arillery] came in view on a slight eminence at the distance of from seventy-five to one hundred yards beyond it."[142] Nevertheless, undeterred by the daunting sight of so many Yankees and bristling cannon in good defensive positions, Work and his troops continued onward through the clover field, charging north with fixed bayonets.

But Work was incorrect in his estimation of his opponent's strength. Actually, there was more than one battery in place in the hope of extinguishing the grand Texans visions of victory. In fact, the First Texas now confronted the overpowering might of "three Union batteries [that shortly] opened on them with double canister." Facing southeast from the Hagerstown Road sector, a section of guns of Company B, Fourth United States Artillery, continued to rake the open field north of the cornfield's northern edge. Combined with enfilade musketry in front and from the flank by the Seventh Wisconsin to the west, this fire continued to tear into the Texans' left flank, taking additional soldiers from the ranks.

Loaded with double loads of canister to inflict maximum damage, these twelve-pounder Napoleons sent hundreds of whizzing canister balls into the Texas Rebels. Positioned in a pasture that covered a rise and sandwiched in between the other two batteries, the artillery of Captain Ransom's Battery of four Napoleon twelve-pounders, possessing the advantage of high ground in the northern part of the clover field's center about one hundred yards behind the Pennsylvania Reserves and directly north of the First Texas, knocked down additional attackers from the surging ranks.[143]

One Texan described the horror of the artillery hell that exploded in the faces of the charging Lone Star State men: "There were shot, shells, and Minie balls sweeping the face of the earth; legs, arms, and other parts of human bodies were flying in the air like straw in a whirlwind."[144] Private James Rook, First Texas, had his left arm taken off and the wooden stock of his .577-caliber Enfield rifled musket shattered when both were "struck by an artillery shell" while he was firing his rifle. Exhibiting state pride, the private's musket was distinguished by a Texas star brand and the five letters of the word *Texas* at each point of the star that had been cut into the stock.[145]

The large clover field (about the same size, around thirty acres, and in the same precise rectangular shape as the Miller Cornfield) stretched northward, and then a plowed field extended north to the southern edge of the North Woods. These once obscure places in Washington County had suddenly become important and strategic plots of land for which so many young men now gave their lives so freely to fulfill bright visions and dreams.

A young Confederate of the western theater wearing a traditional "battle shirt," which was more common among Rebels from the West (especially the Trans-Mississippi Theater), and with his musket by his side. This photo was taken at a Rebel encampment, perhaps in Texas, by a visiting photographer, before the long journey to Virginia. *Author's collection.*

The large size of the clover fields both north and south of the cornfield gave the impression that the "patch of green corn [was located] in an old clover field," in Lieutenant Colonel Work's words.[146]

The broad, open stretch of the clover field north of the Miller Cornfield now presented an obstacle for the First Texas's assault, which continued to far outpace the rest of the brigade's units during the sweeping attack north, despite continuing to suffer from an enfilade fire from the west. In fact, the nearest regiments of Wofford's Texas Brigade were at least two hundred yards (perhaps more) distant to the right rear, and Law's Alabama, Mississippi and North Carolina regiments were about the same distance to Work's left rear.

These prized possessions of farmer Miller—the plowed field, the clover field and the cornfield, from north to south—had been neatly laid out in meticulous fashion (a distinctive trademark of industrious German farmers, who might well have been mistaken for educated surveyors in their precision), rectangular in shape and roughly about identical in size. All the while, the elated Texans charged directly at the fast-firing four guns of Battery C, Fifth United States Battery, under the capable Captain Ransom, a graduate of Norwich University in 1851, paying a high price for their audacity and courage.

In overall tactical terms, Lieutenant Colonel Work continued to be very concerned because he was now fully "aware that my regiment had advanced 150 or 200 yards further than the regiment upon my left," the Eighteenth Georgia. This disadvantageous situation ensured that the continuation of the First Texas's advance would be enfiladed from the northwest, which was now the tragic predicament of the Texas Brigade's left wing, which continued to be hit by a blistering flank fire.[147]

Meanwhile, additional First Texas soldiers dropped to the increasing fire streaming from the north. Two brothers, Privates James Polk Knight and William Henry Knight, of the Texas Guards, Company H, were cut down. According to the thinking of such diehard Texas Rebels, even if they were to fall, it was best that these two Anderson County brothers went down together in a desperate bid to win a decisive success for the sake of the home folks back in the Lone Star State.[148]

The host of confounding tactical dilemmas now faced by Work's troops did not dissuade the First Texas survivors from continuing to go for broke. All that mattered to these battle-hardened men was one final offensive effort to overrun the roaring guns of Ransom's Battery C, Fifth United States Artillery. After all, these veterans who had captured numerous Federal artillery pieces during their attacks at Gaines's Mill and Second Manassas instinctively knew what to do without being told or ordered by officers—a byproduct of the ample experience and the unique relationship between the Texas enlisted men and their officers. It was a combination of the legacies of Texas culture, western society and the southwestern frontier experience that continued to propel Work's men onward. This situation allowed the common soldiers to utilize a greater degree of initiative and flexibility to enhance the overall chances for success. The Texans realized that not a second was to be wasted on this blood-soaked morning. Lieutenant Colonel Work recalled from the hectic activity among the bluecoats how it was "evident that [this section of guns] was limbering up and in the act of withdrawing," as the charging Texans were close to overrunning the final Federal defensive line.[149]

Meanwhile, the frontier instincts of the men in the ranks continued to rise to the fore. The breathless Texas soldiers directed their efforts at capturing the guns of Battery C, Fifth United States Artillery, exposed on the open ground of the pasture, while chasing the Yankees who had been hurled them from the rail fence bordering the cornfield's northern edge. With a good many of the finest officers cut down, the howling Texans continued to attack across the clover field and ever closer to the stone wall that flamed with musketry.

Behind the fence directly before the First Texas, the men of the Eleventh Pennsylvania Reserves prepared to deliver punishment from shotgun blasts of "buck and ball" (a large-caliber bullet and three buckshot) with their .69-caliber smoothbore muskets, when Work's soldiers got close. In a symbolic showdown, these Pennsylvania boys had old scores to settle with the Texas Rebels after the beating that they had suffered at Second Manassas. In that battle, the Texas Brigade's attack had collapsed the Union line and then smashed the Eleventh Pennsylvania Reserves to pieces, when "our men wer[e] Shot down lik[e] Sheap" by the Texans, in one survivor's words. Meanwhile, the Texas Rebels continued to push ever-farther north and deeper into the vortex of Antietam's storm.

Despite some First Texas soldiers having halted along the cornfield's northern edge because of the thick clouds of smoke, lack of visibility and confusion of battle, Company K's soldiers (Texas Invincibles) from Sabine, Augustine, Nacogdoches and Newton Counties were among the attackers who continued to charge onward to overrun the guns at all costs. With yells that sent a chill down the backs of the boys in blue, especially the Eleventh Pennsylvania Reserves, Work's attackers surged a greater distance across the clover field in a desperate attempt to capture Captain Ransom's guns. Corporal Orlando Thacker Hanks was one of these foremost soldiers in Company K's attack, emphasizing how "onward we went" through the clover field and straight toward the wall of stone and rails now held by large numbers of Yankees. Some of the foremost First Texas Rebels, desperate to overrun Captain Ransom's Battery C, Fifth United States Artillery, reached within one hundred feet of the guns. Meanwhile, other determined Texans on the far left charged even closer (ten to fifteen feet) to the section of guns of Company B, Fourth United States Artillery. Then, these artillery pieces erupted one final time with canister to literally blow away the foremost Texans. After discarding his bugle, fifteen-year-old Johnny Cook won a Medal of Honor for defying the surging Texas Rebels, who seemed about to capture his regular battery, with spirit.

But the Texans' deep penetration and General Hooker's and General Meade's foresight and excellent timing in hurling their last reserves into the face of the Lone Star State counterattack were about to pay high dividends. Exactly where they should have been and at exactly the right time to face the day's most successful Confederate counterattack, as Lee had envisioned, the disciplined soldiers of the Eleventh Pennsylvania Reserves withheld their fire with "buck and ball" until they could distinctly see onrushing Texan legs beneath the smoke that covered the clover field. This most desperate offensive effort of the First Texas soldiers was swept by a tremendous blast of musketry that erupted from the Pennsylvania Reserves, who suddenly rose up like a wall of blue from behind the stone and rail fence. Hell itself exploded into the faces of Work's onrushing soldiers when within only twenty yards away of their goal.

Unleashed at point-blank range, this concentrated fire erupted down the length of the rock and rail fence, rippling down the blue line. A sheet of flame exploded from hundreds of .69-caliber smoothbores and hurled deadly discharges of "buck and ball." This sweeping volley, in the words of the Pennsylvanians' commander, "had the savage impact of double rounds of canister." In the words of Corporal Orlando Thacker Hanks, the attacking First Texas soldiers, with their trademark "Texas yell," charged "within thirty yards" of the makeshift line of light works, which included pulled-up fence rails now lined with large numbers of Keystone troops. These sturdy Pennsylvanians were too much for the Lone Star State soldiers, who were completely exposed in the open field: "We could go no further [because] they were too strong for us, cutting us down almost like grain before a cradle"—little more than a slaughter on the body-strewn clover field.[150] Seeing a good many of his boys now lying dead and wounded, Lieutenant Colonel Work described how the large number of Federal defenders in "our immediate front [were behind the] tumbled-down rock fence just at the outer (Northern) edge of the corn patch and was pouring a galling and deadly fire into [our] ranks."[151]

Highly motivated to defend the sacred soil of the invaded homeland, these Eleventh Pennsylvania Reserves were hardy mountain boys who were as tough and rugged as their beloved Alleghenies. Most of all, they were motivated by the desire to win a decisive victory, march into Richmond and hang Jefferson Davis from the nearest tree. Ironically, this sturdy Pennsylvania regiment had been captured (more than six hundred men went to prison in Richmond) at Gaines's Mill after the Texas Brigade's charge smashed through all resistance. Even worse for unit pride, the regiment's cherished battle flags, both the state banner of green silk and United States flag, had been displayed in Richmond as trophies.

Still refusing to retire and forsake the dream of a decisive success, the surviving First Texas soldiers stubbornly stood their ground in the open. Here, in angry defiance at having been frustrated for the first time this morning, they exchanged a hot fire with the Ninth Pennsylvania Reserves on the left, the Eleventh Pennsylvania Reserves before them and the Twelfth Pennsylvania Reserves to the right.

Despite heavy losses, the Texas Rebels delivered a good deal of punishment of their own. They were rewarded for their steadfastness and accuracy by the invigorating sight of additional Pennsylvania boys tumbling from the ranks. Despite the advantage of the Pennsylvania soldiers blasting away with "buck and ball" at close range, Work's men inflicted a good amount of damage of their own. Three color bearers of the Ninth Pennsylvania Reserves were cut down. However, the Eleventh Pennsylvania Reserves took the brunt of the First Texas's fire. Swept by accurate musketry, groups of Eleventh Pennsylvania soldiers broke for the rear after several color bearers were shot down. So many bluecoats fell back that panicked artillerymen, fearing that the Pennsylvanians' shaky line would break, hurriedly limbered their guns (on the left of Captain Ransom's Battery C, Fifth United States Artillery, which was left alone before the First Texas) and withdrew before being overrun. Incredibly and against the odds, the First Texans once again did the impossible, as "a portion of the Pennsylvanians' line at this point was breached" by Work and his hard-fighting men.[152]

All the while, the blistering fire of the section of guns from Company B, Fourth United States Artillery, near the Hagerstown Road just to the northwest, and Captain Ransom's United States Battery in Work's front, savagely culled the Texans' ranks with canister. Rolls of musketry (especially the lethal "buck and ball" from the Eleventh Pennsylvania Reserves), including the Seventh Wisconsin's enfilade fire to the west, and shotgun blasts of canister and shells were hurled into the Texas Rebels, who had attacked north a good distance beyond the cornfield, back to the rail fence along the cornfield's northern border. Nothing could now survive before this concentrated fire of artillery and musketry from multiple directions. Indeed, the First Texas soldiers paid a frightfully high price for having been the foremost targets in leading the way during the day's deepest penetration, especially because they had been the first Rebels to not only reach, but also to emerge from the cornfield's northern edge and into the open clover field without support on either side.

Even once back behind the rail fence on the cornfield's northern edge and after their reluctant withdrawal, the Texas Rebels stayed close together in this advanced position, holding firm against the odds. Despite a murderous fire, the Lone Star State men resisted the natural temptation to retire to the relative safety of the cornfield. But these men were a band of brothers determined to stay together through thick and thin, dying together if necessary. These veterans would not abandon their advanced position and their comrades. The storm of lead made the green leaves of the cornstalks to the Texans' rear rustle, while tall stalks snapped in half when cut by bullets and canister. In Company K (Texas Invincibles), Lieutenants James Waterhouse and Sam Patton were killed while encouraging their boys, who had seen their deepest penetration broken, to do their best against the odds.

But despite the spiraling casualty rate, the Texas Rebels were far from beaten on this morning. Incredibly, they refused to relinquish their hard-earned gains. Survivors were determined to hold firm as long as possible along the cornfield's northern edge, especially after having seen the guns of the battery position on Captain Ransom's left (Battery C, Fifth United States Artillery) retire in a hurry. For all that these foremost Texans knew, sizeable reinforcements might well be on the way, answering their commander's urgent appeals for assistance. Consequently, Work and his men continued to hold fire in the hope of receiving reinforcements so that they could once again resume the offensive. To increase speed in loading and firing Enfield rifles, steel ramrods were propped up against fence rails by the surviving Texas Rebels. All the while, Union projectiles deflected off fence rails (now the only protection for the Texans), sent wooden splinters flying and kicked up spouts of dust around the surviving band of Work's men.

Work and his sweat-stained boys knew better than to advance into the open clover field without sufficient support or the arrival of reinforcements. Here, along the split-rail fence bordering the cornfield's northern border, what relatively little was left of the First Texas made its determined last stand. The Texans blasted away at their tormentors until rounds in cartridge boxes ran low. In desperate haste, Lone Star State survivors then scoured the leather cartridge boxes of their dead and wounded comrades to gather additional rounds.

A common Southern soldier, very likely a teenager, of the western theater. The freckles on his face reveal his youth and his experience in open campaigning in summer weather. *Author's collection.*

Work later reflected on the turning point of the attack. The lieutenant colonel believed that he had found the cause of the first tactical setback ever suffered by the First Texas, which left him somewhat incredulous. Without saying a word or issuing an order, the exuberant First Texas soldiers "of its own notion and of one accord, unheeding the reiterated command of Forward, Load and Fire at Will, [had] c[o]me to a halt and began shooting down horses and artillerists with the hope and expectation of capturing [Captain Ransom's Battery C, Fifth

United States Artillery], unmindful of the fleeing Federal infantry in our immediate front who had taken refuge behind a tumbled-down rock fence just at the outer (Northern) edge of the corn patch and was pouring a galling and deadly fire into its ranks."[153]

In hindsight, Work was convinced that his veterans, in the excitement of victory, had instinctively focused on the wrong target of opportunity, artillery (Ransom's Battery and the section of Battery B, Fourth United States Artillery to a lesser degree, because Battery C, Fifth United States Artillery was positioned on a rise directly before the First Texas), instead of defending infantrymen. But the common soldiers' focus remained on gaining possession of the Union guns, which were always the most tempting target of the Texans, who blasted away at artillerymen and horses. They still hoped to eventually capture the regular battery of Captain Ransom, especially if reinforced. However, a standoff situation of riflemen versus artillerymen was another no-win scenario, because the accurate fire of the Texans only drew a concentrated artillery fire that was now directed at the Texans' flimsy rail fence shelter.

By concentrating their efforts on silencing the booming artillery while simultaneously suffering under the scorching fire of the fresh regiments of Pennsylvania Reserves and steadying their Enfield rifled muskets on the fence rails for better aim, the Texans' lethal work of destruction continued unabated. Under the hot mid-September sun, these veterans from the Lone Star State blasted away as rapidly as possible. Ransom's Battery C, Fifth United States Artillery, was now exposed on the open ground of the clover field before Work's soldiers and lost accordingly. However, with the section of Battery B, Fourth United States Artillery located near Hagerstown Road, the First Texans on the far left helped to inflict the highest loss of any "long arm" command to date with a flank fire—another glowing testament to the accuracy of the Texans' fire. A total of forty out of one hundred of Lieutenant Stewart's gunners were killed or mortally wounded in the slugfest. But it was the battery positioned directly before Work's men that took the brunt of the Texans' wrath. The sharpshooting First Texans also shot down a large number of horses of Captain Ransom's battery to ensure that the guns could not be quickly withdrawn, making them vulnerable to a counterattack if Work's troops were reinforced as they fully expected. Two Union artillerymen were killed and another thirteen fell wounded in Ransom's Battery C, Fifth United States Artillery.[154]

However, the high price paid by the Union artillerymen was not in vain. What veteran artillery units such as Battery B, Fourth United States Artillery, and Battery C, Fifth United States Artillery, had accomplished this morning was the blunting (especially by Captain Ransom's Battery) of Hood's counterattack—a tactical accomplishment that can hardly be overestimated, as so much was at stake this morning. By any measure, this was the finest day for the Union army's artillery, especially during the intense fighting for possession of the Miller Cornfield. The artillery of "Little Mac" McClellan's army now exceeded its lofty reputation won during the decimation of Lee's attackers at Malvern Hill during the final showdown of the Peninsula Campaign on July 1, 1862.[155]

Significantly, the First Texas's charge had been stopped by a concentrated fire of musketry and artillery (flank fire from Lieutenant Stewart's guns and a frontal fire from Ransom's cannon) rather than Work's orders or any other Southern leader, including their brigade commander, Colonel Wofford, or division commander, General Hood. Once again demonstrating a never-say-die attitude, the Texas soldiers still possessed plenty of fighting spirit, after having taken cover behind the rail fence along the cornfield northern edge. In the minds of Work's veterans, the struggle had only fairly begun for them on this Wednesday morning. The survivors continued to fight back with spirit that would have made the men of the Alamo and San Jacinto proud. Meanwhile, additional Union artillerymen and frightened artillery horses, which whinnied and reared in pain when hit by bullets, fell to lethal Texas marksmanship.

All the while, the First Texas soldiers continued to rapidly load and fire at the fresh troops of the Pennsylvania Reserves, who possessed full cartridge boxes, and at the rallied soldiers of the Iron Brigade and Colonel Phelps's New York Brigade. Both sides stubbornly held their ground, blasting into each other, refusing to budge and lengthening the spiraling casualty lists. Corporal Hanks, Company K, First Texas, described how during the furious exchanges of gunfire: "I noticed a [Pennsylvania] fellow on his knees peeping through an opening made by two rails placed on end forming a kind of triangle. He was about thirty yards distant and had on a double breasted shirt. I had a good gun and drew directly at his breast. I thought to myself, 'If we whip I am going to see if I killed you.'" But, continued Hanks, "I did not get to investigate [because] Just at that time when I was raising my gun to my face to fire again, a bullet passed, struck me in the left side, close up under the arm, coming out under my shoulder blade near my back bone [and later] a bullet passed through my hatrim [*sic*], just over my right ear"—still another close call on a morning of many near brushes with death.

Meanwhile, additional bluecoat gunners of Captain Ransom's Battery went down to the Texans' blistering fire. Familiar with firearms since childhood days while hunting the Lone Star State's forests and on the plains of central Texas, Work's veterans methodically picked off artillerymen exposed in the open clover field. For these veterans, it was like shooting turkeys off their treetop roosts at twilight along an east Texas creek, bayou or river. Now the slaughter among the Federal artillery was reaching new heights. One Texas soldier described the effectiveness of the blazing Texas rifles, which proved successful in "forcing [the Yankees] to abandon a battery [to the left of Ransom's guns] and take shelter in the ravine north of the field."[156]

Despite the solid wall of blue before them and the roaring Union artillery, Work and his men continued to defiantly confront hundreds of fresh Pennsylvania Reserves. Another Texas Brigade member described with pride what had been accomplished this morning against the odds: "The 1st Texas had advanced some distance beyond the remainder of the brigade toward the north side of the cornfield, breaking two lines of the enemy and forcing them to abandon a battery."[157] Work also maintained a defiant advanced position along the rail fence at the cornfield's northern edge because of still another reason besides awaiting reinforcements. By this time, Captain Woodward had reported to Work with a belated order to halt his offensive effort because of the lack of support on either side.

Almost as if possessing a desire to protect so many of his fallen soldiers, including friends and neighbors, Work now remained in his advanced defensive position (the farthest point north of any Army of Northern Virginia unit), as "where I last halted, and where my dead and wounded fell, I halted in consequence of an order or direction to that effect from someone in the rear, said by Captain Woodward to have been [Major] W[illiam] H[enry] Sellers," who had a horse shot from under him this morning. Conveying the general's directives and attempting to rally hard-hit troops in other sectors, Major Sellers made timely contributions while serving as Hood's capable chief of staff. Earlier, he had provided good assistance in sorting out the tactical confusion when the Fifth Texas and Law's troops became entangled before the attack. In Hood's opinion, Major Sellers was "competent to command a brigade under all circumstances." Sellers had issued this order for a halt, after learning how far north the First Texas had advanced on its own.[158]

Now firing from behind the rail fence along the cornfield's northern edge, the First Texas Rebels blasted away from prone positions, raking Union infantrymen and artillerymen without mercy. Work's soldiers gamely fought against fate and far too many Yankees to overcome this morning. However, such defiance in the face of overwhelming numbers was almost suicidal. One Texan, who watched his comrades drop like fallen leaves, attributed the recent setback to the heavy volume of fire and seemingly too many Yankees to count: "Our men were mowed down like grass, and our ranks being so terribly thinned, it [had been] thought prudent to order a halt [and when] the halt was ordered, and what few of the [First Texas] men that were left had laid down for protection from the perfect hail-storm of bullets that were making the air hideous with their noise, there stood Major Dale, seemingly as cool and collected as if nothing was going on."[159]

Despite the staggering losses, the First Texas soldiers continued to rapidly load and fire with their trademark accuracy from the cornfield's northern edge, buying time for the arrival of possible reinforcements. Additional bluecoats went down to a well-aimed fire, rekindling hopes among the most determined and optimistic Texans for a successful outcome, if only they were reinforced in time. Powder-stained lips cracked in the day's heat and from biting off the top of so many paper cartridges, which steadily dwindled in numbers.

Meanwhile, the Texans' Enfield rifles became so heated that they were fouled, slowing the process of loading and the rate of firing—a severe disadvantage not experienced by the relatively fresh Pennsylvania Reserve troops before them during this slugfest. So many shots were fired by Work's soldiers that some .577-caliber muskets could no longer be used and had to be tossed aside. These men then reached down and grabbed the muskets from fallen comrades, splashed in red and moaning in pain, to continue firing during the close-range duel between the two opposing lines in this showdown between the Texans aligned along the rail fence that bordered the cornfield's northern edge and the fast-firing men of the Pennsylvania Reserves behind the rock and rail fence to the north.

With the momentum spent and most of Work's men either killed or wounded by this time, the only source of inspiration (besides leading officers, who continued to implore their survivors to hold firm against the odds) for the ever-dwindling band of First Texas survivors was the sight of the beautiful Lone Star State flag, shredded by bullets, that proudly stood in the line's center. As with the defenders at the Alamo, these

A dark-haired Rebel wearing a stylish civilian vest (a popular garment in his day) under his gray uniform coat. *Author's collection.*

diehard soldiers were prepared to go down together rather than forsake this advanced position gained after so much sacrifice or fall back before even a new line of bluecoats.

The Keystone State soldiers also concentrated their fire at the hated symbols of rebellion, the Lone Star State flag and the Confederate flag, which waved above the surviving band of Texans. Additional good fighting men fell from the fire of soldiers from Eleventh Pennsylvania Reserves' companies like the Connoquenessing Rangers (D), Cambria Guards (A) and the Washington Blues (I). Lieutenant John C. Kuhn was one victim of the Texans' blistering fire, falling mortally wounded. All the while, the fresh Pennsylvanians seemed determined to shoot down every Texas boy in sight along the rail fence.

Additional First Texas color bearers—Galveston-born Private Charles H. Kingsley, Company L (Lone Star Rifles from Galveston), who was hit in the leg and fated to be captured and eventually die in a Yankee prison in his mid-twenties, and Corporal James K. Malone, of Irish heritage and a member of Company A (Marion Rifles)—fell to the murderous fire. As fate would have it, of all Confederate regiments on the field this morning, none were subjected to a heavier or deadlier fire from so many different directions than the increasingly vulnerable men of the First Texas, which continued to gamely fight on its own without support on either side.[160]

Nevertheless, these hard-bitten Texans continued to give as good as they received during the exchanges of musketry. One of the early photographers of Texas, who had left a family photographic studio in Galveston to serve in the First Texas, was dark-haired Solomon Thomas "Tom" Blessing. This talented Galveston photographer of Company L (Lone Star Rifles) described how he "was near our regimental flag when I saw the bearer fall. My first impulse was to pick it up, but then thought I could do more good shooting" at the Yankees, who now seemed too numerous to count.[161]

FATAL SITUATION

With all offensive momentum now spent, no reinforcements arriving and casualties having already reached unacceptable levels, Work faced a most challenging of tactical dilemmas that forced him to rethink the situation. In Work's words, "just at the farther side [north] of the corn-field was the point where I was in great doubt as to the proper move to be made by me."[162]

Lieutenant Colonel Work's increasing concern grew because of the continued lack of support on either side—a recipe for certain disaster, if not annihilation, especially after the arrival of the Pennsylvania Reserves—that continued to leave the First Texas extremely vulnerable to enfilade fires from two directions simultaneously, while eliminating any thought of resuming the offensive beyond the cornfield's northern edge. With losses so high and the persistent lack of reinforcements so infuriating, Work now understood how this bloody fight had become a case of simple survival. He lamented how his regiment's rapid advance had been "so diverging as to leave a wide interval between the right flank of the Eighteenth Georgia and my left, thus exposing both regiments to attack—the Eighteenth upon the right and the First Texas upon the left flank [and] I was aware at the same time that a heavy force of the enemy was massed upon my left and felt confident that in case I moved farther to the front I would be attacked upon my left and rear and annihilated."[163]

Fearing the worst-case scenario for his lonely regiment taking a severe beating, Work was correct in his estimation, as the deteriorating situation could hardly have been more serious. The Eighteenth Georgia had veered farther to the left, or west, to join the Hampton Legion in attacking a section of Company B, Fourth United States Artillery, at the pike. This change of direction had been made without Work's knowledge, leaving the First Texas even more alone and entirely unsupported on the left to the west for the day's remainder. Consequently, the First Texas's left continued to be enfiladed from an even heavier fire (artillery and musketry), streaming from the northwest.[164]

Ironically, the fact that the First Texas soldiers had halted (on their own because of high losses and the arrival of the Pennsylvania Reserves and supporting artillery) had been a wise choice, especially without support on the left—a spontaneous decision that prevented almost certain disaster. Work's initial goal had been to capture the guns of Battery C,

Fifth United States Artillery, before the savvy common soldiers wisely decided otherwise, after having made the final desperate attempt to overrun the prized guns.

But after ascertaining the true situation despite the clumps of dead and wounded bluecoat artillerymen and horses lying around the United States guns, the lieutenant colonel reasoned correctly, resisting the temptation to launch another bid to capture the section of guns of Battery C, Fifth United States. Work later acknowledged that the newfound wisdom was born of the brutal realization that he and his men had been virtually abandoned by all other Confederate units: "Had I moved forward to carry the enemy's battery I would have exposed the regiment to attack from three different directions, to wit, from the front from infantry and artillery and upon the left and rear from infantry."[165]

Additionally, Work was belatedly informed of the disastrous tactical situation: "I am told, also by some of the men that had I advanced a little farther to the front[,] my right flank would have become exposed to attack, and am assured that some distance to my front and obliquely to my right was a large force of the enemy."[166]

Even worse, a heavy concentration of Yankees, including the Nineteenth Indiana and Seventh Wisconsin, loomed threateningly to the First Texas's left, stretching in lengthy lines to the west, after the withdrawal south of the Eighteenth Georgia and Hampton's South Carolina Legion. These Federals unleashed a blistering enfilade fire that tore through the cornstalks from the west, raking the First Texas's exposed left, which continued to hang in midair on the northern part of the cornfield, where rows of stalks had been flattened by the stream of projectiles and the furious combat. Faced with this tactical dilemma of the first magnitude, still clinging precariously to the cornfield's northern edge without any realistic chances for resuming the attack, Work again dispatched a dependable messenger, acting regimental adjutant J. Winkfield Shropshire, originally a sergeant of the Marion Rifles of Company D, on the double to the left.

On the final urgent mission to secure assistance in a crisis situation, he was sent by Work to locate Colonel Wofford, if he even could be found in the smoky confusion of the ravaged cornfield. Acting Adjutant Shropshire carried with him an urgent appeal from Work that reported the alarming news of a lone regiment's desperate situation: "[U]nless the regiments upon my left [Hampton's South Carolina Legion and the Eighteenth Georgia] were moved up quickly to my relief and support upon the left, I would be

A bearded Texas soldier holding a bowie knife, a traditional weapon of the southwest frontier, over his chest in an appropriate display of combativeness. Photo found in east Texas. *Author's collection.*

forced to abandon my position and withdraw." However, like the other messengers dispatched before him, Work's acting adjutant failed to reach Colonel Wofford. He shortly became a fatality of the fighting that continued to swirl through Antietam's greatest killing ground. Therefore, at the very epicenter of the struggle for possession of the embattled cornfield, Work and what little remained of his First Texas remained on their own at the field's northern edge, continuing their own private war against the odds.[167]

As fate would have it, the narrow window of opportunity and the slim margin remaining to exploit any additional tactical gains had been entirely slammed shut by this time. But as if all of the disadvantages were not enough, the worst was still to come for the First Texas's survivors. Indeed, a vicious fire suddenly exploded from the rear, striking Texas Rebels from behind. Ironically, this rear fire stemmed from the disastrous situation on the Texas Brigade's left, which had been started by Iron Brigade troops who had been earlier defeated and hurled from the cornfield by the First Texas. Formerly defeated regiments like the Sixth Wisconsin, which had been driven out of the cornfield by Work's attackers nearly all the way to the high ground around Miller House, had not only rallied but also now played a leading comeback role. Clearly, these Iron Brigade soldiers were some of the most resilient fighting men ever faced by the Texans.

This comeback offensive effort by the Iron Brigade was rather remarkable. Born in Ohio on the Fourth of July 1838, Major Dawes had rallied two hundred of his Sixth Wisconsin troops of the Iron Brigade by waving the regimental colors before his troops. Then, General Gibbon, "grimed and black with powder," implored Major Dawes and his Wisconsin soldiers forward to the rallying cry of "we must save these guns"—the section of the Company B, Fourth United States Artillery. The rallied Badgers surged ahead and down the turnpike to once again face the Texas Brigade troops, the Fourth Texas, Eighteenth Georgia and Hampton Legion troops, engaging them once again in vicious combat.[168]

The advance of these Iron Brigade reinforcements was most timely because this exposed regular artillery unit had almost half of its men killed and wounded and most of its horses shot down by this time. As if still teaching the artilleryman's art at West Point, General Gibbon fired his "last shot" at the Texas Brigade attackers, southwest of the First Texas, from one of these guns, hurling loads of double-shot canister that smashed through crumbling resistance.[169]

As noted, the offensive effort of the Texas Brigade's left near the Hagerstown Road had collapsed by this time. Iron Brigade troops of the Seventh Wisconsin and the Nineteenth Indiana, as well as Brigadier General Marsena R. Patrick's New York Brigade of four regiments (the Twenty-First, Twenty-Third, Thirty-Fifth and Eightieth New York) marched across the pike and then south to the road's west side. Here, they had fired into the left flank of the South Carolina, Fourth Texas and Georgia boys, causing even more damage to these already hard-hit Texas Brigade units on the west. This blistering enfilade fire had forced the Texas Brigade's left to fall back to escape the severe punishment.

Because these fast-paced tactical developments had resulted in a disastrous chain reaction along the turnpike to the west, Work's regiment was placed in even in a more advanced and isolated position than ever before after the withdrawal of the South Carolina, Fourth Texas and Georgia soldiers to the southwest and all the way out of the nightmarish cornfield. Following on the heels of the Texas Brigade's left wing's withdrawal through the cornfield and penetrating farther south parallel to the Hagerstown Road were the advancing ranks of the Nineteenth Indiana and the Seventh Wisconsin and Patrick's New York brigade. These invigorated attackers now surged east through the battered cornfield to send a scorching fire streaming into the left flank and rear of the First Texas. This was the first time that the exhausted First Texas soldiers suffered from a vicious rear fire, catching them completely by surprise. Consequently, this fire from flank and rear combined with the renewed offensive effort of these resurgent New York, Wisconsin and Indiana Federals to sandwich Work and his band of men in a deadly vise that was closing rapidly around them.

Clearly, the tide had turned permanently against the Texans in this bloody sector, despite the fact that this murderous enfilading fire was eventually subdued when the Iron Brigade men and Patrick's Brigade were enfiladed by "Old Jube" Early's resurgent Virginia troops of Stonewall Jackson's command. More importantly, in preparation for delivering a killing blow, thousands of Yankees, including the fresh regiments of the Pennsylvania Reserves, now stood before the Texas Brigade's thinned ranks. In the words of one shocked Fourth Texas soldier, who described why the offensive effort of the Texas Brigade's left had been shattered, after "[r]eaching the road again, with a fence on each side, we found Hooker's [First] Corps, 18,000 strong, in front of us, and to our right was a battery of at least six guns, and the most effective I ever stood before."[170]

As fate would have it, what little remained of his First Texas continued to receive most of the severe artillery fire from blasts of double-shot canister and the rolling volleys of the rallied Second and Sixth Wisconsin and fresh Pennsylvania reinforcements—punishment delivered from three sides. Private Joseph Benjamin Polley, Fourth Texas, wrote of the cruel fate that befell Work's survivors: "The brunt of the battle on that part of the Confederate line occupied by Hood's Brigade at Sharpsburg fell upon the First Texas, and they bore it like the heroes they are."[171]

By this time, a seemingly endless number of Yankees, both Pennsylvania Reserves (especially the Eleventh Pennsylvania Reserves directly in front and sandwiched between two other regiments of the Pennsylvania Reserves) and rallied troops, held the ground before the First Texas. This concentration was far too great not only for the Rebels to achieve any additional gains but also to survive. The row of blazing Union guns, worked at a fast pace by expert artillerymen (especially Captain Ransom's United States Battery directly in front), continued to batter the foremost unit of Hood's Division, the exposed First Texas, with a vengeance. Chaplain Davis explained this suicidal situation in which the "enemy poured a perfect hurricane of grape and canister from their batteries, while their infantry, which had been heavily reinforced, rained missiles of death from their small arms into our [gray] columns."[172]

All the while, the porous rail fence at the northern edge of the cornfield provided precious little shelter for the spunky First Texas soldiers, particularly when they were swept with a combined flank, frontal and rear fire, especially from artillery. The fire from the south was the most devastating, hitting ill-fated Texas boys from the rear. Nevertheless, the surviving band of First Texans remained in its advanced position, busily loading and firing rapidly from prone positions and from behind a rail fence now swept by artillery projectiles and volleys of musketry. As usual, the most devastating artillery punishment was forthcoming from double loads of canister. These field pieces, especially of Captain Ransom's Battery, were essentially giant shots that hurled hundreds of grape-sized iron balls that swept the Texans' fence line in a deadly swath twenty-five yards wide, even at a distance of 400 yards. Unfortunately for the dwindling band of Work's defenders, Captain Ransom's artillery on the rise was now closer at around 150 yards and hence much deadlier.

When the Federal guns scored a direct hit with shells (either before the gunners switched to canister or ran out of canister shot as the fight progressed), "the rails of the fence flew high in the air." Along with the flying fence rails, which were snapped in two or shattered to pieces, the body parts of First Texas Rebels also flew through the air, proving that Captain Ransom's guns were highly effective "infantry killers." Horrified by the sight, one Union officer saw a Texan "arm go 30 feet in the air and fall back again" in one fiery explosion. This Federal officer was sickened by the sight of the slaughter and never forgot the horror: "It was just awful."[173]

From Grimes County, Sergeant William E. Barry, Company G (Grimes County Greys), Fourth Texas, witnessed the continued decimation of the First Texas's ranks, before he was cut down and captured. Born in 1838, only two years after the Texas Revolution's conclusion thanks to Houston's miracle victory at San Jacinto, he described how "[o]n one brief occasion, I saw the fragments of the legs of one poor [First] Texan's body flying in the air, having been torn and dismembered by a shell." Private Barry lamented the ruin of the First Texas, now literally a dying command, writing how "[t]hese brave men were mowed down like the corn surrounding them."[174]

Fighting against a cruel fate, Work's stoic soldiers, who now continued to die long after victory was no longer possible, steadily dropped in gory heaps from multiple fires. Among the victims were three Perry brothers of Company E (Marshall Guards) who hailed from a well-to-do slave-owning family, as well as a cousin. These Harrison County soldiers of the Marshall Guards paid a high price for their desperate bid to win it all this morning. Alabama-born Corporal Harwood Earl Perry, age eighteen, was one brother who was cut down. Known as "Earl," he was fatally wounded in the leaden tempest. His first cousin, Lieutenant Clinton Perry, was likewise killed at the head of his Company E soldiers, who seemed bent on fighting to the bitter end, regardless of the frightful odds. Brothers of "Earl," George F. and Eugene Osceola Perry (named in honor of the great Seminole chief who had long defied the United States Army and West Point's finest officers in Florida's depths during the 1830s), were both seriously wounded. All three young brothers (dark haired and handsome) were cut down, two fatally in the holocaust that raged across the projectile-swept northern edge of the Miller Cornfield that had become a grim killing ground.

Eugene somehow survived the nightmarish combat of the cornfield, but he was fated to be killed at the Battle of the Wilderness in May 1864, when General Ulysses S. Grant's Army of the Potomac mounted its final offensive to capture Richmond. Earl, Eugene and Clinton Perry had attended the prestigious Kentucky Military Institute, located just outside Louisville, Kentucky: educations that helped to enhance the overall combat prowess of the First Texas. At the war's beginning, they had departed from the respected school to enlist together in the Marshall Guards (Company E). Now two of these young men, Clinton and "Earl" Perry, from Harrison County (drained by the Red and Sabine Rivers and located on the Louisiana border in northeast Texas), along with a good many of their "dear friends gave their lives for Texas in the extreme foremost fighting line" at the northern edge of the Miller Cornfield.[175]

A Fourth Texas soldier, Private Polley, described the horror for the young men and boys of the Texas Brigade, especially the First Texas and its swift decimation at the northern edge of the cornfield: "The Texas Brigade was now only a skirmish line [while] The earth and sky seemed to be on fire, and it looked like here would be the Thermopylae of the Texas Brigade. With sublime courage the 1st Texas held their advanced position in the cornfield against overwhelming numbers."[176]

Aligned on favorable ground, from the Hagerstown Road to the elevated vantage point on which Ransom's Battery was perched before the First Texas, Federal artillery continued to hurl forth double loads of canister that punished what little remained of the Texas Brigade. The guns of Battery B, Fourth United States Artillery, along the pike continued to riddle the ranks of Hampton's Legion and the Eighteenth Georgia, while to the left, other Federal guns hurled canister into the First Texas and the Fifth Texas, which was far distant from Work's right flank, still dangerously in midair.[177]

All the while, Work's Texans were severely punished at a steady rate by "a fire of musketry...from my left and rear," causing severe havoc along the thin fence line that bordered the cornfield's northern edge. Additional First Texas boys were hit by bullets pouring from the east, north and south, dropping

A tintype of a Texas soldier in a six-button shell jacket and with his musket by his side. Found in east Texas, this photo was taken in a small room by an unknown photographer who had set up shop at a Confederate encampment. *Author's collection.*

to the vicious crossfire. Company K (Texas Invincibles), First Texas, was especially decimated, with the hail of Yankee bullets creating more widows or orphans in the communities, gulf ports and log cabins across east Texas.[178]

Clearly, this disastrous situation was simply untenable for the remaining band of First Texas soldiers. The fire from the rear brought the greatest terror to surviving Texas Rebels, revealing that all distant support on the regiment's left and rear had disappeared: indications that now raised the distinct possibility that the entire First Texas could be surrounded by the encroaching Union legions.

The ever-dwindling group of Work's survivors now risked the cruel fate of being annihilated by the advancing units of Hooker's Corps after the Texas Brigade's left wing, located somewhere in the expanse of the cornstalks to the southwest, had been repulsed and forced to withdraw. Ironically, however, this scorching flank and rear fire was the price paid by the First Texas for the greatest tactical success and deepest penetration of Hooker's line by any unit of Hood's Division. In a haunting paradox not lost to them, Work's survivors continued to suffer the consequences of their successful advance, especially when combined with the withdrawal of Hampton's South Carolina Legion, Fourth Texas and the Eighteenth Georgia.

Work explained how his regiment's fatal situation could not be altered: "Had the Eighteenth Georgia and Hampton's Legion not met with the most obstinate and stubborn resistance from a superior force to their left, they would have supported me promptly and effectively upon my left" for a resumption of the tactical offensive. With the Hampton Legion, Fourth Texas and Eighteenth Georgia having been repulsed and now withdrawing farther south before the advancing Iron Brigade's Nineteenth Indiana and Seventh Wisconsin and Patrick's Brigade, the First Texas soldiers continued to hold out on their own against the odds. All the while, they remained completely without any support whatsoever on the left to ensure that the regiment was in the process of dying alone and for no gain.[179]

Throughout the entire morning, no reinforcements had been forthcoming to the First Texas, now the most vulnerable and heavily pressured unit of the Army of Northern Virginia. Despite their best efforts, which had cost so many lives of the regiment's best and brightest, Work and his followers remained in a hopeless situation and seemingly trapped in a doomed position that was about to collapse at any moment. All of the hard-fighting regiment's significant tactical gains were about to be forfeited because of the lack of support, after having achieved so much success.

THE SACRIFICE OF MAJOR "MATT" DALE

The regiment's acting lieutenant colonel (Work was now acting colonel after Colonel Alexander "Alex" T. Rainey had been cut down during the attack at Gaines's Mill), young Major Matthew "Matt" Dale, took action in a critical situation. He departed from what little remained of his battered right wing in a risky attempt to seek out Work to request specific instructions during the height of the crisis.

While the air was filled with whizzing projectiles, Dale dashed west through the relatively few remaining green stalks of the cornfield not yet flattened by shot, shell and bullets and across a ground littered with the dead and dying men of both sides. The major ran a deadly gauntlet along the cornfield's northern edge and was miraculously not hit. For the ambitious young man of promise from the agricultural community of Palestine and the Neches River country of Anderson County, it now must have seemed like ages ago when he had been the fiery pro–states' rights editor of the *Trinity Advocate* and a respected Anderson County representative in the state legislature at Austin, located on the upper reaches of the Colorado River.

With bullets zipping through the cornstalks and raising little spurts of dust along the dry ground, young Dale finally reached Lieutenant Colonel Work near the First Texas's center, which was no small accomplishment under such deadly circumstances. Clearly, Major Dale's luck was holding true. Here, the regiment's two leading officers attempted—with considerable difficulty, having to shout to be heard above the din of battle—to discuss the First Texas's dire situation along the cornfield's embattled northern edge, while the fire from multiple directions, including the rear, continued to claim the lives of additional soldiers. He presented the horrifying information to the commanding officer that almost every last soldier of the entire regiment's right wing was now either killed or wounded.

Above the roaring gunfire, Dale yelled to Work that "none would survive unless the regiment was withdrawn" to escape this man-made hell. Lieutenant Colonel Work never forgot the tragic moment when the handsome Major Dale "was conferring with me as to the propriety of advancing or at once withdrawing" south to fight another day. An irreplaceable loss then occurred, and one that was just a matter of time.[180] Work described the painful moment that he never forgot:

> *Just as messenger* [Private Charles] *Hicks had left me on his mission, Major Matt Dale, commanding the rigt* [sic] *wing, came to me at my station at the center and reported that nearly every man of the right wing had been shot down, killed or wounded, and not a man would be left alive unless we withdrew at once. The roar all about us of nearby small arms and of artillery more distant was so deafening that the Major, in making his report, had to place his mouth to my ear. Just as he concluded and whilst we still were standing breast to breast, he with his right side and I with my left towards front, he was stricken by a bullet, straightened, stiffened and fell backwards prone upon the ground, dead.*[181]

Lamenting the loss of a good friend and one of the regiment's best officers, Chaplain Davis described the severe blow suffered by the First Texas when Major Dale "was thus standing [when] the fatal bullet penetrated his body in a vital part, and he fell, and in a few moments breathed his last. No braver or better man fell on the field of Sharpsburg. We can ill afford to spare such a man and such an officer—but he is gone....He was a kind, generous and magnanimous friend, a noble and devoted patriot, a faithful and wise statesman, and a heroic and gallant soldier. One had but to know him well to know the number of his virtues."[182]

Instead of dampening spirits, Dale's fall only heightened the determination of the survivors to keep fighting to the bitter end along the fence line along the cornfield's northern border. They now fought so that the popular major and other revered comrades would not have died in vain. Indeed, the major's death had the dual effect of angering and inspiring Work's soldiers. With the relatively few rounds remaining in cartridge boxes, the men of the First Texas wanted to kill even more Yankees to avenge his loss.[183]

ANTIETAM'S GREATEST KILLING FIELD

As if the grisly spectacle of Major Dale's death and the stunning news that the regiment's right wing had been all but wiped out were not enough of a shock, Captain Woodward, who long had benefited from Dale's solid leadership when he had served as Woodward's top lieutenant in his Anderson County Reagan Guards (Company G), now reached Work with additional bad news. In Work's words: "Immediately [after Major "Matt" Dale's death]—scarcely a minute—Capt. John R. Woodward [the now acting major in Dale's absence, who would be killed at Gettysburg in less than a year, now in command of the left wing] came to me with a like report as to that wing [and] the regiment [now] no longer had the ability either to advance or resist attack effectively," as combat capabilities were no more.[184] Despite the determination to hold firm around their bullet-shredded battle flags that still stood in defiance at the fence bordering the cornfield's north side, the First Texas's left and right were now so decimated that solid resistance was no longer possible.

What could no longer be denied was that the First Texas was virtually wiped out by this time. More than half of Work's soldiers had been killed or wounded. Work finally concluded "that it was madness to advance with the few men left [but he] remained [in position] awaiting orders and information as to what my movements should be, being unwilling to withdraw as long as I had the ability to hold my then position without [orders] to do so."[185]

Nevertheless, the dwindling band of First Texas soldiers continued to hold firm to their toehold along the cornfield's northern edge while additional soldiers went down. No Texans had ever experienced such a nightmarish battlefield situation in Virginia or anywhere else.

Large-caliber bullets from Yankee muskets continued to inflict terrible damage, with the soft lead changing direction upon impact and widening the wound. These chucks of lead shattered bone to leave gaping wounds and massive bleeding, especially when arteries were cut, that could not be stopped. If not bleeding to death on the field, a Texas soldier with a shattered limb faced a crude amputation—a hasty operation by overworked Confederate surgeons that often led to death. Given these ugly realities for the victim, perhaps an instant death in the cornfield was actually a blessing in disguise of sorts for unfortunate Texas Rebels with badly shattered arms and legs. However, even the best surgeons could do nothing for men shot in the stomach, head or chest—almost always a death sentence. This tragic fate had befallen many First Texas men, who were now lying behind the inadequate cover of the rail fence.

Sergeant Russell C. Mitchell was another excellent soldier who went down in the hail of projectiles. He suffered a nasty head wound from an exploding shell. The sergeant was nicknamed "the Lawyer" by his more homespun and less educated Company I comrades of the Crockett Southrons. Of Irish descent from Ulster Province, North Ireland, and with family memories of the Emerald Isle, Mitchell was the grandfather of a shy, diminutive female novelist from Atlanta, Georgia: Margaret Mitchell, the author of America's most famous Civil War novel, *Gone with the Wind*. Of course, this literary feat by his gifted granddaughter was only possible in the twentieth century because Sergeant Mitchell recovered from his head wound suffered in the cornfield. Lucky to have survived one of the war's greatest slaughters, he was then detailed as a nurse at a hospital in strategic Atlanta. Thanks to a strange fate, Mitchell never returned to Company I, First Texas. The sergeant remained in Atlanta, where he started his life anew far from Antietam's killing fields and a cruel fate that could not be overcome.

Embodying never-say-die attitudes despite the staggering losses, the remaining men of Work's regiment were bent on fighting to the bitter end from behind the fence line also because of what the common soldiers held close with pride: the Texas Brigade had yet to retreat in battle. Consequently, these hardened Lone Star State veterans were determined not to break that distinguished record by giving an inch of ground. Caught in the cauldron of the bitter struggle for possession of the cornfield, one Texas Brigade soldier described how "the earth and sky seemed to be on fire, and it looked like here would be the Thermopylae of the Texas Brigade. With sublime courage the First Texas held their advanced position in the [northern edge of the] cornfield against overwhelming numbers" and steadily decreasing chances for survival.[186]

By this time, Colonel Wofford had already given up all hope of achieving any kind of success, as did all regimental commanders of the Texas Brigade except the determined Work. Incredibly, he still refused to relinquish the ground that his regiment had gained. Colonel Wofford finally concluded with justifiable bitterness and regret how "by this time, our brigade having suffered so greatly, I was satisfied they could neither advance or hold their position much longer without reinforcements."[187]

Wofford had galloped to the rear to inform General Hood of the extent of the crisis that was destroying his prized brigade. Ever the fighter, Hood nevertheless hesitated to give the painful withdrawal order, because it meant throwing away the hard-won tactical gains that were so promising in potential terms. Nevertheless, the battered Texas Brigade units, except the First Texas, continued to give ground out of urgent necessity with the resurgent Federals steadily advancing in overwhelming numbers.

Because of the lack of ammunition and high casualties, the outnumbered Confederates now faced certain annihilation. Leading the way to the First Texas's right, the withdrawal of the Fifth Texas, under Captain "Ike" N.M. Turner, who was left with no choice because his "men were out of ammunition," withdrew, starting a chain reaction. The Fourth Texas, to the First Texas's southwest, also retired. The handsome Lieutenant Colonel Benjamin Franklin Carter described the tactical situation: "I discovered… that if I fell back the troops on my right [the First Texas] who had entered the corn-field would be surrounded [therefore] we held this position for some time [and] until the troops [the Fifth Texas] in the corn-field on my right were falling back."[188]

With the foremost Rebels to the regiment's right and left continuing to fall back under the relentless pounding, Work's advanced position at around the midway point of the cornfield's northern edge could not be held much longer. After all, this suicidal stand no longer made any tactical or practical sense. Nevertheless, these last remaining Texas Rebels gamely continued to fire their last remaining cartridges in a close-range exchange with the Pennsylvania Reserves and rallied units, including the Iron Brigade.[189]

Against the odds, the First Texas somehow managed to maintain the most advanced position for the longest period of time. This struggle along the cornfield's northern edge now had only one possible outcome, after the withdrawal of the Texas brigade's remainder that left Work's regiment even more isolated. Incredibly, "All of Hood's regiments had retired except the 1st Texas," which continued to wage its own personal war against too many Yankees to count.

The First Texas at this time was now surrounded on three sides by the advancing Federal units, whose lines extended as far as the eye could see. It now seemed that the Alamo's tragic story was about to be played out again in this obscure spot in Washington County.

The slugfest along the northern edge of the Miller Cornfield had turned into just another bloody repeat of past battles, where the Texans had been unable to fully exploit a breakthrough because of lack of timely support. All the while, the First Texas continued to wither away from the vicious flank and crossfire. A remote cornfield more than 1,500 miles from the state capital at Austin was destined to become a final resting place for a large percentage of the First Texas's manpower.

First Texas soldiers continued to frantically rummage through the cartridge boxes of their dead and wounded comrades while bullets splintered fence rails. So many men had been cut down that some soldiers did not have to search for extra rounds in cartridge boxes. Private James M. Polk recalled, "I didn't take time to load my gun, for there were plenty of loaded guns lying on the ground by the side of the dead and wounded men" of both sides. Racing the clock in an increasingly desperate situation, additional men searched for cartridges deeper into the cornfield, where the bodies lay thick among the trampled cornstalks. One Texas Rebel explained, "After breaking through and thoroughly routing two successive columns of the enemy, their ammunition was exhausted. Unwilling to abandon the advantage so bravely won, scouting squads gathered from the field the cartridges of the dead both friend and foe—and with this supply endeavored to hold their ground until relived by fresh troops."[190]

The regiment's acting major after Major Dale's death, Captain Woodward, dispatched messengers four different times to request support before it was too late. But no reinforcements—not even a single company—were forthcoming to the First Texas, which seemed fated to be wiped out to a man. Colonel Wofford could not be found on this field of death to give the order to withdraw.[191]

Work's ambition (unrealistic at this time) of receiving support on either side of his First Texas and reinforcements from the rear to continue the attack beyond the cornfield in a last-ditch effort to turn the left flank of Hooker's Corps faded away. The golden dream of reaping a decisive victory was doomed to be an unfulfilled one for the surviving Texans. However, not one of Work's messengers ever reached Wofford, leaving him without orders or instructions in the most critical of situations.

As explained by Alabama-born Chaplain Davis, a fiery Presbyterian man of God who saw this war as a great moral crusade and the Yankees as unholy Philistines who needed to be vanquished at all costs, "Again and again, Hood sent for aid [from D.H. Hill's division in the center], while his little devoted band of heroes were struggling with the many thousands of the enemy, who were pouring in…long after every prospect to the eye of the observer of their final success had fled [but] They had never been beaten upon the field, and knew not how to give ground. They were out-numbered twenty to one. But there they stood, amid the storm of death, until they became the astonishment and admiration of their enemies."[192]

Angry over the loss of so many good fighting men in his elite brigade, Hood later wrote with bitterness to his commander, Georgian Major General James Longstreet, "[T]he major-general commanding is aware of the number of messages received from me asking for reinforcements," but none came for his division, slaughtered while awaiting the succor that never arrived.[193]

Meanwhile, this very personal war for the few surviving First Texas men against superior Union might continued unabated, defying fate and postponing the inevitable. One Federal was indeed astonished at the Texans' sheer tenacity in this nightmarish struggle against the odds, writing, "It is beyond all wonder, how men, such as these rebel troops are—can fight as they do. That those ragged and filthy wretches, sick, hungry, and, in all ways miserable, should prove such heroes in the fight, is past explanation. Men never fought better."[194]

What could not be denied by this time was the rather remarkable fact that as long as Work and his soldiers stubbornly fought back from behind the rail fence along the cornfield's northern, the Miller Cornfield was denied to the army of the much-touted "Young Napoleon," who might well be the next United States president if decisive victory was won today. Throughout this morning, these realizations were not lost on the surviving young men and boys from Texas, helping to fuel their determination to hold firm to their precarious toehold at the cornfield's northern end. Despite having been repulsed and now on the verge of annihilation, they had already achieved a strategic success by denying McClellan a decisive victory.

With a mixture of sadness and bitterness, Work recognized the old familiar and tragic pattern that had ensured past Confederate defeats, a persistent failure that seemed to be omnipresent for the hard-fighting common soldiers, who continued to die in overwhelming numbers: "[T]he necessity of having supports promptly and quickly upon the field [to exploit gains] if required to carry strong positions in a few more engagements, and, after carrying them, hold them unaided and alone, this regiment must soon become annihilated and extinct without having accomplished any material or permanent good."[195]

In this regard, Lieutenant Colonel Work was not guilty of exaggeration. Swept by multiple fires, the First Texas was all but extinct by this time. But what had not died this morning was the faith of the men in the ranks for eventually achieving decisive victory on some future battlefield, when the gods of war were less cruel and the Federals less strong. By this time, only a mere handful of First Texas men were left alive. Nevertheless, the survivors still blazed away along the north border of the cornfield, stubbornly holding their ground. Some Texas soldiers had now emptied more than seventy cartridges in attempting to reverse the hands of fate—forty rounds for each cartridge box. During the tenacious struggle for possession of the cornfield, Hood summarized without hyperbole how this was "the most terrible clash of arms, by far, that has occurred during the war."[196]

The most inspirational First Texas leaders were already dead, including young Matt Dale. Major Dale's death came as a severe blow to this elite command. Lamenting the loss of the model Christian warrior who fought with his heart like a crusader battling Islamic warriors in the Holy Land, Chaplain Davis wrote how the entire brigade mourned "the loss of the gallant Major Dale of the 1st Texas, who fell in the thickest of the fight."[197]

In the Miller Cornfield, the color guard troops who protected the Lone Star State flag with their lives continued to be slaughtered at an unprecedented rate. Lieutenant Colonel Work had remained near the colors, as usual, to inspire his men to greater exertions. He already had watched in horror while John Hanson, James Day, Charles H. Kingsley and James K. Malone fell in rapid succession while carrying the tattered

A Confederate soldier in a dark-colored militia uniform and wearing long hair in the popular Texas frontier style. Found in Texas. *Author's collection.*

flag above the omnipresent cornstalks and into the heart of the raging storm during the attack. However, Work wrote with admiration how "after the fall of these [first four color bears], still others raised the colors" to reinvigorate the command's fighting spirit. After the color guard had been shot down, four additional men who carried the Lone Star State flag at the First Texas's head were also cut down during this vicious struggle.[198]

Even the Yankees were awed by the bravery of these steadfast flag guardians of the First Texas. Educated at the Mound Prairie Institute along with his two brothers, who also served with distinction in the First Texas, Lieutenant Robert "Billy" Hugh Gaston of the Texas Guards (or the Anderson County Guards), Company H, went to the rescue of the fallen colors at a time when it was especially important for the silk banner to be raised during the attack. Astonished Yankees "had seen [Lieutenant Gaston] leap forward to grab the Brigade [First Texas] flag as the color-bearer fell to the ground."[199] In an August 1, 1861 letter to his sister, "Billy" Gaston had felt a solemn reverence for the regiment's sacred banner, describing how "President Davis presented [us] with a beautiful banner [which] was made by Mrs. [Louis T.] Wigfall.... It is the finest one I have ever seen."[200]

For his heroics in inspiring the First Texas onward during the most successful charge of Hood's Division, Lieutenant Gaston, the son of a distinguished Texas state legislator who hailed from Mount Sylvan, Smith County, Texas, had been killed. In Gaston's case, the common soldiers' admiration for sheer courage had not been enough to make the Federals hold their fire.[201]

Serving in the company named for the former Tennessee congressman who fell at the Alamo, Private Henry Waters Berryman of the Crockett Southrons (Company I)—whose brother was one of the regiment's most resourceful foragers and a good fighting man, Lieutenant Newton "Newt" Monroe Berryman, who fell wounded in Antietam's tempest—wrote in a September letter only days after the battle how "the flag that was presented to us by Mrs. Davis and Mrs. Wigfall was [targeted by the Yankees] on the field. Just as fast as one man would pick it up he would be shot down. Eight men were killed and wounded in trying to bring it off the field."[202]

The fighting photographer and self-styled artist Solomon Thomas Blessing also saw the flag go down, lamenting the sight of its fall. He wrote how the cherished banner "was made from the wedding dresses of Mrs. Jefferson Davis and Mrs. Louis T. Wigfall, and presented to the regiment."[203]

Revealing his reverence for so many sacrificed color bearers who had led the way, Captain David King Rice, leading Company K (Texas Invincibles), First Texas, wrote shortly after the battle, "There had been eight men shot down with it [the regimental colors], when we entered a cornfield, following the retreating foe" in triumph.[204] In fact, even more young men and boys of the First Texas were killed defending the Lone Star State flag than this grisly total. Corporal William David Henderson Pritchard, of Company H (Texas Guards), described how the tattered colors were "wrapped around the dead body of the last of 16 men who had fallen with it that bloody day."[205]

At the cornfield's northern edge, the unceasing salvos of Union artillery and musketry continued to take a greater toll on the First Texas's survivors. Ironically, issued in 1862, a Southern pamphlet advised Confederate fighting men to "[l]et your beard grow so as to protect your throat and lungs," foolish advice that had accomplished absolutely nothing to save any Texas soldiers in the Miller Cornfield. Captain Richard W. Cotton, leading Company I (Crockett Southrons), went down when a bullet struck him in the head. Other Lone Star State soldiers fell to the iron fragments from exploding shells that burst overhead and then fell around them. With canister and shell, veteran Yankee artillerymen continued to concentrate their murderous fire on the

A view of the Antietam battlefield in the Dunker Church sector north of Sharpsburg. *DeGolyer Library, Southern Methodist University, Lawrence T. Jones III Texas Photography Collection; Civil War: Photographs, Manuscripts and Imprints.*

lone Confederate regiment that lay on the verge of annihilation. Shells exploded around them, and double loads of canister and volleys of musketry swept the fence. One Texan described in horror, "I saw the fragments of the legs of one poor [1st] Texan's body flying in the air, having been torn and dismembered by a shell....These brave men were mowed down like the corn surrounding them."[206]

Another Texas soldier described the ultimate tragic reality of the slaughter in the Miller Cornfield, writing how there was "no protection, and it seemed impossible for a rat to live in such a place....The dead and wounded were in every direction [and] were lying in every direction."[207]

For all practical purposes, the First Texas was now all but extinguished as a viable command—every four of five members of Work's regiment had been cut down this morning. Lee's best fighters, these young men and boys now lay in twisted, bloody clusters of mangled bodies among the battered cornstalks.

AN UNPRECEDENTED SLAUGHTER

A lengthy list of Texas soldiers of the "Ragged First" who were either killed or wounded in one of the war's most nightmarish struggles told the tragic story of a regiment's destruction—nearly 50 killed and almost 150 wounded in the bitter contest for the cornfield. This was the highest loss of any Texas Brigade regiment. Hereafter and for ample good reason, simply the mention of the Miller Cornfield prompted trauma for the few remaining regimental members who somehow survived the war's most severe blood-letting on an unparalleled day of slaughter.

Acting Adjutant J. Winkfield Shropshire was badly wounded (it was thought mortally at first), when he fell before he could deliver Work's desperate message requesting support. In attempting to supply the First Texas with extra rounds when survivors urgently needed additional cartridges to maintain a steady fire, Ordnance Sergeants M.A. Dunham, still not fully recovered from a nasty Second Manassas wound, but yet at the forefront, and W. Park Mynatt, who was fated to die in this war, both went down wounded while performing beyond the call of duty.

By this time, entire companies of the First Texas had been utterly annihilated, completely knocked out of action by the spiraling losses. Company F lost every Woodville Rifles soldier in its ranks. Among the men of this company from Tyler County in northeast Texas, the following Company F members fell wounded in the cornfield: Lieutenant Sam A. Wilson; Sergeant James E. Perryman; and Privates S. Engleking, Amos G. Hanks, William F. Holmes, W.A. Roundtree and William F. Scott, who died on September 17. Among the killed were Lieutenant J. Perry Runnels, Private Oscar Felps and Private Charles Hicks, who, like Shropshire, was fatally cut down when attempting to deliver Work's desperate message for assistance.

The second-hardest-hit company of the First Texas, Company A, was wiped out except for a single very lucky survivor. The Marion Rifles (Company A) had lost its leader, Captain George T. Todd, a former private who had risen up through the ranks by his own ability and initiative. He fell wounded from the iron fragments of an exploding shell, along with ten of his men who were likewise wounded, including Sergeant J.C. Hill; Corporal James K. Malone; and Privates George Washington Armstrong, Frank E. Blackburn, T.E. Brewer, Green Baker, Ben R. Lane and E.P. Derrick, who was destined for death at Gettysburg, where Lee's s next Northern invasion proved as equally ill-fated as the first. Private Willis Whitaker lost an arm and nearly his life. Four soldiers of the Marion Rifles from Marion and Cass Counties were killed in the bitter struggle amid the tall cornstalks: Sergeant James C. Hill and Privates James A. Joyner and C.D. and Tom Jones. Along with Private Stephen Hempstead, who was captured, Private H.J. Epperson was wounded, captured and then fated to die in a dirty Yankee prison camp.

The Livingston Guards of Company B were also hit hard, paying a high price for attempting to do the impossible against so many Yankees and well-served pieces of artillery. Eleven Company B men fell wounded, including two mortally, in the cornfield: Lieutenant John L. Shotwell; Sergeant Charles W. Butler, from Livingston, Polk County, and Sergeant John Victory; and Privates M.B. Anderson, George Washington Barfield, B.L. Bowling, Rufus R. Choate, George H. Johnson, W.O. Pankey, Sam L. Ward and Sam J. Woodward. Meanwhile, Corporal C.R. Dunham, who also cut down, was captured after the cornfield was regained by the Yankees.

As fate would have it, only two survivors were now alive in the decimated ranks of Company C. Among the Palmer Guards (Company C) from the bustling town of Houston, Lieutenant F.L. Hoffman, of German descent, and Private G.L. Gage were killed. Another three soldiers from Houston (named for the hero of San Jacinto who won the independence of the Texas

Republic) fell wounded in the swirling combat: Privates George Washington McMannus, who had been named after the "Father of the Country," William T. Stamper and Charles Watson. Private Watson survived the operation that resulted in the amputation of his leg, but he died only three days after the battle. Captain David King Rice was not even listed among the First Texas wounded, despite a jagged fragment of shell striking his hip and leaving a deep, bloody gash. Clearly, Rice was one of the fortunate ones on this bloody Wednesday morning, having survived with four bullets holes through the blanket roll wrapped around his shoulder.

In the decimated ranks of Company D, nine men of the Marion Rifles (also known as the Star Rifles) were killed: Privates Edward "Ed" B. Brown, Raddy Connally, W.C. and W.R. Jackson, Abe S. Therrell, William Snow, William Sartin, Jake Durrum and J.R. Connally (of Irish descent and affectionately known by his friends as "Ruddy," which was in keeping with his brother's nickname of "Raddy"). Unfortunately, however, Texas sources that tell about the stories of Irish Confederates, especially at Antietam, are few and far between, obscuring the lives and sacrifices of the sons of Erin like the Connally boys.

Another eight Company D boys from Marion County were wounded by bullets, shells and bayonets, including Sergeant William A.T. Oliver; Sergeant Andrew Jackson Wood, who was named after America's seventh president of Scotch-Irish descent and an American Revolutionary War veteran from South Carolina; Sergeant E.C. Powell; and Privates James P. Dunklin, H.C. McCoy, Jack P. Wood, Miles J. Foster and Lucian W. Thomas, who was captured and fated to die in a Northern prison. But unlike so many of his comrades, Private Bartlett beat the odds, surviving his leg's amputation in a painful procedure that was managed with deliberate speed by a capable Union surgeon to prevent blood loss and enhance chances for recovery.[208]

Only three survivors of cornfield remained alive in Company E ranks to tell the tale of the disaster that had befallen the First Texas. Four soldiers of the Marshall Guards (Company E) were killed: Lieutenant Clinton E. Perry, Howard Earl Perry, Corporal Harwood Earl Eugene Perry and Private William M. Campbell. Privates Eugene Osceola Perry and Sidney Franklin Perry, who was known affectionately as "Bose," were wounded.

A good many members of Company E (Marshall Guards) fell wounded, including Lieutenant Berry W. Webb, who was an inspirational and respected leader. Among these Company E wounded men who hailed from Harrison County were Privates T.W. Willingham, Robert L. Clark, C.H. Fields, Marcus Gillette, Joseph F. Rudder, John W. Smith, Samuel T. Watson, George F. Heard, W. Samuel Brazeal, Robert J. Marshall, J.D. Campbell and James H. Hendrick, who died of his wound. Private E.M. Ewing was captured.[209] Having been cut to pieces during the bitter struggle for possession of the Miller Cornfield, Company F was simply no more. Not a single member of the Woodville Rifles escaped the combat. Every Tyler County soldier was killed, wounded or captured in what was truly a holocaust for the First Texas.

But no company of the First Texas was affected more in terms of the total number of fatalities than the Reagan Guards of Company G from Anderson County. From the long list of casualties, this unit could no longer be called the Anderson County Invincibles. The fine command lost seven killed: Lieutenant Matt Dale (acting major); Sergeant Manley M. Files; Corporals Zeb Cantley and Basil "Bass" A. Hallum; and Privates James Aspley, Smith Bottoms, Richard Butler, John "Jack" Cone, M.M. Eeles, W.P. Hoover, Calvin R. McFarland and the Posey boys, Privates Andrew Jackson "Joe" and Ed Posey.

Another ten Company G soldiers from Anderson County were wounded, including Charley Wright, who had his arm blown off by an artillery projectile. Other wounded members of the crack Reagan Guards included Lieutenants Elbert S. Jemison and T. Jeff Rose; Sergeant Matthew James Aspley; Privates Silas L. "Sebe" Blackshear, James W. Mathews, James Ward, F.J. Watts and Jim M. Corder, who was mortally wounded; and Corporal Z.W. Cantley, known as "Zeb."

The Texas Guards, or Anderson County Guards, of Company H lost three killed and thirteen wounded. Fatalities of Company H included Sergeant James H. Marshall and Privates Antonio Anderson, James G. Tippen and Caleb McBride. William Hollingsworth was also among the killed. Two brothers fell wounded, Nathan Hollingsworth and Joseph C. Hollingsworth, who was fated to die of his wound in mid-October. Well-educated Lieutenant Robert Hugh Gaston, one of the finest natural leaders of Company H, was killed while carrying the regimental colors.

Among the wounded men of Company H were Sergeant James R. Jones; Corporals Haywood G. Hickman and Eldred F. Ezell; and Privates W.A. Roundtree, Canada S. Bolton, John A. Counts, George Washington Culpepper, William G. Derrough, Felix M. Embry, Leander L. Evans, William L. Williams and William F. Scott, who died of his wound.

Company I (Crockett Southrons) lost six men killed on this morning in Washington County. Other soldiers killed from this excellent company included Corporal Drury Hale and Privates Felix W. Box, Allen A. Congleton, Thomas Jefferson Cook, Levi J. Fitts, W.M. Payne and Wiley A. House.

On the bloodiest morning of the Civil War, Company I lost more officers than any other First Texas company. Captain Richard W. Cotton died of his head wound before the end of this sad September. Captain John H. Wootters was wounded, along with Lieutenants Albert A. Aldrich, Henry N. Jomes and Newton "Newt" Monroe Berryman—who also had been wounded in the assault on Malvern Hill—and Private Tom A. Boone. Other wounded members of the Crockett Southrons included Corporal William D. Pritchard and Privates John S. Harwell, brainy Russell C. "Lawyer" Mitchell, H.C. Patrick, John H. Sheridan, M. Youngblood and Malachiah Reeves.

Company K, the Texas Invincibles, lost two officers killed, Lieutenants James Waterhouse and Samuel F. Patton. In addition, Sergeant Sam F. Patton, an inspirational leader of the boys in the ranks, was killed. Among the privates killed in the living nightmare of the Miller Cornfield was Jesse M. Hale, known as "Jess." Counted among the long list of wounded, Captain John M. Massey was cut down along with eight of his men, including Corporal Orlando Thacker Hanks, who remained defiantly in the fight to the bitter end, despite his severe wound; Sergeant J.O. Noble; and Privates Stephen M. Day, William W. Gray, Edward G. "Ned" Miller, Henry E. Mosely and William O. Quinn, of Scotch-Irish heritage. Private Andrew Jackson Wilson, who had been named for the son of a hopeful Irish immigrant from South Carolina and victor of the Battle of New Orleans, which had propelled him as the people's choice to the presidency, was captured.

In the decimated ranks of the Lone Star Rifles (Star Rifles) of Company L, Lieutenant James C.S. Thompson was killed. Along with twenty of his men, Captain William A. Bedell fell wounded the morning of September 17. Reflecting how the flow of Jewish immigration from Europe to America, including Texas (especially port cities like Galveston), had increased three times in the decades before the Civil War, a number of Jewish Rebels of Company L were included in the fallen: Privates Henry Cohen, who was wounded, and Jacob Frank, who was killed. Other Company L fatalities included Sergeant Stephen A. Carpenter and Privates Joel Bowman, S. Carpenter, George Bass, Robert Jacoblef and William Zimmer, a German perhaps also of the Hebrew faith.

A view of Antietam battlefield looking west from Sharpsburg, Maryland. *DeGolyer Library, Southern Methodist University, Lawrence T. Jones III Texas Photography Collection; Civil War: Photographs, Manuscripts and Imprints.*

Among the Company L wounded soldiers were Corporal John Hanson and Privates Joseph Alsbrook, William Hoskins, Samuel (Solomon) Thomas "Tom" Blessing, John P. Gillis, Charles B. Halleck, Austin W. Jones, Charles H. Kingsley, William Leach, John M. Smith, James Nagle, Henry Schultz, Fred Schwarting, James Welch, William Young, Henry B. McGan and John O. Rourke, a soldier of Irish heritage who was fortunate to survive the ghastly amputation of his arm. Privates John Coffee and Michael Garrity were taken captive on this day of broken dreams.

The Sumter Light Infantry of Company M lost four killed and another eighteen wounded—the highest number of casualties in any First Texas company. Ironically, its eleven survivors ranked highest in number of lucky soldiers of any First Texas company who were spared the slaughter. Among these wounded men of the Silver Greys were Captain Howard Ballenger and Lieutenant William T. Sanford, both attorneys from Trinity County. Other wounded men of Company H included Corporal R.O. Bennett; Sergeant W.C. "Button" Evans; and Privates William J. Townes, James Day, James Bass, Richard O. Bennett, John R. Carlton, E.B. Eaves, J.T. "Turner" Evans, Oliver McBride, J.M. Motes, E. Pope, A. Walter, William J. Goodson and John Lancaster, who died of his wound. In addition, Private H. Charles

Stewart also "probably died" of his wound, paying the high sacrifice for his states' rights beliefs.

In total, Company M suffered seven fatalities, with two wounded men who later died: Lieutenant Sanford and Privates Jeff Bowman, Joshua "Josh" Boon, Vondra J. Wisby, Wade Turner, Thomas Jefferson "Jeff" Bowman, James W. Story and Sergeant S.D. "Shady" Roach.[210]

Lieutenant Colonel Work now looked over what little was left of his regiment, and he was sickened to realize that the best and brightest men of his regiment had been cut down in "the bloodiest patch of land in America." Certainly what little remained of the battered First Texas along the northern edge of the Miller Cornfield was a true "Spartan band," in the words of Corporal Hanks, Texas Invincibles (Company K), who was fortunate to survive a number of close calls. In a letter, one New Englander, Private Roland E. Bowen, was stunned by the extent of the carnage of the Miller Cornfield: "[I]t seemed as if the ground was almost covered with dead and wounded, a large majority of wich [*sic*] were Confederates. It appears that Hooker had fought one of the most desperate fights on this field that has been fought since the commencement of the Rebellion."[211]

ESCAPING TO FIGHT ANOTHER DAY

On this tragic morning, there was no time for the survivors to mourn their devastating losses, including their own relatives, especially brothers, in part because not enough First Texas survivors remained alive to even do so. Meanwhile, two brigades of General Meade's Division and the rallied Iron Brigade launched a greater counterattack in a final united effort to sweep the remainder of the First Texas and the rest of severely depleted Hood's Division from the field. With renewed confidence, this mighty host of bluecoats moved south to lay claim to the cornfield, where at least ten thousand on both sides had been cut down in short order.

Meanwhile, from its position nearly 200 yards southwest of the First Texas at the opposite side of the cornfield in its southwestern corner, the Fourth Texas, the Hampton Legion and the Eighteenth Georgia continued to withdraw to seek shelter from the leaden storm. Three of General Law's regiments, the Second and Eleventh Mississippi and the Sixth North Carolina, which had fought about 150 to 200 yards to the right in the cornfield's northeast edge, likewise fell back to escape the advancing Union juggernaut.

The lonely First Texas remained between the two widely separated sections of Hood's Division. Counterattacking troops of the Iron Brigade and Patrick's New York Brigade continued to push the Texas Brigade's regiments, to the First Texas's left and rear, farther rearward. And to the First Texas's right, Meade's units hurled Law's Alabama, North Carolina and Mississippi regiments southward and from the slight shelter of the cornfield. Now the First Texas was left even more alone and isolated on this day of destiny, after Colonel Wofford and General Law had ordered their respective brigades rearward, before they were destroyed.

Knowing that the day was won in this crucial sector, an overwhelming number of Union attackers continued to punish the First Texas with repeated volleys. With flank and rear fires dropping additional men, and in the face of an overpowering counterattack from the front, "the 1st Texas lay dying": a tragic testament to a dream deferred. Lieutenant Colonel Work "determined…at once to withdraw, as I had but a handful of men left all of whom must have been slain or captured had I remained longer [therefore,] I at once gave the order to fall back."[212]

Despite having received no orders from either Colonel Wofford or General Hood to withdraw, and after having engaged in the nightmarish struggle for the Miller Cornfield from around 7:00 a.m. to 9:00 a.m., Work dispatched Captain U.S. "Scott" Connally, who was destined to die of disease in barely a month and was now leading the few remaining men of the Star Rifles (or the Marion Rifles) from Marion County, Company D, to retire what little remained of the First Texas's right wing now that the popular Major "Matt" Dale was dead. In his most painful directive issued during the war, Work finally did what he and his surviving men had long believed was an impossibility for the leader of an elite combat regiment: he ordered the first withdrawal of First Texas soldiers in this war.

Meanwhile, Captain Woodward was instructed to withdraw the diminutive band of survivors of the regiment's left wing. In the words of the lieutenant colonel, who had witnessed the horror of having seen his fine regiment cut to pieces, "As the regiment no longer had the ability either to advance or resist attack effectively, and in addition, as its line of retreat was in momentary danger of being cut off by the Federals who were firing into our left from the rear, I directed Captain Woodward to retire the left."[213]

RAISING THE TEXAS FLAG ONCE AGAIN

In the hard-pressed center, Work remained with his dwindling band of survivors. Still another First Texas color bearer was cut down. Now torn by bullets, canister and iron shell fragments, the colorful flag of the Lone Star State once again dropped among the rows of corn. By this time, the silken Texas banner was already stained with the blood of previous color bearers. Nevertheless, at least six Texans immediately scrambled forward to raise the fallen colors to inspire their comrades to take heart and continue the fight against impossible odds.

Amid the drifting smoke and whizzing bullets, Work watched with pride as the Lone Star State flag once again went up, rising above the remaining few upright cornstalks for all to see. The black powder–stained faces of the survivors stopped their frantic activity in biting off cartridge tops, ramming down bullets and taking aim to momentarily glance up at the inspiring sight of their raised banner. Now rejuvenated by the invigorating sight, the Texans felt a new surge of adrenaline that boosted their resolve to still defy the odds. This new infusion of fighting spirit caused survivors to fire faster at the encroaching bluecoats with renewed vigor. Work then dashed east through the hail of bullets to assist Captain Connally, of Celtic-Gaelic heritage, in retiring the regiment's right wing under a blistering fire, while Captain Woodward withdrew the regiment's left wing, before every single First Texas soldier was cut down. Work described how he "proceeded to withdraw the right wing" to save what few of his men were still alive by this time.

With fatal resignation and much bitterness over the futile losses of so many good men and officers slaughtered in the thirty-acre field of corn of farmer Miller, Lieutenant Colonel Work, assisted by Captain Woodward on the left and Connally on the right, led the battered First Texas south. But still no regimental member of Work's command faltered or lacked defiance in firing back at their tormentors, even after the three regiments—the Ninth, Eleventh and Twelfth Pennsylvania Reserves of Colonel Robert Anderson's Third Brigade of Meade's Third Division—immediately before them counterattacked. Turning to face and occasionally fire to knock another Pennsylvania soldier out of their lengthy formation, Work's survivors slowly moved back during a quarter-mile withdrawal through the green rows that were still standing, with much confidence and verve.

There was no panic during the Texas withdrawal, as might be expected under such an emergency situation and after such high losses. Indeed, a large part of the Texas Brigade's lofty reputation rested on the fact that these members of Lee's Grenadier Guard had not panicked or run on any battlefield. Withdrawing south in stubborn defiance and repeatedly turning to fire at their tormentors, the First Texas soldiers upheld that hard-won reputation despite taking the highest percentage loss of any unit on the war's bloodiest day, while thousands of other troops (North and South) who had suffered far less already had fled in panic. By any measure, this was a remarkable battlefield feat under the circumstances and had few parallels in the annals of American military history.

Instead of fleeing wildly after suffering staggering losses and an unprecedented beating, Work's survivors still yelled defiant words and curses at the encroaching bluecoats. In addition, the surviving Texans continued to unleash their distinctive Comanche war cry from the Southwest frontier in response to the cheers of the attacking Pennsylvania Reserves of Meade's Division, all while firing back at their pursuers.[214] One Yankee soldier watched the sight in amazement, noting that this was the first time that "the first Union troops to have ever seen the backs of Hood's famous Texans."[215]

Having suffered a wound this morning, the dark-haired and blue-eyed William Robert Hamby, born in 1845 and a member of Company B (Tom Green Rifles), Fourth Texas, never forgot with a measure of pride how: "I saw them broken, shattered, and falling back before overwhelming numbers, the few who were left giving the Rebel yell with more spirit than the hurrahs of the Union troops advancing upon them."[216]

In retiring south, Work planned to take his survivors back (if they could make it) to the inviting shelter of the West Woods from which they had emerged earlier with such confidence to launch their desperate bid to save the day on Lee's shattered left flank: a remarkable tactical feat that had been accomplished against the odds. Consequently, the relatively few First Texas survivors thus walked away with a sense of pride and satisfaction in not only gaining a Pyrrhic victory but also ensuring that Lee's Army was not destroyed and lived to fight another day for the dream of an independent republic—an often forgotten turning point of the bloodiest phase of the Battle of Antietam. However, there was no time to bask in achievements, as it now seemed as if no First Texas soldier would escape the cornfield alive. Indeed, the First Texas soldiers remained under heavy fire from multiple directions, a true gauntlet of death.

From the ranks of Company M (the Sumter Light Infantry) at a point where the ground "was littered with dead and wounded," Private J.T. "Turner" Evans of Polk County went down with a smashed hip. Fortunately, Private William J. "Bill" Townes came to the rescue of his friend. Under a severe fire, Townes "ran with him about a half mile," carrying him rearward through the cornstalks and over the clumps of bodies with Private Evans on his back while bullets made the air sing. After having learned the hard way that they could not count on anyone (including other members of not only the Texas Brigade but also of Hood's Division) but themselves, the boys of the Sumter Light Infantry (Company M) from Trinity County were sticking together to the bitter end. Private Townes was shortly wounded, cut down like so many of his comrades. Thanks to the timely actions of Townes, Private Evans managed to escape the hellish prisons (deadlier even than the battlefield), such as at Alton, Illinois, or Point Lookout, Maryland. Disabled for active duty thereafter, Evans eventually returned to Texas. Here, he then enlisted in a mounted company and fought Native Americans on the frontier to protect the vulnerable people on the Texas frontier—the Texans' forgotten other war—while Hood's men fought and died in disproportionate numbers in faraway western Maryland.[217]

Despite taking a severe wound in the left side, Corporal Hanks was one of the few men left standing in the decimated ranks of Company K, the Texas Invincibles. But like so many First Texas soldiers on this morning, he suffered multiple wounds. In Corporal Hanks's words, "While I was moping along to the rear and being among the last, a bullet passed through my hat brim [but] I made it back a short distance and was carried to a field hospital."[218]

A FINAL TRAGIC LOSS

One final drama remained to be played out in the First Texas, and one that was almost more painful to the survivors than even the loss of so many comrades. During the regiment's lengthy withdrawal through the cornfield and when making a final stand in a desperate attempt to slow the close pursuit of the Eleventh Pennsylvania Reserves, the surviving Texas Rebels were swept with an especially devastating close-range volley of deadly "buck and ball." This accurate volley from a row of .69-caliber smoothbore muskets of the Pennsylvanians was directed at a band of only sixteen Texas men, who stood close together to make a final defensive stand around the tattered Lone

Star State flag—an audacious, but forgotten, last stand in order to allow their hard-pressed comrades time to escape south.

Fourteen soldiers instantly fell in a gory pile after the Pennsylvanians' heavy volley swept through them. Along with one other survivor left alive after this murderous volley, Corporal William David Henderson Pritchard of Company I suddenly found himself standing alone in the trampled corn and among the pile of bodies. But the corporal had not escaped unscathed. This blast of "buck and ball" from soldiers of the Pennsylvania Reserves left him wounded in the face and covered in blood. Corporal Pritchard, the second to last soldier to carry the bullet-shredded banner this morning, dropped the Lone Star State flag in severe pain, clutching his injured face splashed with blood. Then, while bent over to retrieve the fallen colors, a bullet smashed through his breast and tore downward into his stomach. The mortally wounded Corporal Pritchard went down beside the cherished Lone Star State flag in a symbolic falling.

The only survivor of the final fiery blast of the Pennsylvanians' musketry was Private Samuel (Solomon) Thomas "Tom" Blessing. He was the twenty-two-year-old photographer (along with his two brothers—never Confederate soldiers like their youngest brother) who had worked in Houston and Galveston during the 1850s and was a native Marylander of the so-called Wigfall Mess of friends, relatives and comrades. A strange fate had seemingly brought Private Blessing to this point in Washington County, as he had only recently temporarily "deserted" the regiment to briefly visit his family not long after crossing the Potomac and entering Maryland. Now the Company I (Crockett Southrons) soldier, who feared that his photographic career might end forever in an obscure cornfield in the middle of nowhere, watched as a new color bearer, who had immediately picked up the flag after Corporal Pritchard's fall, was likewise cut down by a murderous fire.

One of the early Texas pioneers of photography, Private Blessing described how "[v]ery shortly I fell, shot through the leg and a buckshot in the hand," which left painful wounds and a lifelong scars. The badly wounded Corporal Pritchard and Private Blessing, who also went down with wounds in "both hips," could only now watch the sickening spectacle as the Ninth Pennsylvania Reserves surged forward in triumph. Like its sister Eleventh Pennsylvania Reserves, the Ninth Pennsylvania Reserves was a confident command, having recently "drove the jonies off [South] Mountain," in one soldier's boastful words. In still another success in sweeping the last Rebels out of the cornfield, the elated Keystone State victors then took possession of the

Lone Star State flag, as there was no one was left standing to either defend or save the precious banner. Taking pride in making this unique distinction, Springfield, Massachusetts–born Captain David King Rice, commanding the Palmer Guards of Company C and the nephew of Rice University's founder, William Marsh Rice, wrote in a letter immediately after the battle how "our regiment lost its flag, but it was not taken from us." Around the prized battle flag, at least seventeen First Texas soldiers were lying together, dead, dying or wounded.[219]

When troops of the Ninth Pennsylvania Reserves reached the site of their destructive volley and the widespread decimation of their "buck and call," they were astonished by the extent of the bloody carnage. Amid the lengthy rows of corn that were cut flat by the hail of projectiles, dead and wounded Texans were clumped together in a sickening pile. Perhaps some downed Texans, stained in blood, asked a Pennsylvania soldier for assistance or water, if even able to speak at all. The dream of another easy victory over the often-defeated Army of the Potomac—once embraced by so many naïve Confederates, who had only recently believed that they could vanquish any number of Federals—was over. Born in Fayette County, southwest Pennsylvania, in January 1845 and raised in the small town of Connellsville, Pennsylvania, as the oldest of eight children of John and Sarah Kemp Johnson, Private Samuel Johnson, Company G, Ninth Pennsylvania Reserves, picked up the fallen First Texas colors. For his "capture" of the Lone Star State flag, Private Johnson received the Medal of Honor.[220]

The loss of the regimental battle flag of the "Ragged First" was a heartfelt one that came as a severe blow to the entire regiment. After all, President Davis had presented this beautiful banner to the First Texas during the summer of 1861, when every Texan believed that the war would be short and inevitably end in glory. At that time, the colonel had solemnly promised that "the flag would never trail in the dust in retreat." But that sacred pledge was broken in the surreal horror of the nightmarish fighting in the Miller Cornfield. Private Johnson found the bullet-scarred battle flag, which was known as "Mrs. Wigfall's Wedding Dress" banner, "wrapped around the body of the last of sixteen men," who gave their lives in defense of the Lone Star State flag to allow their comrades to safely withdraw from the great killing ground of the Miller Cornfield.[221]

SLIPPING AWAY FROM A NIGHTMARE

After running a gauntlet of fire and death for about a quarter mile, the surviving First Texas men finally escaped the hellish cornfield to once again reach the clover field to the south. Here, along the cornfield's southern edge, Lieutenant Colonel Work formed up the few of his traumatized First Texas soldiers now left standing, who were most fortunate to still be left alive. He recalled, "Falling back to the Southward limit of the corn patch, I directed the few who had emerged from the corn to rally upon a squad of perhaps thirty men who were gathered about a Confederate battle flag some thirty or forty yards to the Northwest of us and resisting the advance of Federal infantry, whilst I remained to forward on others as they might appear from…the corn."[222]

At this point, for the first time, it was ascertained by the First Texas's survivors that their prized Lone Star State flag was missing. The beautiful colors and their steadfast band of guardians (the color guard of the elite soldiers), who were the regiment's most respected men after the leading officers, had never left the expansive cornfield. Captain David King Rice, commanding Company C (Palmer Guards), wrote shortly after the battle, "After fighting awhile, we were ordered out, and only had 46 men, and none of them knew the flag was left until too late, the corn being so dense that it could be seen but a short distance when flying."[223]

Shocked by the startling realization that the cherished battle flags—the Confederate and Lone Star State banners—were missing, a frantic Captain Woodward "cried out substantially," in Lieutenant Colonel Work's words, "The flags, the flags. Where are the flags?"[224]

As if to answer his own agonizing question, Woodward immediately sprinted alone back into the cornfield, where so many of his men now lay in deathly silence or groaning in pain from multiple wounds. He must have felt that he was reentering hell itself. Significantly, and to Woodward's great credit, the respected captain embarked on his one-man mission without ordering anyone else to perform this dangerous task.

The sweat-stained captain, destined in time to become regimental major and die of a battle wound far from Texas in 1863, demonstrated that he was an exceptional natural leader by undertaking such a dangerous mission on his own. Work watched as Captain Woodward, who only six months before had been serving on a recruiting mission to Texas and might have remained safely in the Trans-Mississippi Theater instead of now returning to the eastern theater, suddenly "rushed back into the corn to recover" the flags.[225]

But Woodward's risky dash to rescue the fallen colors was briefer than he had anticipated. "He had proceeded but a short distance when he came face to face with the advancing enemy, and returned without them," wrote Work of the brave attempt to redeem the regiment's honor and reputation. Indeed, the regimental colors of the First Texas and the distinctive Lone Star State flag were already in Federal hands. The victors proudly exulted over these colorful banners as magnificent trophies of war.[226]

Along with Woodward's futile bid to retrieve the fallen banners in the cornfield, Work's orders for a final defensive stand below the cornfield likewise could not be carried out: "Simultaneously with Woodward's dash in the corn patch, the squad of [First Texas] men rallied about the battle-flag [suddenly] gave way" before overwhelming numbers of attackers, who could hardly believe that they had the much-feared Texans on the run.[227]

Stained with streaks of black powder and the blood of comrades who were no more, these soldiers from the rural countryside of Texas and towns like Galveston, St. Augustine and Houston were swept southeastward through the clover field by masses of Pennsylvania Reserves pouring from the northwest. Now the escape route to the safety of the protective West Woods was blocked by overwhelming numbers of Keystone State soldiers. Realizing that their "line of retreat was cut off by the advancing Federals" and facing still another crisis on a morning of seemingly endless challenges and no-win situations, the versatile Lieutenant Colonel Work quickly developed another tactical plan on the fly.[228]

Surveying the field through the drifting smoke, he now saw that "to the Eastward there was an open but uphill route to a lengthy rail fence, running approximately North and South, which fence was constructed of split slabs from six to eight inches in width and some two inches thick morticed with posts [and] I directed the few [First Texas men] with me to flee to that fence."[229]

With the First Texas's bloody struggle for possession of the cornfield over but never forgotten by any survivor, Work led his band of men farther south toward the relative safety of the rail fence along the dusty Smoketown Road. In many ways, this was a timely strategic and symbolic withdrawal, now that the Miller Cornfield was in Union hands. No troops of the Army of Northern Virginia had accomplished more to deny the enemy possession of the Miller Cornfield or paid a higher price in pursuit of the lofty but impossible goal than the ill-fated Texas soldiers, who had gone to hell and back in a forlorn hope on a nightmarish September morning.

The survivors of the First Texas withdrew farther away from the war's greatest killing ground, where the command had seen its finest and cruelest day to date—a haunting paradox. With pride in what he and his men had accomplished against overwhelming numbers and the best fighting men of the Army of the Potomac, Captain Rice, who led the Palmer Guards of Company C with distinction, wrote, "To the credit of our brave Texas troops, not one man left the field until he was ordered to do so." Fortunately, for the First Texas men who had beaten the odds by merely staying alive on the bloodiest morning of the war, "the attention of the Federals was directed to the battle-flag squad fleeing toward the woods [for] we seemed to escape their notice until we had accomplished about half of the distance to the fence."[230]

Work described still another close call, "[T]hey began firing upon us.... Their bullets when striking the hillside ground raised puffs of dust, just as in the beginning of a shower do[es] large drops of rain on a dusty [Smoketown] road [but] not a man of us received a wound. Capt. Woodward's canteen, swinging against his left side and hip, was shot through from back to front. The scabbard of my light dress sword was stricken in such a way as [it] threw the lower end between by legs from in front and gave me a fall....Before arising I removed the belt from about my waist and upon regaining my feet carried it in my hand the balance of the way."[231]

Finally, Work and his surviving seventeen men took advantage of the slight shelter of the rail fence along the Smoketown Road that ran northeast along the cornfield's southern edge. Here, "Upon reaching the fence some crawled through between slabs and others climbed and bounded over." Fortunately, at this point, the Smoketown Road "which from long usage and rain washing had been worn and cut to a depth of from three to four feet leaving precipitous sides"—a natural trench that provided shelter from the storm. "To the right and left of where we reached it we found [about sixty] men of various commands...the base of the road was littered over with castaway rifles and cartridge boxes, cast away by other fugitives who had continued on in quest of greater safety [and now we had] the greatest plenty both of arms and ammunition," wrote a thankful Work, whose life had been spared by God, he believed.[232]

Now, and for the first time all day, the First Texas soldiers finally gained a much-needed resupply of ammunition. But many other Rebel troops from other commands did not demonstrate a comparable fighting spirit to Work's men. Lieutenant Colonel Work and Captain Woodward became "sternly busy in requiring all of these other fugitives to take rifles and ammunition, 'fall in' and open fire upon the advancing enemy, [while] the members of the 1st Texas were pouring into them a deadly and telling fire, every shot counting [until] soon the Federals were not only repulsed but routed."[233]

With the Yankees of the Pennsylvania Reserves in their immediate front repulsed for the moment and "having disappeared from view," the Texans finally breathed a sigh of relief. Work led his lucky First Texas survivors and their "fugitive" comrades (about seventy-five men in total) east and then south through the clover field littered with the fallen victims. "Whilst thus retreating Southward we were discovered by General Hood, who [now] conducted the squad [toward] the woods to the Southwestward," where the remainder of Hood's Division had rallied. In a symbolic gesture, Hood arrived to personally lead this hard-hit band of Rebels, including the First Texas, back to the West Woods.

What little remained of the First Texas eased into the screening shelter of the West Woods from where these crack soldiers had come only a relatively short time before, but now seemed like a lifetime ago, after having endured some of the war's vicious combat this morning. Some First Texas boys recited silent prayers learned in childhood days, giving thanks for having survived the greatest carnage on a single morning to date. Hood's Division was now little more than "Hood's Squad," as Lieutenant Colonel Work dubbed it with a veteran's grim sense of humor, perhaps to compensate for the nightmares stemming from his experiences in the Miller Cornfield.

By that time on this unforgettable morning of supreme sacrifice and carnage, and the Battle of Antietam had only begun on September 17. However, the fighting was still not over for the First Texas. Shortly, along with the pitiful remainder of Hood's once magnificent division, these weary men were sent out as skirmishers to cover a wide front in defense of the West Woods.[234]

The only surviving Perry boy of the four relatives who entered into the cornfield in the ranks of the Marshall Guards (Company E), Private Eugene Osceola Perry, who lost two brothers killed in the Miller Cornfield and who himself died in battle later in 1864, felt terribly alone at this time. Like other

A view of where the Second Corps, Army of the Potomac, attacked south toward the Dunker Church and the Sunken Road during the second phase of the battle of Antietam. *DeGolyer Library, Southern Methodist University, Lawrence T. Jones III Texas Photography Collection; Civil War: Photographs, Manuscripts and Imprints.*

First Texas survivors, he felt anguish over the morning's events. Private Perry was tormented by the loss of so many comrades and relatives.[235]

Alabama-born Lieutenant William Henry Gaston of Company H (Texas Guards) summarized the events of the day in a sad letter to his father: "We were overpowered by the Enemy and compelled to give up the battlefield leaving behind our killed and wounded with some prisoners & were not permitted to go on the field after the battle. Consequently, I cannot tell the result of the missing."[236]

Most of all, Lieutenant Gaston was haunted by the sad fact that one of the missing was his own brother, Lieutenant Robert "Billy" Hugh Gaston. They had grown up together and attended the Prairie Mound Institute in the distant homeland. A tortured Gaston wrote back home to Anderson County to his parents, Robert Kilpatrick Gaston and Letitia Suddeth-Gaston, in a pitiful November letter regarding Robert's unknown fate: "I have been inquiring and hunting for him ever since he was lost. I can hear nothing from him. I feel that he was slain although I cannot give him up yet. There is some chance for him to be alive yet. He may have been badly wounded and still in the hands of the enemy." But such was not the case. Lieutenant Gaston was killed in the cornfield in a desperate attempt to rescue the fallen colors of the First Texas.[237]

Before the fighting shifted south to Lee's center, Confederate fortunes on the weak left continued to be in serious jeopardy. More than seven thousand troops of Manfield's Twelfth Corps, which had reinforced the First Corps, had driven a wedge between what little remained of Hood's battered division on the left and D.H. Hill's Division defending the center of Lee's overstretched battle line. Acting commander of the Twelfth Corps after General Mansfield was killed, Brigadier General Alpheus Starkey Williams from Detroit, Michigan, known affectionately as "Old Pap" to his troops, had hurled every unit of his command into the fray. Combined with rallied and counterattacking First Corps troops, the offensive effort of the Twelfth Corps succeeded in delivering the blow that outflanked the Confederates in the cornfield. General Williams was stunned by how the grim "toll was greatest in the Cornfield."[238]

At long last and after so much sacrifice on both sides, the bloody cornfield of farmer Miller was finally swept clean of the last lingering Confederate troops, except the multitudes of dead, dying and wounded men that covered the ground as far as the eye could see. Symbolically, the Texas men were the last soldiers of the Army of Northern Virginia to depart this vast field of death. Yankees who finally took possession of the cornfield were stunned by the extent of the carnage. In disbelief, General Hooker, who suffered a wound on this day, described the sickening spectacle: "[E]very stalk of corn in the northern and greater part of the field was cut as closely as could have been done with a knife, and the slain lay in rows precisely as they had stood in their ranks a few moments before. It was never my fortune to witness a more bloody, dismal battle-field."[239]

Nowhere were the dead piled higher or lay thicker than in the most advanced Confederate position, once held by the First Texas with such tenacity, at the cornfield's northern end. One Texas Brigade soldier recalled the horror, "Our dead lay in rows upon the ground, where they had fought a fruitless fight."[240]

Sickened by the extent of the surreal carnage, an Iron Brigade soldier of the Second Wisconsin wrote, "I thought I had seen men piled up and cut up in all kinds of shape but never anything in comparison to that field." Another Wisconsin Yankee of the same command was shocked by the sight of "the dead [who] were piled in windrows on both sides." Known as the "Little Colonel," Lieutenant Colonel Edward Bragg, Sixth Wisconsin, who fell wounded in the bloody struggle for the cornfield's possession, described the horrific field where the First Texas fought and died: "The battlefield was too terrible to behold without a shock. I never want to see another such. I counted eighty Rebels in one row along the fence in front of us, lying so thick you could step from one to the other, and this was only in one place. In others they lay in heaps, mowed down, and many of our brave boys with them."[241]

Young Lieutenant Robert Gould Shaw, who was destined to be killed in leading the Fifty-Fourth Massachusetts in the attack on Fort Wagner just outside Charleston, South Carolina, on July 18, 1863, wrote of Antietam's greatest killing ground in a letter to his mother after having viewed the piles of dead and wounded of the Texas Brigade and General Hood's Division: "[T]he Brigade advanced through a cornfield in front, which, until then, had been occupied by the enemy; it was full of their dead and wounded.... Beyond the cornfield was a large open field [the clover field south of the cornfield], and such a mass of dead and wounded men, mostly Rebels, as were lying there, I never saw before; it was a terrible sight."[242]

Despite the cornfield's capture and the decimated Lone Star State command's withdrawal from the field of death and broken dreams, the tragic drama that was the unforgettable story of the First Texas's cruel decimation at Antietam was far from over. Lieutenant William E. Barry, Company G (Grimes County Grays), Fourth Texas, was captured at the cornfield. After the battle, he stood in sullen silence as an exhausted prisoner after having been turned over to Union cavalry for escort to the rear and then eventually to a Northern prison camp.

Barry described one of the unforgettable scenes at Antietam that stayed with him for life:

> *I saw approaching from the Federal front a part of infantry soldiers, one of whom was waving a flag that I immediately identified as that of the First Texas. When the party came up, the* [cavalry] *major* [in command] *asked what flag it was and where it had been captured. The reply of the man who held it was: "I did not capture it, Major—I found it in the cornfield." The major then asked me if I knew the flag. "Yes," said I as the soldier handed it to me. "I know it well; it is the* [Lone Star State] *flag of the First Texas regiment." And kissing it reverently I returned it to the soldier and asked him where he got it. He repeated his statement that he had found it in the cornfield, and then told me that thirteen men lay dead within touch of it, and that the body of one of the dead* [Lieutenant Richard Hugh Gaston, who was the brother of Captain William Henry Gaston] *lay stretched across it.*[243]

Perhaps the best explanation of the Texas Brigade's accomplishments was written by native South Carolinian General Stephen D. Lee, a respected West Pointer who was saddened by the harrowing sights: "I witnessed the glory the brigade won at Sharpsburg. I saw them sweep the enemy from their front; I saw them almost annihilated, and even then I saw them contribute the greater part to the repulse of Hooker's [First] Corps, then of Mansfield's

[Twelfth] Corps....I saw them broken, shattered, and falling back before overwhelming numbers, the few who were left giving the Rebel yell with more spirit than the hurrahs of the Union troops advancing upon them."[244]

One surviving Texas Brigade member placed the magnificent offensive role and frightfully high sacrifice in the cornfield in a proper historical perspective that has been long ignored:

> *The wild charge of the Light Brigade "through the valley of death" at Balaklava is one of the proudest but saddest memories of the British army. It has been immortalized in story and in song, and yet the percentage of losses sustained by the "Six Hundred" does not equal that of many organizations at Sharpsburg, either Federal or Confederate. The killed and wounded of the "Six Hundred" at Balaklava was less than forty per cent of those engaged in the charge. In the battle of Sharpsburg, September 17, 1862, the 1st Texas Regiment lost over eighty per cent in killed and wounded, including nine color bearers.*[245]

One of the few fortunate survivors of the slashing counterattack through the cornfield, Private John N. Scott, Company G (Reagan Guards), First Texas, also drew on appropriate historical analogies to place the Texans' offensive role and tactical accomplishments in a proper historical perspective, with a distinctive Napoleonic hue: "Hood and his Texans held the gap like Marshall [Jean] Lannes at Friedland....It was the contest in the...cornfield that Lee said was the hottest on any battlefield" of the war.[246]

Most of all, what the Texas Brigade, and especially the First Texas, achieved (saving the Army of Northern Virginia) astounded the fighting men of both sides on the early morning of September 17: "[It] may well have been the grandest charge of the entire war."[247] More importantly, as planned by General Lee, who had chosen the right soldiers to serve as his last strategic reserve, this sweeping counterattack, with the Texas Brigade (along with the rest of Hood's Division) spearheading the way, had been calculated to inflict the mortal wound on the Army of the Potomac that might bring decisive victory, foreign recognition and a dramatic reversal of the war's course—a desperate offensive gamble against the odds to not only reverse the day's fortunes, but also to win it all. This great dream of the possibility of reaping a decisive victory north of the Potomac that would bring peace was what had fueled and driven the Texans ever onward and straight into hell itself on the bloodiest day of the Civil War.[248]

Bitter Epilogue

The vicious fighting at Antietam on the morning of September 17 is only one part of the story. North of Sharpsburg along the Hagerstown Turnpike and in the trampled fields of the Miller farm, the struggle sputtered to an end out of exhaustion and a frightful attrition. General Jackson's Command and Hooker's First Corps had virtually destroyed each other during the fierce struggle in only three hours on a single morning. The intense combat then flowed farther south from north of Sharpsburg to rage anew on other killing fields to the south. The focus on the next phase, or the second of three distinct phases of the Battle of Antietam, drifted south to the center of Lee's thin battle line, which was anchored along a narrow sunken road ("Bloody Lane") located just northeast of Sharpsburg.

After the savage contest for possession of the Sunken Road, the struggle then shifted even farther south to the Rohrbach Bridge (Burnside's Bridge) to Lee's right flank, which was anchored on the lower stone bridge over Antietam Creek, by the early afternoon. Throughout the day, Lee's diminutive army narrowly survived the series of hammer blows that fortunately for Southern fortunes were not simultaneous. On this day of unprecedented carnage, more than twenty-three thousand Americans became casualties. Eighteen generals were either killed (a total of six equally divided on both sides) or wounded. Lee's Army of Northern Virginia was fortunate to have narrowly escaped to fight another day, ensuring that the Confederacy's struggle would continue in the years ahead.

Brigadier General Robert Toombs evolved into a capable brigade commander. He saw his finest day on the afternoon of September 17, when his veteran Georgia Brigade defended the Rohrbach Bridge (Lower Bridge/Burnside's Bridge) and thwarted the repeated assaults of the Ninth Corps on the far right of Lee's overextended battle line. *Library of Congress.*

However, if not for the amazing success of the Texans' slashing counterattack that had turned the tide north of Sharpsburg, then there would have been no second and third phases of the Battle of Antietam. In overall tactical terms on this day of decision, the enormous sacrifice paid by the First Texas on Lee's left flank staved off decisive defeat and saved the Army of Northern Virginia, all while paving the way for Lee's men to hold firm during the battle's second and third phases. All in all and although this fact has been largely overlooked, the offensive effort of the Texas Rebels played the leading role in saving the day to ensure the army's survival, when the Army of Northern Virginia's very life (and that of the Confederacy) was at stake.

The bloody high-water mark of Lee's first invasion of the North and the apex of Southern fortunes in 1862, Antietam was one of the decisive battles of the Civil War. Although generally unrecognized for its supreme importance compared to Gettysburg, which has cast a giant historical shadow to this day, the Battle of Antietam actually sounded the overall death knell of the Confederacy through significant political and military developments. Thanks to Union victory at Antietam and Lee's failure to achieve strategic gains north of the Potomac, the Union war effort was revitalized politically and morally by President Lincoln's Emancipation Proclamation (previously written by the president, who had waited for a key Union success before issuing the historical document) immediately after the withdrawal of Lee's Army to Virginia. Now the war to determine America's destiny was to be fought to the bitter end without political compromise or settlement, especially now that slavery had been targeted for destruction. Gaining the advantage to prosecute the war to the bitter end because of what happened at Antietam, the North now possessed the higher moral ground in contrast to the Confederacy's bid for self-determination that was now doomed to an unkind fate.

With the North's newly declared strategic objective of destroying slavery, France and England never became allies of the Confederacy, thanks to the Battle of Antietam. The infant Confederacy, without sufficient manpower or resources to survive modern warfare over an extended period, was fated to wither and die in a lengthy war of attrition. While the young men and boys of the Confederacy fought and died in vain in unprecedented numbers on the gory battlefields across America, this largely agrarian Southern nation had already become obsolete in a more progressive, liberal and industrialized world that had already moved forward.[249]

TRAGIC LEGACY

During some of the best fighting seen in the Army of Northern Virginia to date, Brigadier General John Bell Hood's Division and the Texas Brigade had accomplished the impossible on September 17. Winning a dramatic but Pyrrhic victory at great cost, these relatively few men in gray and butternut from the Lone Star State had played the leading role in successfully blunting the most powerful assaults of "Fighting Joe" Hooker's First Corps, including that of the Army of the Potomac's best combat unit (the Iron Brigade), to save the day during the battle's crucial first phase.

For all practical purposes, during one of the most dramatic reversal of fortunes seen on any Civil War battlefield, the First Corps' victorious onslaught was suddenly and unexpectedly delivered a stunningly destructive blow by the counterattack of Hood's Division (Lee's only strategic reserve). The Texans' slashing counterattack stopped the Union legions by denying them possession of the crucial high ground around the Dunker Church, ensuring that this all-important strategic position was kept out of Major General George B. McClellan's hands when the Army of Northern Virginia's life was at stake as never before. Ironically, if not for the Texans' sparkling success in turning the tide, "Little Mac" McClellan (and not Lincoln) might well have become the next president in November 1864, forever altering the course of American history—a political development that perhaps could have led to a negotiated peace and the existence of two American nations to this day.

But the impressive tactical success in saving Lee's left flank to ensure that the Army of Northern Virginia was not destroyed amid the farmlands of Washington County came at a fearful price for a good many young men and boys from Texas and the South. General Hood's crack division, perhaps the best combat unit in either army, was virtually no more, losing nearly 1,400 men in the struggle for possession of the cornfield. Having felt the sharp sting of the hard-fighting Texans once unleashed, "Fighting Joe" Hooker's First Corps lost nearly 2,600 soldiers in the bloody sector. Around 10,000 on both sides fell in the struggle north of Sharpsburg in only several hours.

On the night of September 17 at General Lee's headquarters, fully aware how narrowly the Army of Northern Virginia had escaped annihilation, the commanding general asked a gloomy Hood for the latest information about the exact location and condition of his crack division that was the pride of the army: "Great God, General Hood, where is the splendid division you had this morning?" To this, and much like General George Edward Pickett's embittered response after the disaster of "Pickett's Charge" on the third day of Gettysburg, Hood only spoke a few anguished words that told eloquently about the ultimate horror of the bitter struggle for possession of the Miller Cornfield: "They are lying on the field where you sent them. My division has been wiped out."[250]

By far the greatest slaughter (in overall percentage terms) of any unit of the Army of Northern Virginia had occurred in the ranks of the First Texas, which had been destroyed. Attesting to the fact that the First Texas, in Private Joseph Benjamin Polley's words from a letter, bore "the brunt of the battle on that part of the Confederate line occupied by Hoods' brigade," the First Texas lost more men than its sister regiments, the Eighteenth Georgia or the Fourth Texas. While the Georgia regiment lost 101 of its 176 soldiers, the First Texas lost more of its members than the entire number of Eighteenth Georgia soldiers who fought on September 17. And the First Texas lost only 14 fewer soldiers than the total number of Fourth Texas troops—a total of 200, of which 107 fell as casualties. The First Texas lost, at least, a staggering 186 men (45 killed and 141 wounded) from the 226 soldiers who had so confidently entered the Miller Cornfield to do or die in "the hardest and deadliest struggle of the day."[251]

Saddened, if not traumatized, by the devastating losses to what once had been the hardest-fighting regiment of Lee's most combative brigade, an appalled Lieutenant Colonel Philip Alexander Work penned with marked sadness, "The loss of the 1st Texas in the corn patch fight on the 17th was fifty killed and one hundred and thirty six wounded of a total strength of only 226."[252]

One of the few survivors of Company C (Palmer Guards), Captain David King Rice wrote shortly after the regiment's awful decimation in only a relatively short time: "I do believe that troops ever fought against such odds. I went into the fight with 23 men, and only escaped with myself and [the] Orderly Sergeant, all the rest being either killed or wounded. Hoffman was among the killed beyond a doubt, he died nobly doing his duty. You may judge of our fighting, when I tell you we took 296 men into the fight, and only brought out 46. Among the killed and wounded there was 21 officers, our Major [Matt Dale] being among the killed. Six officers was all that was left to the regiment at the time our regiment reformed with the rest of our brigade."[253]

Eighteen-year-old Private Henry Waters Berryman, Company I (Crockett Southrons), First Texas, penned in a sad September 22 letter to his Cherokee County, Texas family the grim reality of the virtual annihilation of an elite command of American fighting men, who fought and died for what they believed was right:

> *We had another big fight, one of the hardest contested fights that has ever been fought in the East. This fight commenced on the 16th and ended the evening of the 17th of September. It was near a little town in Maryland called Sharpsburg, of course the Texas Brigade was in it and in the hottest part of the battlefield. Poor Tom Cook was shot down and left on the field. It is not known whether he was killed or not. Our Lt. saw him fall, but he says he did not think he was killed. Newt* [brother Newton "Newt" Monroe Berryman, also of Company I] *was slightly wounded in the thigh, it did not break the skin. I think that it must have been done by a spent grape* [canister] *shot. It bruised his leg and makes him a little lame. Tom Boone was wounded slightly in the foot by a piece of shell.... Malachia Reeves...was slightly wounded in the head. William Pritchard was wounded in the face with a buck shot, also in the breast. It struck him about the middle while stooping, ranged downward and lodged in the skin of his belly. The ball has been taken out. His wound looks pretty bad but he is able to walk about....Lawyer Mitchell was wounded on the head with a piece of shell, his skull is supposed to be fractured....Captain Cotton was shot in the head, he is still living, some hopes of his getting well....J.R. Jones...was shot through the thigh* [and] *Sam Stuart was wounded and left on the battlefield....There were only three men* [of Company I] *to come out unhurt. The Regiment only had three stacks of arms, our Major* [Dale] *was killed and left in the hands of the Yankees.*[254]

At the end of his letter, young Private Berryman added a brief update concerning the tragic fate of the popular captain of the Crockett Southrons of Company I, who failed to survive the brutal combat in the Miller Cornfield: Captain Richard W. "Cotton [who] is dead."[255]

In playing the leading role in reversing the tide at Antietam on Lee's left until the Texans rose magnificently to the challenge, the Texas Brigade had been cut to pieces to the point of oblivion—a total of 560 men out of 854 Texas Brigade members killed, wounded or missing. The Texas Brigade lost more than 60 percent of its strength in only a matter of two hours.

As mentioned, no regiment of the Texas Brigade or the Army of Northern Virginia lost as severely as the First Texas—an unprecedented loss in overall percentage terms in the annals of not only of the Civil War, but also in American history. The casualty rate of at least 82.3 percent of the total strength of the 226 First Texas men who had entered the battle with confidence of turning the tide of battle was the highest percentage loss of any regiment, North or South, in a single day's combat during the four years of war. In making the deepest penetration into the cornfield and beyond, the First Texas alone lost 45 killed and another 141 wounded. Only about 40 men, sickened by the unprecedented slaughter, walked away from the cornfield to tell the tale. It was no exaggeration that in less than an hour, the First Texas had earned the "front-rank spot for bloodletting in the Civil War."[256]

Thankful to have served in the Fourth Texas instead of Work's more thoroughly decimated regiment, one soldier wrote of the unparalleled sacrifice: "The First Texas went into battle with 226 men, and lost in killed and wounded, 186, a loss of eighty-two per cent. As one flag-bearer would fall, another would seize the flag, until nine men had fallen beneath their colors [and it was here that] the First Texas lost more men, killed and wounded, [and] in proportion to numbers engaged, than any other regiment engaged, either Federal or Confederate, in any other battle of the war."[257]

However, the fearful losses were not disproportionate to the overall importance of the vital role played by the First Texas in spearheading the counterattack that saved the day north of Sharpsburg. Private "Joe" Polley, Fourth Texas, summarized how "[t]he brunt of the battle of the 17th on that part of the line occupied by the Texas Brigade, fell upon the First Texas, and its men bore it like the heroes they were. By their bravery on that field of carnage they proved that, given the same opportunity, either one of the Texas regiments could be depended on to do all that mortals may to punish a foe and wrest from him a victory."[258]

In fact, the First Texas's terrible losses were actually higher than the long-accepted and outdated figure of 82.3 percent casualties. After the war, Lieutenant Colonel Work detailed in a letter how some of his soldiers had been absent from the regiment when the Texans were suddenly called into action to do the impossible in regard to reversing the tide. Therefore, instead of 226 First Texas men having entered into the living nightmare that was the Miller Cornfield, there were, in all likelihood, only 211 First Texas men present. If so, then the First Texas at Antietam actually lost not 82.3 but nearly 90 percent of its strength.[259]

By comparison, the highest percentage of loss suffered by a Federal regiment, the Twelfth Massachusetts Volunteer Infantry of Brigadier General George Lucas Hartsuff's Third Brigade, Brigadier General James Brewerton Rickett's Second Division, First Corps, at Antietam was 67 percent. Not surprisingly, this loss was suffered by the New England regiment during the bitter struggle for possession of the cornfield.[260]

In the end, what little was left of the hellish thirty-acre Miller Cornfield became the graveyard of the First Texas and the most tragic of places where the loftiest dreams and ambitions died in record time. At least one account has maintained that a total of 234 First Texas soldiers entered the cornfield with fixed bayonets, and this elite western regiment "came out with only 34 unhurt, the greatest loss sustained by any regiment on either side during the entire war."[261]

For the First Texas survivors, adding to the shame of defeat was the loss of their cherished battle flag, the beautiful Lone Star State banner that had inspired these men during the crisis. However, one bittersweet realization that brought some comfort to Work and his surviving men was that the regimental banner was not captured by the Yankees, as in the case of most Confederate battle flag captures during the height of combat. In truth, only the regiment's thorough decimation and the deaths of a good many color bearers had resulted in the capture of the Lone Star State flag. Most importantly for them, these westerners in gray and butternut had fully demonstrated their cherished "right to stand by the side of those who fought and conquered on the red field of San Jacinto" on April 21, 1836.[262]

One of the Union's most celebrated accomplishments in the struggle in the Miller Cornfield was the capture of the coveted Lone Star State flag of the First Texas. Ironically, Private Samuel Johnson won his Medal of Honor for what was mistakenly officially cited as his capture of the colors of the "First Texas Rangers" (of course, no Texas Rangers served in the eastern theater) instead of the First Texas Confederate Regiment.

Significantly, Chaplain Nicholas Davis described the capture of the Lone Star State flag:

> *The First* [Texas], *carried its old flag through every battle, until at Sharpsburg, when the Ensign was shot down, unnoticed in the cornfield, as the regiment was changing its position to prevent being flanked, and it fell into the hands of the enemy, who, we learn from some of our men that were made prisoners, rejoiced over it exceedingly—mounting it upon a music wagon, and running up the Stars and Stripes over it, drove it through the camp, to the tune of "Yankee Doodle," and then to* [Major General] *McClellan's headquarters, when they delivered themselves of several "Spread Eagle" speeches on the subject of capturing a Texas flag. Well, let them make the most of it, for it is the first Texas flag they have got, and I guess many of them will bite the dust before they get another.*[263]

SAD LEGACY

In the days ahead, the fallen soldiers of the First Texas and the Texas Brigade were buried haphazardly by Union burial details in unmarked graves in and around the Miller Cornfield. Today, not a single gravestone of a Texas soldier marks the area where so many Lone Star State men fell in this hardest-fought sector at Antietam, which appears the same today as it did in September 1862. Only one of these First Texas men received a proper burial. Because of his outstanding heroism and self-sacrifice for a greater good, this lone First Texas soldier who received the only decent burial of the Texas Brigade was Lieutenant Robert "Billy" Hugh Gaston of the Texas Guards (or the Anderson County Guards) Company H.

Having embarked on a suicidal mission, the young lieutenant's courageous attempt to save the First Texas's fallen colors impressed the Federal soldiers who shot him down. Therefore, in tribute to his gallantry, Lieutenant Gaston received the distinction of having been "accorded an honorable burial by them [the men of the Pennsylvania Reserves] with a headmark placed over his grave extolling his conspicuous bravery" in the Miller Cornfield.[264]

Clearly, the price paid for saving the day was frightfully high for the First Texas, fighting and dying in a picturesque agricultural paradise and within sight of the bluish South Mountain just to the east. The Army of Northern Virginia continued to struggle to preserve the fragile life of a new republic in the years ahead only because the Texas Brigade had turned the tide on September 17. As penned by one Texas survivor of the saddest day of his life: "On the 18th [of September] we buried our dead. This don't look like a defeat, but when the roll call [is made] and find that two-thirds of our brave Texas boys have gone down in battle and that their remains now lie buried in soldiers graves on the field of Sharpsburg, we are hardly prepared to boast of it as a victory."[265]

The once high hopes for the Confederacy's invasion of Maryland and then Pennsylvania had been dashed forever by the unparalleled carnage during the bloodiest single day of the Civil War. Here, along with the South's best and brightest of an entire generation of young men, Confederate ambitions died on the obscure farmlands, especially the Miller Cornfield, located just west of Antietam Creek and north of Sharpsburg.

A saddened Chaplain Davis described the appearance of the surviving men of the decimated Texas Brigade not long after the battle: "Their clothes were ragged, and many of their feet were bare; and in their coats, pants and hats could be seen many marks of the bullet. They had many times performed long marches, and fought hard battles, without rations. The weather was warm and dry, and the dust had settled thick over their clothes. But they were cheerful and lively, and as resolved to fight to the bitter end.... They had marched long and fought hard—they had buried many comrades on different fields [but they still believed that] 'a people could never be conquered who were determined to be free.'"[266]

Johann August Heinrich Heros Von Borcke, a Confederate cavalry officer who had been born in today's Germany, marveled at the unbreakable fighting spirit of Hood's troops before and after the climactic showdown at Antietam: "It was astonishing to see men without shoes, whose lacerated feet often stained their path with blood, limping to the front to conquer or fall with their comrades."[267]

For good reason, surviving Texas soldiers, including Lieutenant Colonel Work, were long haunted by the lost opportunities of Antietam that faded away forever with the setting sun of September 17, leaving a red glow over a scene of unspeakable horrors and piles of bodies. A more significant victory might well have been achieved at Antietam had the First Texas and the Texas Brigade received the sufficient and timely reinforcements that had been repeatedly requested by desperate officers, who sought to exploit the tactical opportunity and gains to the fullest. One Fourth Texas soldier explained the enticing possibility of winning it all: "If the reinforcements had reached the firing line before the Texas Brigade and Law's Brigade were forced to abandon their advanced positions, the Federals would have been swept from the field and another triumph would have been added to the list of Confederate victories."[268]

A golden opportunity to reverse the war's course had been lost north of Sharpsburg after the Texas Brigade had turned the tide; General Hood, perhaps Lee's best division commander, certainly believed as much like his men. He lamented in his battle report that "our victory on the left would have been as thorough, quick, and complete as upon the plains of Manassas on August 30," if reinforced at the critical moment.[269]

As Hood's men realized during Lee's first invasion of the North when the greater opportunities of Pennsylvania beckoned as never before, a decisive Confederate victory won at Antietam could have reversed the war's course. While the initial news of Lee's invasion had brought England closer to official recognition of the Confederacy's experiment in nationhood, President Lincoln's Emancipation Proclamation sounded the death knell for any possible direct involvement of the European powers, including France, in supporting the Confederacy.

In the frustrated words of a veteran Texan in the ranks, the war's bloodiest battle was just another "fruitless fight" for Lee and his men, a tragic pattern that was fated to be repeated year after year, until the end finally came for the depleted Army of Northern Virginia at Appomattox Court House on Palm Sunday 1865.

For ample good reason, perhaps no one was more outspoken about the lost opportunity at Antietam than Lieutenant Colonel Work. North of Sharpsburg, the First Texas and the Texas Brigade had largely fought alone in a desperate bid to grasp destiny and fulfill the cherished dream of a long life for their people's republic. Like no other regiment, the First Texas played a key role in denying the Federals a decisive victory on that awful mid-September morning.

Regarding the lost Confederate opportunities at Antietam, a universal lament now consumed the relatively few surviving members of Hood's Division. These veteran soldiers had been seared by the cornfield's horrors, their hearts darkened by the sacrifice of so many lives in vain. No one was more livid about the lack of support for his hard-fighting division and the Texas Brigade's tragic fate, which fought and died on its own, than Brigadier General John Bell Hood.[270] As could be expected, Colonel Wofford was also disgusted about the high sacrifice and missed opportunity. He wrote, "These brave officers [of the Texas Brigade] all fell while gallantly leading their small bands on an enemy five times their number. They deserved a better fate than to have been, as they were, sacrificed for the want of proper support."[271]

In spearheading the fierce counterattack of not only the Texas Brigade but also Hood's Division to blunt the assault of "Fighting Joe" Hooker's massive First Corps, the First Texas also bought precious time to gain an opportunity for Stonewall Jackson to launch a counterattack on Lee's left to turn the Army of the Potomac's right flank—an often overlooked tactical opportunity.[272]

After the first phase of the Battle of Antietam concluded on the north, the ever-opportunistic Jackson contemplated launching a counterattack in a bid to win the day. He had even received permission from Lee to do so. Jackson was determined to exploit the opportunity bestowed by the Texas Brigade's counterattack to the fullest, declaring in no uncertain terms, "We'll drive McClellan into the Potomac!" Won by the Texas Brigade with an unparalleled sacrifice, this often forgotten tactical opportunity still provided Lee with an option of launching an offensive effort north of Sharpsburg that might have brought success.[273]

Most of all, the unsurpassed battlefield performance and sacrifice of the Texans, especially the First Texas, was not lost to General Lee, who was forever thankful to his most unconventional fighting men who had saved his army from certain destruction. Only days after Hood's troops performed like no other Confederate soldiers at Antietam, Lee paid the ultimate compliment to the Texas Brigade and its unparalleled sacrifice. Knowing that such elite troops were absolutely necessary if the Army of Northern Virginia was to achieve decisive victory and win the war, General Lee wrote to the Texas Senator Louis T. Wigfall to inquire about securing additional Texas regiments to bolster the combat prowess of the Army of Northern Virginia: "I need them very much [as] I rely upon those we have in all our tight places, and fear that I have to call upon them too often. They have fought grandly and nobly, and we must have more of them...With a few more regiments such as Hood now has, as an example of daring and bravery, I could feel more confident of the campaign."[274]

A young Texas Brigade private wrote of his undying determination that most of all applied to the bloody showdown at Antietam in a letter home, "We can not be whipped, though they may kill us all." Perhaps Private Henry Waters Berryman—a member of the Berryman clan of the Crockett Southrons of Company I, First Texas, and who hailed from the little Texas town of Alto, which had been founded on the Old San Antonio Road around 1849 and was named for the highest ground between the Neches and Anglina Rivers—said it best. Summarizing the savage struggle for possession of the Miller Cornfield, he emphasized how, "I can't say we were whipped, but we were overwhelmed. The Texas Brigade stood up and fought without any reinforcements three or four fresh Yankee Brigades until all of her men had fallen, or most of them. They always take the Texians to the hottest part of the field, but her best men have fallen now and they will be more particular now, I reckon where she is carried hereafter."[275]

Because no timely support was forthcoming to the First Texas from other Texas Brigade units, from Hood's Division or from Major General Daniel H. Hill's Division, Lieutenant Colonel Work's soldiers fought and died in vain largely on their own against the odds, stubbornly maintaining the army's most advanced position in the cornfield far longer than anyone could have reasonably expected. Far from their homes and families in east and southeast Texas, which faced dire threats from Union invasions and Indian attacks, the young men and boys from Texas were sacrificed like cannon fodder at an unprecedented rate on the morning of September 17. The First Texas was virtually wiped out not unlike their legendary Texas heroes (Lieutenant

Colonel William Barret Travis, David Crockett and Jim Bowie) at the Alamo in an earlier people's revolution against another centralized government.

Symbolically, the 186 casualties suffered by the First Texas in the wreckage of the hellish cornfield was the exact number of slain defenders at the Alamo—one of the strange paradoxes of the Battle of Antietam. Ironically, while the Alamo's citizen-soldiers have been long immortalized as a supreme example of heroic sacrifice for God and country, the Texans' far more important fight on the morning of September 17 has been largely forgotten. Here, in a sun-baked patch of corn in Washington County, the First Texas soldiers were motivated by the heroic examples (both the Alamo and San Jacinto) of the Texas Revolution, a cherished legacy that the Texas Rebels successfully emulated during their counterattack and the vicious struggle for possession of the Miller Cornfield.[276]

One Union officer never forgot the sight presented by "the bloody cornfield where lay two or three hundred festering bodies, nearly all of them rebels, the most hideous exhibition I had yet seen. Many were black as Negroes, heads and faces hideously swelled, covered with dust until they looked like clods."[277] This was a tragic ending for the best and brightest of the Texas Brigade, especially the devastated First Texas.

In a letter written by one war-weary Texas Brigade soldier that caught the representative mood of the relatively few survivors not long after the nightmarish battle, "You said in our last letter that you hoped the Texians thirst for Yankee blood had been partly quenched. I can speak for the three reg. in Va. Their thirst has not only been partially quenched, they have been in so many fights and have suffered so much they would be willing never to go in another fight."[278]

However, the war was only beginning for the Texas Brigade. The replacement battle flag of the First Texas was adorned with a wide black border to honor the multitude of soldiers cut down in the cornfield. The Lone Star State soldiers who had achieved so much against the odds on the morning of September 17 were not forgotten by the survivors, who continued to fight on year after year. Even Union veterans, officers and enlisted men, were amazed by what the Texas Brigade soldiers had accomplished in the Miller Cornfield: "That those ragged, filthy, wretched, sick, hungry and in all ways miserable men…should prove such heroes in the fight, is past explanation. Men never fought better" in the annals of American military history.[279]

The Texans' superior combat performance at Antietam resulted in hundreds of forgotten casualties and a good many grieving families and widows across Texas. In a November 28, 1862 letter to his distressed "Pa" that revealed the full extent of the personal trauma and tragedy of an American family, Lieutenant William Henry Gaston naturally focused on the sad subject of the fate of his missing brother, Lieutenant Robert "Billy" Hugh Gaston:

> *I wrote you soon after the fight* [at Antietam] *& gave you all the information that I could about Robert. I have been inquiring and hunting for him ever since he was lost. I can hear nothing from him. I feel that he was slain although I cannot give him up yet. There is some chance for him to be alive yet. He may have been badly wounded and still in the hands of the enemy. There have been some of my boys* [the Texas Guards of Company H] *sent back from Maryland that I thought was killed. They saw nothing of Robert but say he may be there somewhere as our boys are scattered all over Md. I hope he may turn up someday. I have felt miserable since he has been gone and it is with deep regret that I have to communicate his loss to you....If Robert can be found I will find him....If killed we will have to give him up for a time* [before his body could be found and returned to Texas].[280]

William Henry Gaston was fated to experience no peace of mind until his missing brother, who was last seen charging through the Miller Cornfield, was found.

Such unprecedented sacrifices were accepted by the surviving soldiers and family members with a stoic fatalism and a sense of moral courage, because they believed strongly that God was on their side. In a prophetic letter that spoke eloquently of the extent of his determination to succeed at any cost, Lieutenant Robert "Billy" Hugh Gaston had earlier sworn to his parents that it was far better "to die on the battlefield than to stay at home & ever have the finger of scorn pointed at us as those who were afraid to contend for their rights."[281]

Like so many other comparably determined Texas Brigade soldiers, young Lieutenant Gaston backed up his words with his heroic actions on the battlefield and his life, which he willingly sacrificed for what he believed was right—the commitment of the common soldiers (mostly yeomen farmers without slaves) to ensure a long life for their infant republic. Clearly, there was nothing at all ragged about the remarkable combat performance of the "Ragged First" Texas on the morning of September 17, 1862.[282]

In future decades, all that remained of one of the most dramatic and important charges of the Civil War were the scattered bones, decaying shreds of butternut and gray uniforms and perhaps a silver or iron Texas star (representing the Lone Star State and worn with pride on hats) that were occasionally turned up by farmers while plowing the new rows in the dark soil of the cornfield during springtime. A disproportionate percentage of young men and boys from Texas had saved the day for their outgunned army and fledgling nation by making the supreme sacrifice against the odds. In attempting to reverse the war's course at any cost, a good many Texans met a cruel fate on the nightmarish ground of the war's greatest killing field on the bloodiest day of the Civil War, the Miller Cornfield. Here, among the rows of high-standing cornstalks, Antietam's most savage fighting was described without exaggeration by one fortunate survivor as having been as fierce as "a thousand storms in the region of Hades" during "the greatest fight since Waterloo [which was] contested…with an obstinacy even equaled to Waterloo."[283]

Appendix

Order of Battle

Organization of the Army of the Potomac at Antietam
Major General George Brinton McClellan, Commanding

Escort
Captain James B. McIntyre
Independent Company, Oneida Cavalry (New York)
Company A, 4th U.S. Cavalry
Company E, 4th U.S. Cavalry

Volunteer Engineer Brigade
Brigadier General Daniel P. Woodbury
15th New York Engineers
50th New York Engineers

Regular Engineer Battalion
Captain James C. Duane

Provost Guard
Major William H. Wood
Companies E, F, H and K, 2nd U.S. Cavalry
Companies A, D, F and G, 8th U.S. Infantry

Company G, 19th U.S. Infantry
Company H, 19th U.S. Infantry

Headquarters Guard
Major Granville O. Haller
Sturges's Rifles (Illinois)
93rd New York Infantry

Quartermaster's Guard
Companies B, C, H and I, 1st U.S. Cavalry

First Corps
Major General Joseph Hooker (w)
Brigadier General George Gordon Meade

Escort
Companies A, B, I and K, 2nd New York Cavalry

1st Division
Brigadier General Abner Doubleday

1st Brigade
Colonel Walter Phelps Jr.
22nd New York
24th New York
30th New York
84th New York
2nd United States Sharpshooters

2nd Brigade
Lieutenant Colonel J. William Hofmann
7th Indiana
76th New York
95th New York
56th Pennsylvania

3rd Brigade
Brigadier General Marsena R. Patrick
21st New York
23rd New York
35th New York
80th New York

4th Brigade
Brigadier General John Gibbon
19th Indiana
2nd Wisconsin
6th Wisconsin
7th Wisconsin

1st Division/First Corps Artillery
Captain J. Albert Monroe
1st Battery, New Hampshire Light Artillery
Battery D, 1st Rhode Island Light Artillery
Battery L, 1st New York Light Artillery
Battery B, 4th United States Artillery

2ND DIVISION
Brigadier General James Brewerton Ricketts

1st Brigade
Brigadier General Abram Duryea
Colonel Peter Lyle
97th New York
104th New York
105th New York
107th Pennsylvania

2nd Brigade
Colonel William A. Christian
26th New York
94th New York
88th Pennsylvania
90th Pennsylvania

3rd Brigade
Brigadier General George Lucas Hartsuff (w)
Colonel Richard Coulter
16th Maine
12th Massachusetts
13th Massachusetts
83rd New York
11th Pennsylvania

2nd Division/First Corps Artillery
Battery F, 1st Pennsylvania Light Artillery
Battery C, Pennsylvania Light Artillery

3RD DIVISION
Brigadier General George Gordon Meade
Brigadier General Truman Seymour

1st Brigade
Brigadier General Truman Seymour
Colonel R. Biddle Roberts
1st Pennsylvania Reserves

2nd Brigade
Colonel Albert L. Magilton
3rd Pennsylvania Reserves

2nd Pennsylvania Reserves
5th Pennsylvania Reserves
6th Pennsylvania Reserves
13th Pennsylvania Reserves
4th Pennsylvania Reserves
7th Pennsylvania Reserves
8th Pennsylvania Reserves

3rd Brigade
Lieutenant Colonel Robert Anderson
9th Pennsylvania Reserves
10th Pennsylvania Reserves
11th Pennsylvania Reserves
12th Pennsylvania Reserves

3rd Division/First Corps Artillery
Battery A, 1st Pennsylvania Light Artillery
Battery B, 1st Pennsylvania Light Artillery
Battery G, 1st Pennsylvania Light Artillery
Battery C, 5th United States Artillery

SECOND CORPS
Major General Edwin Vose Sumner

ESCORT
Company D, 6th New York Cavalry
Company K 6th New York Cavalry

1ST DIVISION
Major General Israel B. Richardson (mw)
Brigadier General Winfield Scott Hancock

1st Brigade
Brigadier General John C. Caldwell
5th New Hampshire
7th New York
61st New York
64th New York
81st Pennsylvania

2nd Brigade
Brigadier General Thomas Meagher
29th Massachusetts
63rd New York
69th New York
88th New York

3rd Brigade
Colonel John Rutter Brooke
2nd Delaware
52nd New York
57th New York
66th New York
53rd Pennsylvania

1st Division/Second Corps Artillery
Battery B, 1st New York Light Artillery
Batteries A & C, 4th United States Artillery

2nd Division
Major General John Sedgwick (w)
Brigadier General Oliver Otis Howard

1st Brigade
Brigadier General Willis Gorman
Colonel Joshua T. Owen
Colonel DeWitt C. Baxter
15th Massachusetts
1st Minnesota
34th New York
82nd New York
1st Company, Massachusetts Sharpshooters
2nd Company, Minnesota Sharpshooter

2nd Brigade
Brigadier General Oliver Otis Howard
69th Pennsylvania
71st Pennsylvania
72nd Pennsylvania
106th Pennsylvania

3rd Brigade
Brigadier General Napoleon J.T. Dana (w)
Colonel Norman Hall
19th Massachusetts
20th Massachusetts
7th Michigan
42nd New York
59th New York

2nd Division/Second Corps Artillery
Battery A, 1st Rhode Island Light Artillery
Battery I, 1st United States Artillery

3RD DIVISION
Brigadier General William Henry French

1st Brigade
Brigadier General Nathan Kimball
14th Indiana
8th Ohio
132nd Pennsylvania
7th West Virginia

2nd Brigade
Colonel Dwight Morris
14th Connecticut
108th New York
130th Pennsylvania

3rd Brigade
Brigadier General Max Weber (w)
Colonel John W. Andrews
1st Delaware
5th Maryland
4th New York

Unattached Second Corps Artillery
Battery G, 1st New York Light Artillery
Battery B, 1st Rhode Island Light Artillery
Battery G, 1st Rhode Island Light Artillery

TWELFTH CORPS
Major General Joseph K.F. Mansfield (mw)
Brigadier General Alpheus Williams

ESCORT
Company L, 1st Michigan Cavalry

1ST DIVISION
Brigadier General Alpheus Williams
Brigadier General Samuel Wylie Crawford (w)
Brigadier General George Henry Gordon

1st Brigade
Brigadier General Samuel Wylie Crawford
Colonel Joseph F. Knipe
5th Connecticut

2nd Brigade
Brigadier General George H. Gordon
Colonel Thomas H. Ruger
27th Indiana

10th Maine
28th New York
46th Pennsylvania
124th Pennsylvania
125th Pennsylvania
128th Pennsylvania

2nd Massachusetts
13th New Jersey
107th New York
Pennsylvania Zouaves D'Afrique
3rd Wisconsin

2ND DIVISION
Brigadier General George Sears Greene

1st Brigade
Lieutenant Colonel Hector Tyndale (w)
Major Orrin J. Crane
5th Ohio
7th Ohio
29th Ohio
66th Ohio
28th Pennsylvania

2nd Brigade
Colonel Henry J. Stainrook

3rd Maryland
102nd New York
109th Pennsylvania
111th Pennsylvania

3rd Brigade
Colonel William B. Goodrich (k)
Lieutenant Colonel Jonathan Austin
3rd Delaware
Purnell Legion (Maryland)
60th New York
78th New York

TWELFTH CORPS ARTILLERY
Captain Clermont L. Best
4th Battery, Maine Light Artillery
6th Battery, Maine Light Artillery
Battery M, 1st New York Light Artillery
10th Battery, New York Light Artillery
Battery E, Pennsylvania Light Artillery
Battery F, Pennsylvania Light Artillery
Battery F, 4th United States Artillery

Organization of the Army of Northern Virginia at Antietam General Robert E. Lee, Commanding

Longstreet's Corps
Major General James Longstreet

McLaws's Division
Major General Lafayette McLaws

Kershaw's Brigade
Brigadier General Joseph Kershaw
2nd South Carolina
3rd South Carolina
7th South Carolina
8th South Carolina

Cobb's Brigade
Brigadier General Howell Cobb
Lieutenant Colonel C.C. Sanders
Lieutenant Colonel William McRae
16th Georgia
24th Georgia
Cobb's (Georgia) Legion
15th North Carolina

Semmes's Brigade
Brigadier General Paul Semmes
10th Georgia
53rd Georgia
15th Virginia
32nd Virginia

Barksdale's Brigade
Brigadier General William Barksdale
13th Mississippi
17th Mississippi
18th Mississippi
21st Mississippi

Artillery
Major S.P. Hamilton
Colonel H.C. Cabell
Manly's (North Carolina) Battery
Pulaski (Georgia) Artillery
Richmond (Fayette) Artillery
Richmond Howitzers (1st Company)
Troup (Georgia) Artillery

ANDERSON'S DIVISION
Major General Richard H. Anderson

Wilcox's Brigade
Colonel Alfred Cumming
8th Alabama
9th Alabama
10th Alabama
11th Alabama

Mahone's Brigade
Colonel William A. Parham
6th Virginia
12th Virginia
16th Virginia
41st Virginia
61st Virginia

Featherston's Brigade
Colonel Carnot Posey
12th Mississippi
16th Mississippi
19th Mississippi
2nd Mississippi Battalion

Armistead's Brigade
Brigadier General Lewis Armistead
9th Virginia
14th Virginia
38th Virginia

53rd Virginia
57th Virginia

Pryor's Brigade
Brigadier General Roger A. Pryor
14th Alabama
2nd Florida
8th Florida
3rd Virginia

Wright's Brigade
Brigadier General Ambrose R. Wright
44th Alabama
3rd Georgia
22nd Georgia
48th Georgia

Artillery
Major John Saunders
Donaldsonville (Louisiana) Artillery (Maurin's Battery)
Huger's (Virginia) Battery
Moorman's (Virginia) Battery
Thompson's (Grimes's Virginia) Battery

JONES'S DIVISION
Brigadier General David R. Jones

Toombs's Brigade
Brigadier General Robert Toombs
Colonel Henry L. Benning
2nd Georgia
15th Georgia
17th Georgia
20th Georgia

Drayton's Brigade
Brigadier General Thomas F. Drayton
50th Georgia
51st Georgia
15th South Carolina

Pickett's Brigade
Brigadier General Richard B. Garnett
8th Virginia
18th Virginia
19th Virginia
28th Virginia
56th Virginia

Kemper's Brigade
Brigadier General J.L. Kemper
1st Virginia
7th Virginia
11th Virginia
17th Virginia
24th Virginia

Jenkins's Brigade
Colonel Joseph Walker
1st South Carolina (Volunteers)
2nd South Carolina Rifles
5th South Carolina
6th South Carolina
4th South Carolina Battalion
Palmetto (South Carolina) Sharpshooters

Anderson's Brigade
Colonel George T. Anderson
1st Georgia (Regulars)
7th Georgia
8th Georgia
9th Georgia
11th Georgia

Artillery
Fauquier (Virginia) Artillery (Stribling's Battery)
Loudoun (Virginia) Artillery (Rogers's Battery)
Turner (Virginia) Artillery (Leake's Battery)
Wise (Virginia) Artillery (J. Brown's Battery)

Walker's Division
Brigadier General John Walker

Walker's Brigade
Colonel Vannoy H. Manning
3rd Arkansas
27th North Carolina
46th North Carolina
48th North Carolina
30th Virginia
French's (Virginia) Battery

Ransom's Brigade
Brigadier General Robert Ransom Jr.
24th North Carolina
25th North Carolina
35th North Carolina
49th North Carolina
Branch's Field Artillery (Virginia)

Hood's Division
Brigadier General John Bell Hood

Hood's Brigade
Colonel William T. Wofford
18th Georgia
Hampton (South Carolina) Legion
1st Texas
4th Texas
5th Texas

Law's Brigade
Colonel Evander M. Law
4th Alabama
2nd Mississippi
11th Mississippi
6th North Carolina

Artillery
Major B.F. Frobel
German Artillery (South Carolina)
Palmetto Artillery (South Carolina)
Rowan Artillery (North Carolina)

Evan's Brigade
Brigadier General Nathan G. Evans
Colonel Peter F. Stevens
17th South Carolina
18th South Carolina
22nd South Carolina
23rd South Carolina
Holcombe (South Carolina) Legion
Macbeth (South Carolina) Artillery

Artillery

Washington (Louisiana) Artillery
Colonel J.B. Walton
1st Company, Captain C.W. Squires
2nd Company, Captain J.B. Richardson
3rd Company, Captain M.B. Miller
4th Company, Captain B.F. Eshleman

Lee's Battalion
Colonel Stephen D. Lee
Ashland (Virginia) Artillery
Bedford (Virginia) Artillery
Brooks (South Carolina) Artillery
Eubank's (Virginia) Battery
Madison (Louisiana) Light Artillery
Parker's (Virginia) Battery

Jackson's Command
Major General Thomas J. Jackson

Ewell's Division
Brigadier General Alexander Lawton (w)
Brigadier General Jubal Early

Lawton's Brigade

Colonel Marcellus Douglass (k)

Major J.H. Lowe

Colonel John Lamar

13th Georgia

26th Georgia

31st Georgia

38th Georgia

60th Georgia

61st Georgia

Early's Brigade

Brigadier General Jubal Early

Colonel William Smith

13th Virginia

25th Virginia

31st Virginia

44th Virginia

49th Virginia

52nd Virginia

58th Virginia

Trimble's Brigade

Colonel James A. Walker

15th Alabama

12th Georgia

21st Georgia

21st North Carolina

1st North Carolina Battalion

Hays's Brigade

Brigadier General Harry T. Hays

5th Louisiana

6th Louisiana

7th Louisiana

8th Louisiana

14th Louisiana

Artillery
Major A.R. Courtney
Charlottesville (Virginia) Artillery (Carrington's Battery)
Chesapeake (Maryland) Artillery (Brown's Battery)
Courtney (Virginia) Artillery (Latimer's Battery)
Johnson's (Virginia) Battery
Louisiana Guard Artillery (D'Aquin's Battery)
First Maryland Battery (Dement's Battery)
Staunton (Virginia) Artillery (Balthis's Battery)

A.P. HILL'S DIVISION
Major General Ambrose Powell Hill

Branch's Brigade
Brigadier General L. O'Branch (k)
Colonel James H. Lane
7th North Carolina
18th North Carolina
28th North Carolina
33rd North Carolina
37th North Carolina

Gregg's Brigade
Brigadier General Maxcy Gregg
1st South Carolina (Provisional Army)
1st South Carolina Rifles
12th South Carolina
13th South Carolina
14th South Carolina

Field's Brigade
Colonel John Brockenbrough
40th Virginia
47th Virginia
55th Virginia
22nd Virginia Battalion

<u>Archer's Brigade</u>
Brigadier General James J. Archer
5th Alabama Battalion
19th Georgia
1st Tennessee (Provisional Army)
7th Tennessee
14th Tennessee

<u>Pender's Brigade</u>
Brigadier General William D. Pender
16th North Carolina
22nd North Carolina
34th North Carolina
38th North Carolina

<u>Thomas's Brigade</u>
Colonel Edward Thomas
14th Georgia
35th Georgia
45th Georgia
49th Georgia

<u>Artillery</u>
Lieutenant Colonel Reuben L. Walker
Branch (North Carolina) Artillery (A.C. Latham's Battery)
Crenshaw's (Virginia) Battery
Fredericksburg (Virginia) Artillery (Braxton's Battery)
Letcher (Virginia) Artillery (Davidson's Battery)
Middlesex (Virginia) Artillery (Fleet's Battery)
Pee Dee (South Carolina) Artillery (McIntosh's Battery)
Purcell (Virginia) Artillery (Pegram's Battery)

JACKSON'S DIVISION
Brigadier General John R. Jones (w)
Brigadier General William E. Starke (k)
Colonel A.J. Grigsby

Stonewall Brigade
Colonel A.J. Grigsby
Major H.J. Williams
2nd Virginia
4th Virginia
5th Virginia
27th Virginia
33rd Virginia

Taliaferro's Brigade
Colonel James W. Jackson
47th Alabama
48th Alabama
10th Virginia
23rd Virginia
37th Virginia

J.R. Jones's Brigade
Captain John Penn (w) (c)
Captain A.C. Page
Captain R.W. Withers
21st Virginia
42nd Virginia
48th Virginia
1st Virginia Battalion

Starke's Brigade
Brigadier General William Starke
Colonel Leroy A. Stafford
Colonel E. Pendleton
1st Louisiana
2nd Louisiana
9th Louisiana
10th Louisiana
15th Louisiana
Coppens's (Louisiana) Battalion

<u>Artillery</u>
Major L.M. Shumaker
Alleghany (Virginia) Artillery (Carpenter's Battery)
Brockenbrough's (Maryland) Battery
Danville (Virginia) Artillery (Wooding's Battery)
Hampden (Virginia)Artillery (Caskie's Battery)
Lee (Virginia) Battery (Raine's Battery)
Rockbridge (Virginia) Artillery (Poague's Battery)

D.H. HILL'S DIVISION
Major General Daniel Harvey Hill

<u>Ripley's Brigade</u>
Brigadier General Roswell Ripley (w)
Colonel George Doles
4th Georgia
44th Georgia
1st North Carolina
3rd North Carolina

<u>Rodes's Brigade</u>
Brigadier General Robert E. Rodes
3rd Alabama
5th Alabama
6th Alabama
12th Alabama
26th Alabama

<u>Garland's Brigade</u>
Colonel Duncan McRae
5th North Carolina
12th North Carolina
13th North Carolina
20th North Carolina
23rd North Carolina

G.B. Anderson's Brigade
Brigadier General George B. Anderson (mw)
Colonel Risden T. Bennett
2nd North Carolina
4th North Carolina
14th North Carolina
30th North Carolina

Colquitt's Brigade
Colonel Alfred H. Colquitt
13th Alabama
6th Georgia
23rd Georgia
27th Georgia
28th Georgia

Artillery
Major Pierson
Hardaway's (Alabama) Battery
Jefferson Davis (Alabama) Artillery
Jones's (Virginia) Battery
King William (Virginia) Artillery

RESERVE ARTILLERY
Brigadier General William N. Pendleton

Brown's Battalion
Colonel J. Thompson Brown
Powhatan Artillery (Dance's Battery)
Richmond Howitzers, 2nd Company (Watson's Battery)
Richmond Howitzers, 3rd Company (Smith's Battery)
Salem Artillery (Hupp's Battery)
Williamsburg Artillery (Coke's Battery)

Cutts's Battalion
Lieutenant Colonel A.S. Cutts
Blackshears's (Georgia) Battery
Irwin (Georgia) Artillery (Lane's Battery)
Lloyd's (North Carolina) Battery

Patterson's (Georgia) Battery
Ross's (Georgia) Battery

<u>Jones's Battalion</u>
Major Hilary P. Jones
Morris (Virginia) Artillery R.C.M. Page's Battery)
Orange (Virginia) Artillery (Peyton's Battery)
Turner's (Virginia) Battery
Wimbish's (Virginia) Battery

<u>Nelson's Battalion</u>
Major William Nelson
Amherst (Virginia) Artillery (Kirkpatrick's Battery)
Fluvanna (Virginia) Artillery (Ancell's Battery)
Huckstep's (Virginia) Battery
Johnson's (Virginia) Battery
Milledge (Georgia) Artillery (Milledge's Battery)

<u>Miscellaneous</u>
Cutshaw's (Virginia) Battery
Dixie (Virginia) Artillery (Chapman's Battery)
Magruder (Virginia) Artillery (T.J. Page Jr.'s Battery)
Rice's (Virginia) battery, Captain W.H. Rice
Thomas (Virginia) Artillery (E.J. Anderson's Battery)

CAVALRY
Major General Jeb Stuart

<u>Hampton's Brigade</u>
Brigadier General Wade Hampton
1st North Carolina
2nd South Carolina
10th Virginia
Cobb's (Georgia) Legion
Jefferson Davis Legion

Lee's Brigade
Brigadier General Fitzhugh Lee
1st Virginia
3rd Virginia
4th Virginia
5th Virginia
9th Virginia

Robertson's Brigade
Colonel Thomas T. Munford
2nd Virginia
6th Virginia
7th Virginia
12th Virginia
17th Virginia Battalion

Horse Artillery
Captain John Pelham
Chew's (Virginia) Battery
Hart's (South Carolina) Battery
Pelham's (Virginia) Battery

Notes

Chapter 1

1. James Gindlesperger and Suzanne Gindlesperger, *So You Think You Know Antietam?: The Stories Behind America's Bloodiest Day* (Winston-Salem, NC: John F. Blair Publishers, 2012), xv; Stephen M. Hood, *John Bell Hood: The Rise, Fall, and Resurrection of a Confederate General* (Eldorado Springs, CO: Savas Beatie, LLC, 2013), xxiii; Emory M. Thomas, *Robert E. Lee: A Biography* (New York: W.W. Norton and Company, 1995), 255–56; James A. Kegel, *North with Lee and Jackson* (Mechanicsburg, PA: Stackpole Books, 1996), 143–52.
2. Thomas, *Robert E. Lee*, 256.
3. Ibid., 225–56.
4. Jack Dempsey and Brian James Egen, *Michigan at Antietam: The Wolverine State's Sacrifice on America's Bloodiest Day* (Charleston, SC: The History Press, 2015), 26–27; Kegel, *North with Lee and Jackson*, 143–55; Thomas, *Robert E. Lee*, 256.
5. Michael A. Palmer, *Lee Moves North: Robert E. Lee on the Offensive* (New York: Wiley Publishing, 1998),16.
6. Grady McWhiney and Perry D. Jamieson, *Attack and Die: Civil War Tactics and the Southern Heritage* (Tuscaloosa: University of Alabama Press, 1982), 153–57.
7. Ibid., 154; Dempsey and Egen, *Michigan at Antietam*, 26–27.
8. Palmer, *Lee Moves North*, 16; Otis A. Singletary, *The Mexican War* (Chicago: University of Chicago Press, 1960), 71–101; T.R. Fehrenbach, *Fire and Blood: A History of Mexico* (New York: Da Capo Press, 1995), 128–45;

David Donald, ed., *Why the North Won the Civil War* (New York: Collier Books, 1973), 37–41.

9. Dempsey and Egen, *Michigan at Antietam*, 31; Palmer, *Lee Moves North*, 15–17; John D. McKenzie, *Uncertain Glory: Lee's Generalship Re-Examined* (New York: Hippocrene Books Inc., 1997), 95.
10. Robert W. Glover, ed., "From Tyler to Sharpsburg," *The War Letters of Robert H. and William H. Gaston, Company H, First Texas Infantry Regiment, Hood's Texas Brigade* (Waco, TX: W.M. Morrison Publishers, 1960), 1, 5.
11. McKenzie, *Uncertain Glory*, 95; Dean B. Mahin, *One War at a Time: The International Dimensions of the American Civil War* (Washington, D.C.: Brassey's, 2000), 25–57, 122–41; Herman Hattaway and Archer Jones, *How the North Won: A Military History of the Civil War* (Urbana: University of Illinois Press, 1991), 237–44; Thomas, *Robert E. Lee*, 257.
12. Dempsey and Egen, *Michigan at Antietam*, 26–27; Palmer, *Lee Moves North*, 16–17, 22–23, 34–36; Hattaway and Jones, *How the North Won*, 240–42.
13. Clifford Dowdey and Louis H. Manarin, *The Wartime Papers of R.E. Lee* (New York: Bramhall House, n.d.), 292–93; Richard Slotkin, *The Long Road to Antietam: How the Civil War Became a Revolution* (New York: Liveright Publishing Company, 2013), 145–51, 154; Hattaway and Jones, *How the North Won*, 240–42.
14. Harold B. Simpson, *Hood's Texas Brigade: Lee's Grenadier Guard* (Waco, TX: Texian Press, 1970), 160–61; Dempsey and Egen, *Michigan at Antietam*, 26–27; Joseph B. Polley, *A Soldier's Letters to Charming Nellie* (Gaithersburg, MD: Butternut Press, 1984), 80; Joseph B. Polley, *Hood's Texas Brigade: Its Marches, Its Battles, Its Achievements* (New York: Neale Publishing Company, 1910), 112; Slotkin, *Long Road to Antietam*, 156; Edward B. Williams, *Hood's Texas Brigade in the Civil War* (Jefferson, NC: McFarland and Company Inc., 2012), 96.
15. Orlando Thacker Hanks, *History of Captain B.F. Benton's Company 1851–1865* (Austin: Briscoe Center for American History, University of Texas–Austin, n.d.).
16. Simpson, *Hood's Texas Brigade*, 162–63, note no. 20; Compiled Service Records of Confederate Soldiers Who Served in Organizations from the State of Missouri, Record Group 109, National Archives, Washington, D.C. (hereafter CTSR, NA); Polley, *Hood's Texas Brigade*, 128; Sal Gambino, "George A. Branard, Color Bearer, 1st Texas Infantry, Co. L, Hood's Texas Brigade," Find's Treasure Forums message board, http://www.findmall.com/read.php?14,310864,310864.
17. Polley, *Hood's Texas Brigade*, 115; Hanks, *History of Captain B.F. Benton's Company*, Confederate Research Center Archives and Library (CRC); Matt Dale to Brother, June 7, 1862, CRC.

18. Thomas, *Robert E. Lee*, 256; Richard B. Harwell, ed., *The Confederate Reader* (New York: Longarms Green and Company, 1957), 131.
19. Hanks, *History of Captain B.F. Benton's Company*, CRC.
20. Guy R. Everson and Edward W. Simpson Jr., eds., *Far, Far from Home: The Wartime Letters of Dick and Tally Simpson, 3rd South Carolina Volunteers* (Oxford, UK: Oxford University Press, 1994), 147–48.
21. Edward Alexander Porter, *Fighting for the Confederacy: The Personal Recollections of General Edward Porter Alexander* (Chapel Hill: University of North Carolina Press, 1989), 139; Dempsey and Egen, *Michigan at Antietam*, 28.
22. Thomas, *Robert E. Lee*, 259.
23. John A. Lynn, *Feeding Mars: Logistics in Western Warfare from the Middle Ages to the Present* (San Francisco, CA: Westview Press, 1993), 9–25; Martin Van Creveld, *Supplying War: Logistics from Wallenstein to Patton* (Cambridge, UK: Cambridge University Press, 1977), 1–2, 8, 17; Palmer, *Lee Moves North*, 24–25.
24. Mary Lasswell, *Rags and Hope: The Recollections of Val C. Giles, Four Years with Hood's Brigade, Fourth Texas Infantry* (New York: Coward-McCann Inc., 1961), 133.
25. James A. Rawley, *Turning Points of the Civil War* (Lincoln: University of Nebraska, 1989), 106–7; Kegel, *North with Lee and Jackson*, 158–59; Palmer, *Lee Moves North*, 33; Donald, *Why the North Won the Civil War*, 36–41; Dempsey and Egen, *Michigan at Antietam*, 30; William Garrett Piston, *Lee's Tarnished Lieutenant: James Longstreet and His Place in Southern History* (Athens: University of Georgia Press, 1990), 24–25; Hattaway and Jones, *How the North Won*, 240; Slotkin, *Long Road to Antietam*, 163–64.
26. Palmer, *Lee Moves North*, 24–26; Kegel, *North with Lee and Jackson*, 158–59; Piston, *Lee's Tarnished Lieutenant*, 24–25; Slotkin, *Long Road to Antietam*, 163–64.
27. Kegel, *North with Lee and Jackson*, 167–68.
28. Gindlesperger and Gindlesperger, *So You Think You Know Antietam*, 200–201; Dempsey and Egen, *Michigan at Antietam*, 41–42; Kegel, *North with Lee and Jackson*, 167–72; Piston, *Lee's Tarnished Lieutenant*, 24–28; Joseph B. Mitchell, *Decisive Battles of the Civil War* (New York: Fawcett Premier, 1992), 87–89; Slotkin, *Long Road to Antietam*, 218.
29. *Houston Daily Telegraph*, October 15, 1862; Slotkin, *Long Road to Antietam*, 170–72.
30. Palmer, *Lee Moves North*, 24–25; Porter, *Fighting for the Confederacy*, 141–42; Piston, *Lee's Tarnished Lieutenant*, 27–28.
31. Gindlesperger and Gindlesperger, *So You Think You Know Antietam*, xviii; Kegel, *North with Lee and Jackson*, 173–75; Piston, *Lee's Tarnished Lieutenant*, 27–28.

32. John Banks, *Connecticut Yankees at Antietam* (Charleston, SC: The History Press, 2013), 15; Palmer, *Lee Moves North*, 29–30, 33; Thomas, *Robert E. Lee*, 261; Williams, *Hood's Texas Brigade in the Civil War*, 100; Slotkin, *Long Road to Antietam*, 163–64, 168–69.

Chapter 2

33. Simpson, *Hood's Texas Brigade*, 166–68; Philip A. Work, *The 1st Texas Regiment of the Texas Brigade of the Army of Northern Virginia at the Battles of Boonsboro Pass or Gap and Sharpsburg or Antietam, Md. in September 1862*, Confederate Research Center Archives and Library (CRC), Hill Junior College (Hillsboro, TX: Confederate Research Center Archives and Library, Hill Junior College, n.d.); Harold B. Simpson, *Gaines' Mill to Appomattox* (Waco, TX: Texian Press, 1963), 103.
34. Cooper K. Ragan, "Alexander Work, Philip," Handbook of Texas Online, https://tshaonline.org/handbook/online/articles/fwo25.
35. Ted Alexander, *The Battle of Antietam: The Bloodiest Day* (Charleston, SC: The History Press, 2011), 44–45; Simpson, *Hood's Texas Brigade*, 168; Richard McMurry, introduction, *Advance and Retreat* (New York: Da Capo Press, 1995), 57; Work, *1st Texas Regiment*, CRC; George E. Otott, "Clash in the Cornfield: The First Texas in the Maryland Campaign," *Civil War Regiments* 5 (1966): 80–81; David T. Cottingham, *Bridges: Our Legacy in Stone* (Hagerstown, MD: Washington County Board of Commissioners, 1977); Phillip Thomas Tucker, *Burnside's Brigade: The Climactic Struggle of the 2nd and 20th Georgia at Antietam Creek* (Mechanicsburg, PA: Stackpole Publishing, 2000), 64–65.
36. Gerald J. Smith, *"One of the Most Daring of Men": The Life of Confederate General William Tatum Wofford* (Murfreesboro, TN: Southern Heritage Press, 1997), 1–21; James Lee McDonough and James Pickett Jones, *War So Terrible: Sherman and Atlanta* (New York: W.W. Norton, 1987), 134–39; Dempsey and Egen, *Michigan at Antietam*, 28.
37. Smith, *"One of the Most Daring of Men,"* 10–21, 40.
38. Hood, *John Bell Hood*, xxii, 1–8.
39. Smith, *"One of the Most Daring of Men,"* 23–29; *Houston Daily Telegraph*, October 15, 1862.
40. Smith, *"One of the Most Daring of Men,"* 29–36; Compiled Service Records of Confederate Soldiers Who Served from the State of Georgia, National Archives, Washington, D.C.; Hood, *John Bell Hood*, 6–7.
41. Pritchard, "Hood's Brigade," First Texas File, Antietam National Military Park Archives, Sharpsburg, Maryland (hereafter ANMPA).

42. McMurry, *Advance and Retreat*, 47; Slotkin, *Long Road to Antietam*, 211–13.
43. J. Roderick Heller III and Carolynn Ayres Heller, eds., *The Confederacy Is On Her Way Up the Spout: Letters to South Carolina, 1861–1864* (Columbia: University of South Carolina Press, 1998), 55.
44. Glover, "From Tyler to Sharpsburg," 20.
45. Alexander, *Battle of Antietam*, 42–43, 47; Dempsey and Egen, *Michigan at Antietam*, 74; Gindlesperger and Gindlesperger, *So You Think You Know Antietam*, xv; Work, *1st Texas Regiment*, CRC; Otott, "Clash in the Cornfield," 81–82; D.H. Hamilton, *History of Company M, First Texas Volunteer Infantry, Hood's Brigade, Longstreet's Corps, Army of the Confederate States of America* (Waco, TX: W.M. Morrison, 1962), 54; Michael Pittmon to Ted Alexander, November 14, 1996, First Texas File, ANMPA; Williams, *Hood's Texas Brigade in the Civil War*, 100–101; William A. Frassanito, *Antietam: The Photographic Legacy of America's Bloodiest Day* (New York: Charles Scribner's Sons, 1978), 42, 572.
46. James I. Robertson Jr., *Stonewall Jackson: The Man, the Soldier, the Legend* (New York: Macmillan Publishing Company, 1997), 563, 592–609; Mark Mayo Boatner, *The Civil War Dictionary* (New York: David McKay, 1959), 442–43; Williams, *Hood's Texas Brigade in the Civil War*, 101.
47. Porter, *Fighting for the Confederacy*, 145–46; Stephen Sears, *Landscape Turned Red: The Battle of Antietam* (New York: Ticknor & Fields, 1983), 180–81.
48. Palmer, *Lee Moves North*, 30–31; Stephen W. Sears, *George B. McClellan: The Young Napoleon* (New York: Ticknor & Fields, 1988), 95–146; Alexander, *Battle of Antietam*, 40.
49. Robertson, *Stonewall Jackson*, 609.
50. Porter, *Fighting for the Confederacy*, 146.
51. Simpson, *Hood's Texas Brigade*, 168; Porter, *Fighting for the Confederacy*, 150–51; Robertson, *Stonewall Jackson*, 609.
52. Work, *1st Texas Regiment*, CRC.
53. Hamilton, *History of Company M*, 22–23.
54. McMurry, *Advance and Retreat*, 19–20.
55. Ragan, "Philip Alexander Work."
56. Simpson, *Hood's Texas Brigade*, 168–70; Boatner, *Civil War Dictionary*, 371; Otott, "Clash in the Cornfield," 83–84; John Michael Priest, *Antietam: The Soldiers' Battle* (Shippensburg, PA: White Mane Publishing Company, 1990), 15, 18; Robertson, *Stonewall Jackson*, 611; Compiled Service Records of Confederate Soldiers Who Served in Organizations from the State of Texas, Record Group 109, National Archives, Washington, D.C.; Robert Maberry Jr., "Robertson, Jerome Bonaparte," Handbook of Texas Online, https://tshaonline.org/handbook/online/articles/fro28.
57. CTSR, NA.

58. Polley, *Hood's Texas Brigade*, 128; O.M. Roberts, *Confederate Military History, Texas*, vol. 11 (Atlanta, GA, 1899), 314; CTSR, NA.

59. Alexander, *Battle of Antietam*, 49–50; Simpson, *Hood's Texas Brigade*, 169–70; Work, *1st Texas Regiment*, CRC; Otott, "Clash in the Cornfield," 84–85; Boatner, *Civil War Dictionary*, 636–37; Priest, *Antietam*, 15–20; CTSR, NA; Joseph Gibbs, *Three Years in the Bloody Eleventh: The Campaigns of a Pennsylvania Reserve Regiment* (University Park: Pennsylvania State University Press, 2002), xiii, 181; John W. Stevens, *Reminiscences of the Civil War: A Soldier in Hood's Texas Brigade, Army of Northern Virginia* (Hillsboro, TX: Hillsboro Mirror Print, 1902), 99; Rick Eiserman, "We Have Had a Picture Taken," *Civil War Times* 49, no. 4 (August 2011): 44–47.

60. Work, *1st Texas Regiment*, CRC; Priest, *Antietam*, 20; McMurry, *Advance and Retreat*, 42.

61. Simpson, *Hood's Texas Brigade*, 170; Alexander, *Battle of Antietam*, 57; Douglas Southall Freeman, *Lee's Lieutenants: A Study in Command*, vol. 2 (New York: Charles Scribner's Sons, 1944), 206; Priest, *Antietam*, 22–23; Robertson, *Stonewall Jackson*, 609, 611; Slotkin, *Long Road to Antietam*, 70.

62. Simpson, *Hood's Texas Brigade*, 170–71; Otott, "Clash in the Cornfield," 87; Hanks, *History of Captain B.F. Benton's Company*, CRC; Priest, *Antietam*, 51; Matt Dale to brother, June 7, 1862, CRC.

63. Frassanito, *Antietam*, 66; Alexander, *Battle of Antietam*, 52; Dempsey and Egen, *Michigan at Antietam*, 71; Gindlesperger and Gindlesperger, *So You Think You Know Antietam*, xvii, 4–5, 14–15; Porter, *Fighting for the Confederacy*, 150; Williams, *Hood's Texas Brigade in the Civil War*, 103; Slotkin, *Long Road to Antietam*, 173, 253–54.

64. Work, *1st Texas Regiment*, CRC; Otott, "Clash in the Cornfield," 88; Simpson, *Hood's Texas Brigade*, 171; Curt Johnson and Richard C. Anderson, *Artillery Hell: The Employment of Artillery at Antietam* (College Station: Texas A&M University Press, 1995), 47; Hanks, *History of Captain B.F. Benton's Company*, CRC; Williams, *Hood's Texas Brigade in the Civil War*, 105.

65. *Houston Daily Telegraph*, October 15, 1862.

66. Alexander, *Battle of Antietam*, 62; Simpson, *Hood's Texas Brigade*, 171; Alan T. Nolan, *The Iron Brigade: A Military History* (New York: Macmillan Company, 1961), 135–37; Otott, "Clash in the Cornfield," 88–89; Abner Doubleday, *My Life in the Old Army: The Reminiscences of Abner Doubleday* (Fort Worth: Texas Christian University Press, 1998), 1–7; Freeman, *Lee's Lieutenants*, 206; Sears, *Landscape Turned Red*, 180–82; McMurry, *Advance and Retreat*, 38–41; Robertson, *Stonewall Jackson*, 563, 609–11; Hanks, *History of Captain B.F. Benton's Company*, CRC; Scott L. Mingus Sr., *The Louisiana Tigers in the Gettysburg Campaign June–July 1863* (Baton Rouge: Louisiana State University Press, 2009), 1–13.

67. Alexander, *Battle of Antietam*, 62–64; Terry L. Jones, *Lee's Tigers: The Louisiana Infantry in the Army of Northern Virginia* (Baton Rouge: Louisiana State University Press, 1987), 129–31; Otott, "Clash in the Cornfield," 89–90; Freeman, *Lee's Lieutenants*, 206; Boatner, *Civil War Dictionary*, 252; Sears, *Landscape Turned Red*, 185–89; Robertson, *Stonewall Jackson*, 612–13; Priest, *Antietam*, 38; Mingus, *Louisiana Tigers*, xv, 1–13, 108.
68. Jones, *Lee's Tigers*, 131; Alexander, *Battle of Antietam*, 64–66; Sears, *Landscape Turned Red*, 191; Robertson, *Stonewall Jackson*, 563.
69. Otott, "Clash in the Cornfield," 90.
70. Jeffery D. Wert, *A Brotherhood of Valor: The Common Soldiers of the Stonewall Brigade, C.S.A., and the Iron Brigade, U.S.A.* (New York: Touchstone Books, 1999), 172, 178–80; Donald L. Smith, *The Twenty-Fourth Michigan* (Mechanicsburg, PA: Stackpole Books, 1962), 36; Otott, "Clash in the Cornfield," 90; Monroe F. Cockrell, ed., *Gunner with Stonewall: Reminiscences of William Thomas Poague* (Wilmington, NC: Broadfoot Publishing Company, 1987), 45–46; Johnson and Anderson, *Artillery Hell*, 44, 47–48; Sears, *Landscape Turned Red*, 192–93; Priest, *Antietam*, 31–35.
71. Alan D. Gaff, *On Many a Bloody Field: Four Years in the Iron Brigade* (Indianapolis: Indiana University Press, 1996), 184–85.
72. Wert, *Brotherhood of Valor*, 180–81; James I. Robertson, *The Stonewall Brigade* (Baton Rouge: Louisiana State University Press, 1962), 157–58, 162; Nolan, *Iron Brigade*, 138; Sears, *Landscape Turned Red*, 191–93; Priest, *Antietam*, 38.
73. Wert, *Brotherhood of Valor*, 181; Nolan, *Iron Brigade*, 138–39; Smith, *Twenty-Fourth Michigan*, 35–37; Otott, "Clash in the Cornfield," 90; Sears, *Landscape Turned Red*, 192–93, 200; Priest, *Antietam*, 4, 40–42.
74. Gindlesperger and Gindlesperger, *So You Think You Know Antietam*, 31; Smith, *Twenty-Fourth Michigan*, 37; Wert, *Brotherhood of Valor*, 182; Ronald Bailey, *The Bloodiest Day: The Battle of Antietam* (Alexandria, VA: Time-Life Books, 1984), 74; Nolan, *Iron Brigade*, 138–39; Otott, "Clash in the Cornfield," 91; Sears, *Landscape Turned Red*, 193–94; Priest, *Antietam*, 43–44.
75. Bailey, *Bloodiest Day*, 74; Otott, "Clash in the Cornfield," 91; Priest, *Antietam*, 43–44.
76. Wert, *Brotherhood of Valor*, 181–82; Robertson, *Stonewall Brigade*, 10–22, 158; Smith, *Twenty-Fourth Michigan*, 37; Bailey, *Bloodiest Day*, 74–75; Otott, "Clash in the Cornfield," 91; Sears, *Landscape Turned Red*, 194; Priest, *Antietam*, 49; Boatner, *Civil War Dictionary*, 442–43.
77. Jones, *Lee's Tigers*, 131–32; Frassanito, *Antietam*, 126–29, 132–38; Thomas Walter Brooks and Michael Dan Jones, *Lee's Foreign Legion: A History of the 10th Louisiana Infantry* (Gravenhurst, Canada: Watts Printing, 1995),

34; Bailey, *Bloodiest Day*, 74–75; Otott, "Clash in the Cornfield," 91–92; Robertson, *Stonewall Jackson*, 613.

78. Smith, *Twenty-Fourth Michigan*, 37; Bailey, *Bloodiest Day*, 75; Nolan, *Iron Brigade*, 139–40.
79. Simpson, *Hood's Texas Brigade*, 171; Alexander, *Battle of Antietam*, 67; Perry D. Jamieson, *Death in September: The Antietam Campaign* (College Station, TX: State House Press, 1998), 60–61; Wert, *Brotherhood of Valor*, 182; Bailey, *Bloodiest Day*, 74–75; Nolan, *Iron Brigade*, 139; Sears, *Landscape Turned Red*, 197.
80. *War of the Rebellion: A Compilation of the Official Records of the Union and Confederate Armies*, volume 19, part. 1 (Washington, D.C.: United States War Department, 1880–1901), 933 (hereafter *OR*); Roberts, *Confederate Military History*, 314; CTSR, NA; Gambino, "George A. Branard."
81. Hanks, *History of Captain B.F. Benton's Company*, CRC.
82. Ibid.
83. Arlow W. Andersen, *The Norwegian-Americans* (Boston: Twayne Publishers, 1975), 73; Wert, *Brotherhood of Valor*, 21–162; CTSR, NA; Alan Nolan, "The Forging of the Iron Brigade," *Civil War* 11, no. 1 (January–February 1993): 17–22; McMurry, *Advance and Retreat*, 43; Nolan, *Iron Brigade*, 4, 16; Simpson, *Hood's Texas Brigade*, 172; Otott, "Clash in the Cornfield," 92; Slotkin, *Long Road to Antietam*, 205; Sears, *Landscape Turned Red*, 197; Mark Lloyd, *Combat Uniforms of the Civil War* (New York: Mallard Press, 1990), 92; Alan T. Nolan, introduction, *A Full Blown Yankee of the Iron Brigade: Service with the Sixth Wisconsin Volunteers* (Lincoln: University of Nebraska Press, 1999), xi, 13, 26, 28, 35, 43, 47.
84. Wert, *Brotherhood of Valor*, 144–55; Robertson, *Stonewall Brigade*, 147.

Chapter 3

85. McMurry, *Advance and Retreat*, 43.
86. Ibid.; Alexander, *Battle of Antietam*, 62–67.
87. *Kansas State Journal*, October 2, 1862; Nolan, *Iron Brigade*, 134; Simpson, *Hood's Texas Brigade*, 172; Williams, *Hood's Texas Brigade in the Civil War*, 105.
88. Gindlesperger and Gindlesperger, *So You Think You Know Antietam*, 55; Wert, *Brotherhood of Valor*, 182; McMurry, *Advance and Retreat*, 58; Freeman, *Lee's Lieutenants*, 206–7; Simpson, *Hood's Texas Brigade*, 172; Robertson, *Stonewall Jackson*, 613; Williams, *Hood's Texas Brigade in the Civil War*, 105.
89. Freeman, *Lee's Lieutenants*, 207; Simpson, *Hood's Texas Brigade*, 172.
90. Theodore Gerrish, *Army Life: A Private's Reminiscences of the Civil War* (Portland, OR: Hoyt, Fogg and Donham, 1995), 33.
91. McMurry, *Advance and Retreat*, 43.

92. Ibid.; Williams, *Hood's Texas Brigade in the Civil War*, 105.

93. Simpson, *Hood's Texas Brigade*, 172, 177; John H. Worsham, *One of Jackson's Foot Cavalry* (Wilmington, NC: Broadfoot Publishing Company, 1987), 86–87, note nos. 18 and 19; Freeman, *Lee's Lieutenants*, 206–7; CTSR, NA; Johnson and Anderson, *Artillery Hell*, 7, 47; Robertson, *Stonewall Jackson*, 614.

94. Freeman, *Lee's Lieutenants*, 387–89.

95. McMurry, *Advance and Retreat*, 43.

96. Ibid.; CTSR, NA; Thomas W. Cutrer, "Willson, Samuel A.," Handbook of Texas Online, https://tshaonline.org/handbook/online/articles/fwi47.

97. G.T. Todd, *First Texas Regiment* (Waco, TX: Texian Press, 1963), ix–x, 11; CTSR, NA; Otott, "Clash in the Cornfield," 81; Slotkin, *Long Road to Antietam*, 236, 264; Nolan, *Iron Brigade*, 139–40; Daniel S. Gray, *In the Words of Napoleon*, (Troy, MI: Troy State University Press, 1977), 6; Robertson, *Stonewall Jackson*, 612–13; Hanks, *History of Captain B.F. Benton's Company*, CRC; Priest, *Antietam*, 51, 55; John R. Elting, *Swords Around a Throne: Napoleon's Grande Armee* (New York: Da Capo Press, 1997), 183–205, 657; McMurry, *Advance and Retreat*, 43; Slotkin, *Long Road to Antietam*, 146.

98. Glover, "From Tyler to Sharpsburg," 10.

99. Nolan, *Iron Brigade*, 140; E. Scott Carson, "Hampton's Legion and Hood's Brigade," *Confederate Veteran* 16, (July 1908): 342; Robertson, *Stonewall Jackson*, 614; Susannah F. Ural, "A Little Body of Malcontents," *Civil War Times* (June 2014): 68.

100. Smith, *Twenty-Fourth Michigan*, 37; McMurry, *Advance and Retreat*, 58; Work, *1st Texas Regiment*, CRC; Jeffrey D. Stocker, ed., *From Huntsville to Appomattox: R.T. Coles's History of 4th Regiment, Alabama Volunteer Infantry, C.S.A., Army of Northern Virginia* (Knoxville: University of Tennessee Press, 1996), 67–68; Freeman, *Lee's Lieutenants*, 207; Bailey, *Bloodiest Day*, 75–76; Otott, "Clash in the Cornfield," 93; Sears, *Landscape Turned Red*, 197–98; Robertson, *Stonewall Jackson*, 613; Priest, *Antietam*, 51–55; Nolan, *Full Blown Yankee*, 88–90; T.R. Fehrenbach, *Lone Star: A History of Texas and the Texians* (New York: Da Capo Press, 2000), 227–33; McMurry, *Advance and Retreat*, 43; Randy Roberts and James S. Olson, *A Line in the Sand: The Alamo in Blood and Memory* (New York: Free Press, 2001), 3, 48–49, 129; Williams, *Hood's Texas Brigade in the Civil War*, 105–6; Stevens, *Reminiscences of the Civil War*, 74; Frassanito, *Antietam*, 132.

101. Alexander, *Battle of Antietam*, 69; Smith, *"One of the Most Daring of Men,"* 56; Otott, "Clash in the Cornfield," 93, 95; Priest, *Antietam*, 54–55.

102. *OR*, vol. 19, pt. 1, 932.

103. Smith, *"One of the Most Daring of Men,"* 56; Otott, "Clash in the Cornfield," 95; *Houston Daily Telegraph*, October 15, 1862; Priest, *Antietam*, 60.

104. Smith, *"One of the Most Daring of Men,"* 56.
105. CTSR, NA; Otott, "Clash in the Cornfield," 95, 97; Williams, *Hood's Texas Brigade in the Civil War*, 106.
106. CTSR, NA; McMurry, *Advance and Retreat*, 58; Freeman, *Lee's Lieutenants*, 208; Simpson, *Hood's Texas Brigade*, 172–73; *OR*, vol. 19, pt. 1, 932; John J. Hennessy, *Return to Bull Run: The Campaign and Battle of Second Manassas* (Norman: University of Oklahoma Press, 1998), 362–73; Nolan, *Iron Brigade*, 113–30, 140; Bailey, *Bloodiest Day*, 76; Otott, "Clash in the Cornfield," 95; Nolan, *Full Blown Yankee*, 90–91; Sears, *Landscape Turned Red*, 198; Robertson, *Stonewall Jackson*, 614; Priest, *Antietam*, 55; John L. Plaster, *Sharpshooters in the Civil War* (Boulder, CO: Paladin Press, 2009), 11.
107. Polley, *Hood's Texas Brigade*, 124–25, 128, 131; Nolan, *Iron Brigade*, 140–41; *OR*, vol. 19, pt. 1, 933; CTSR, NA.
108. Wert, *Brotherhood of Valor*, 183; Nolan, *Iron Brigade*, 140–41; Priest, *Antietam*, 55.
109. Work, *1st Texas Regiment*, CRC; Donald E. Everett, ed., *Chaplain Davis and Hood's Texas Brigade* (Baton Rouge: Louisiana State University Press, 1999), 127; Simpson, *Hood's Texas Brigade*, 172–73; *OR*, vol. 19, pt. 1, 930, 933; Wert, *Brotherhood of Valor*, 184, 325–26; Nolan, *Iron Brigade*, 140–41; Sears, *Landscape Turned Red*, 199; Williams, *Hood's Texas Brigade in the Civil War*, 108.
110. Smith, *"One of the Most Daring of Men,"* 56; Sears, *Landscape Turned Red*, 199.
111. Freeman, *Lee's Lieutenants*, 208; Nolan, *Full Blown Yankee*, 91.
112. *Confederate Veteran* 22, no. 12, "The Texans at Sharpsburg" (December 1914): 555; Nolan, *Iron Brigade*, 140–41; Bailey, *Bloodiest Day*, 76; Hanks, *History of Captain B.F. Benton's Company*, CRC; Nolan, *Full Blown Yankee*, 91; Slotkin, *Long Road to Antietam*, 147, 150–51; Marquis James, *The Raven: A Biography of Sam Houston* (New York: Blue Ribbon Books Inc., 1929), 238–52.
113. Nolan, *Full Blown Yankee*, 91.
114. *OR*, vol. 19, pt. 1, 932; Williams, *Hood's Texas Brigade in the Civil War*, 104, 106.
115. Nolan, *Full Blown Yankee*, 88.
116. Everett, *Chaplain Davis and Hood's Texas Brigade*, 167; Simpson, *Hood's Texas Brigade*, 168; Polley, *Hood's Texas Brigade*, 131; Nolan, *Iron Brigade*, 140–41; Priest, *Antietam*, 55–58.
117. Carson, "Hampton's Legion and Hood's Brigade," 342; Hanks, *History of Captain B.F. Benton's Company*, CRC.
118. Work, *1st Texas Regiment*, CRC; *OR*, vol. 19, pt. 1, 928, 932; Wert, *Brotherhood of Valor*, 184; Nolan, *Iron Brigade*, 140–41; Bailey, *Bloodiest Day*,

76; Otott, "Clash in the Cornfield," 97; Smith, *"One of the Most Daring of Men,"* 56; Sears, *Landscape Turned Red*, 181; "Col. F.S. Bass," CRC; Williams, *Hood's Texas Brigade in the Civil War*, 105–6.

119. *OR*, vol. 19, pt. 1, 932; Wert, *Brotherhood of Valor*, 184; Nolan, *Iron Brigade*, 140–41; Otott, "Clash in the Cornfield," 97.

120. CRSR, NA; Wert, *Brotherhood of Valor*, 184; Nolan, *Iron Brigade*, 140–41; Henry Waters Berryman to Mother, September 22, 1862, First Texas File, ANMPA; *Houston Daily Telegraph*, October 15, 1862; Susan Williams Benson, ed., *Confederate Scout-Sniper: The Civil War Memoir of Berry Benson* (Athens: University of Georgia Press, 1992), 23–24; Gerrish, *Army Life*, 33; James, *Raven*, 238–52.

121. Todd, *First Texas Regiment*, 1, 11; Sears, *Landscape Turned Red*, 198.

122. *OR*, vol. 19, pt. 1, 932; Nolan, *Iron Brigade*, 140–41; Otott, "Clash in the Cornfield," 98.

123. *OR*, vol. 19, pt. 1, 932; Nolan, *Iron Brigade*, 140–41.

124. Nolan, *Iron Brigade*, 141.

125. Otott, "Clash in the Cornfield," 98.

126. Slotkin, *Long Road to Antietam*, 146–51, 236, 264.

127. *OR*, vol. 19 pt. 1, 932; Nolan, *Iron Brigade*, 140–41.

128. *OR*, vol. 19, pt. 1, 930–32, 934; Work, *1st Texas Regiment*, CRC; CTSR, NA.

129. McMurry, *Advance and Retreat*, 58; *OR*, vol. 19, pt. 1, 932; Simpson, *Hood's Texas Brigade*, 172–74, 176–77; Polley, *Hood's Texas Brigade*, 116, 131; Nolan, *Iron Brigade*, 140–41; Hamilton, *History of Company M*, 23; Gaff, *On Many a Bloody Field*, 185; CTSR, NA; "Texas-Facebook," Internet; Charles E. Brooks, "The Social and Cultural Dynamics of Soldiers in Hood's Texas Brigade," *Journal of Southern History* 67, no. 3 (August 2001): 539–40.

130. Polley, *Hood's Texas Brigade*, 131; *OR*, vol. 10, pt. 1, 932.

131. Gerrish, *Army Life*, 34.

132. Work, *1st Texas Regiment*, CRC; *OR*, vol. 10, pt. 1, 932.

133. *OR*, vol. 19, pt. 1, 930–32; Simpson, *Hood's Texas Brigade*, 174; Nolan, *Iron Brigade*, 141; Otott, "Clash in the Cornfield," 98; Gaff, *On Many a Bloody Field*, 185–86; Sears, *Landscape Turned Red*, 200.

134. Otott, "Clash in the Cornfield," 99–100.

135. Wert, *Brotherhood of Valor*, 184; Robertson, *Stonewall Jackson*, 615.

136. *OR*, vol. 19, pt. 1, 934; Sears, *Landscape Turned Red*, 200–201.

137. Nolan, *Iron Brigade*, 140–42; Gaff, *On Many a Bloody Field*, 185.

138. Sears, *Landscape Turned Red*, 199.

Chapter 4

139. Wert, *Brotherhood of Valor*, 184; Gaff, *On Many a Bloody Field*, 185.
140. Simpson, *Hood's Texas Brigade*, 174–77; Sears, *Landscape Turned Red*, 200–201.
141. Otott, "Clash in the Cornfield," 95; Bailey, *Bloodiest Day*, 78; Work, *1st Texas Regiment*, CRC; Sears, *Landscape Turned Red*, 199–200; Alexander, *Battle of Antietam*, 40; Gaff, *On Many a Bloody Field*, 185; CTSR, NA; Hanks, *History of Captain B.F. Benton's Company*, CRC; Freeman Cleaves, *Meade of Gettysburg* (Norman: University of Oklahoma Press, 1991), 78–79; Gibbs, *Three Years in the Bloody Eleventh*, 2–184.
142. Work, *1st Texas Regiment*, CRC; Wert, *Brotherhood of Valor*, 184.
143. Smith, *"One of the Most Daring of Men,"* 57; Otott, "Clash in the Cornfield," 98; Johnson and Anderson, *Artillery Hell*, 71; Sears, *Landscape Turned Red*, 200–201; Gaff, *On Many a Bloody Field*, 185.
144. *Confederate Veteran*, "Texans at Sharpsburg," 555.
145. Note by O.T. Reilly, Antietam Battlefield guide and shop owner, Sharpsburg, Maryland, on eBay auction of "J. Rook" musket stock, October 2, 2012.
146. Work, *1st Texas Regiment*, CRC.
147. Gindlesperger and Gindlesperger, *So You Think You Know Antietam*, 51; *OR*, vol. 19, pt. 1, 932; Hanks, *History of Captain B.F. Benton's Company*, CRC; Gaff, *On Many a Bloody Field*, 185.
148. *Athens Daily Review*, April 12, 1972; CTSR, NA.
149. Gindlesperger and Gindlesperger, *So You Think You Know Antietam*, 51; Work, *1st Texas*, CRC; Brooks, *Social and Cultural Dynamics*, 535–72.
150. Gindlesperger and Gindlesperger, *So You Think You Know Antietam*, 48, 51; Simpson, *Hood's Texas Brigade*, 177; Bailey, *Bloodiest Day*, 78; Sears, *Landscape Turned Red*, 199–201; Hanks, *History of Captain B.F. Benton's Company*, CRC; Priest, *Antietam*, 66; Slotkin, *Long Road to Antietam*, 236; Gibbs, *Three Years in the Bloody Eleventh*, 156–60, 184; Cleaves, *Meade of Gettysburg*, 78–79.
151. Work, *1st Texas Regiment*, CRC.
152. Priest, *Antietam*, 66–68; Gibbs, *Three Years in the Bloody Eleventh*, 2–185; Cleaves, *Meade of Gettysburg*, 79.
153. Priest, *Antietam*, 66–68; Everett, *Chaplain Davis and Hood's Texas Brigade*, 167; Bailey, *Bloodiest Day*, 78; Otott, "Clash in the Cornfield," 98; Hanks, *History of Captain B.F. Benton's Company*, CRC; Gibbs, *Three Years in the Bloody Eleventh*, 184–85; Gaff, *On Many a Bloody Field*, 185.
154. Nolan, *Iron Brigade*, 144; Otott, "Clash in the Cornfield," 100; Johnson and Anderson, *Artillery Hell*, 71; Priest, *Antietam*, 66–68; Plaster, *Sharpshooters in the Civil War*, 83, 86.

155. Johnson and Anderson, *Artillery Hell*, 7; Gaff, *On Many a Bloody Field*, 185.
156. Polley, *Hood's Texas Brigade*, 131; Otott, "Clash in the Cornfield," 100–101; Hanks, *History of Captain B.F. Benton's Company*, CRC; Priest, *Antietam*, 66–68; Gaff, *On Many a Bloody Field*, 185; Gibbs, *Three Years in the Bloody Eleventh*, 184–85.
157. W.R. Hamby, "Hood's Texas Brigade at Sharpsburg," *Confederate Veteran* 16, no. 1 (January 1908): 19; Priest, *Antietam*, 66–68.
158. *OR*, vol. 19, pt. 1, 934; Polley, *Hood's Texas Brigade*, 117; Smith, *"One of the Most Daring of Men,"* 58; *Houston Daily Telegraph*, October 15, 1862.
159. Everett, *Chaplain Davis and Hood's Texas Brigade*, 167.
160. Otott, "Clash in the Cornfield," 100–101; Gibbs, *Three Years in the Bloody Eleventh*, 25, 184–85; *OR*, vol. 19, pt. 1, 933; CTSR, NA.
161. Evault Boswell, *Texas Boys in Gray* (Plano: Republic of Texas Press, 2000), 97; Lawrence T. Jones III, "Photography in Civil War Texas," Handbook of Texas Online, https://tshaonline.org/handbook/online/articles/kjp04.
162. *OR*, vol. 19, pt. 1, 932.
163. Ibid.; Gaff, *On Many a Bloody Field*, 185.
164. Smith, *"One of the Most Daring of Men,"* 57; Gibbs, *Three Years in the Bloody Eleventh*, 184; Gaff, *On Many a Bloody Field*, 185.
165. *OR*, vol. 19, pt. 1, 932.
166. Ibid., 932–33.
167. Ibid., 933; Smith, *"One of the Most Daring of Men,"* 57; CTSR, NA; Otott, "Clash in the Cornfield," 102; Work, *1st Texas Regiment*, CRC; Gaff, *On Many a Bloody Field*, 185; Gibbs, *Three Years in the Bloody Eleventh*, 183.
168. Smith, *Twenty-Fourth Michigan*, 37–38; Gaff, *On Many a Bloody Field*, 185; Nolan, *Full Blown Yankee*, 91.
169. Smith, *Twenty-Fourth Michigan*, 37–38.
170. *Confederate Veteran*, "Texans at Sharpsburg," 555; Wert, *Brotherhood of Valor*, 184–85; Nolan, *Iron Brigade*, 141; Otott, "Clash in the Cornfield," 102; Gaff, *On Many a Bloody Field*, 185.
171. Polley, *Soldier's Letters to Charming Nellie*, 85; Gibbs, *Three Years in the Bloody Eleventh*, 184–85; Nolan, *Iron Brigade*, 142.
172. Everett, *Chaplain Davis and Hood's Texas Brigade*, 167; Nolan, *Iron Brigade*, 142; Priest, *Antietam*, 66–68; Gibbs, *Three Years in the Bloody Eleventh*, 184–85.
173. Smith, *Twenty-Fourth Michigan*, 38; Bailey, *Bloodiest Day*, 79; Smith, *"One of the Most Daring of Men,"* 57; Plaster, *Sharpshooters in the Civil War*, 90–91; Slotkin, *Long Road to Antietam*, 240–41.
174. W.E. Barry, "Dauntless Courage and Heroic Deeds," in F.B. Chilton, *Unveiling and Dedication of Monument to Hood's Texas Brigade* (Houston, TX: self-published, 1911), 107; CTSR, NA.

175. Harwood Earl Perry, First Texas File, ANMPA; Harold S. Simpson, ed., "Whip the Devil & His Hosts," typescript, First Texas File, ANMPA.
176. Polley, *Hood's Texas Brigade*, 132.
177. Smith, *"One of the Most Daring of Men,"* 57.
178. *OR*, vol. 19, pt. 1, 933; Nolan, *Iron Brigade*, 141; Hanks, *History of Captain B.F. Benton's Company*, CRC.
179. *OR*, vol. 19, pt. 1, 934; Smith, *"One of the Most Daring of Men,"* 57; Nolan, *Iron Brigade*, 141.
180. *OR*, vol. 19, pt. 1, 934; Everett, *Chaplain Davis and Hood's Texas Brigade*, 166; Otott, "Clash in the Cornfield," 102.
181. Work, *1st Texas Regiment*, CRC.
182. Everett, *Chaplain Davis and Hood's Texas Brigade*, 167.
183. Ibid.
184. Work, *1st Texas Regiment*, CRC; Everett, *Chaplain Davis and Hood's Texas Brigade*, 166; CTSR, NA.
185. *OR*, vol. 19, pt. 1, 934.
186. Hamby, "Hood's Texas Brigade at Sharpsburg," 20; CTSR, NA; Otott, "Clash in the Cornfield," 101–2.
187. *OR*, vol. 19, pt. 1, 928.
188. Ibid., 935; Polley, *Hood's Texas Brigade*, 122–23.
189. *OR*, vol. 19, pt. 1, 932–33, 935; Priest, *Antietam*, 66–68.
190. Everett, *Chaplain Davis and Hood's Texas Brigade*, 129–30; Simpson, *Hood's Texas Brigade*, 177.
191. *OR*, vol. 19, pt. 1, 936; Smith, *"One of the Most Daring of Men,"* 57–58.
192. Everett, *Chaplain Davis and Hood's Texas Brigade*, 128; Smith, *"One of the Most Daring of Men,"* 57.
193. *OR*, vol. 19, pt. 1, 923.
194. Ibid., 129.
195. Ibid., 934.
196. Everett, *Chaplain Davis and Hood's Texas Brigade*, 126, 129–30.
197. Ibid., 128.
198. *OR*, vol. 19, pt. 1, 933.
199. Widener to Antietam National Battlefield Site, May 26, 1976, ANMPA; CTSR, NA; Robert W. Glover, "Gaston, William Henry," Handbook of Texas Online, https://tshaonline.org/handbook/online/articles/fga63; Handbook of Texas Online, "Mound Prairie Institute," https://tshaonline.org/handbook/online/articles/kbm30.
200. Glover, "From Tyler to Sharpsburg," 9.
201. Ibid., 1; Widener to Antietam National Battlefield Site; CTSR, NA; Glover, "Gaston, William Henry."

202. Henry Waters Berryman to Mother; Michael Pittmon to Ted Alexander; CTSR, NA; Hamilton, *History of Company M*, 54.
203. Boswell, *Texas Boys in Gray*, 97; Jones, "Photography in Civil War Texas."
204. *Houston Daily Telegraph*, October 15, 1862.
205. Pritchard, "Hood's Brigade."
206. Otott, "Clash in the Cornfield," 101–2; Bell Irwin Wiley, *Embattled Confederates: An Illustrated History of Southerners at War* (New York: Harper and Row Publishers, 1964), 77.
207. John Spencer, *From Corsicana to Appomattox* (Corsicana: Texas Press, 1984), 43.
208. CTSR, NA; Todd, *First Texas Regiment*, xi, 11; Work, *1st Texas Regiment*, CRC; *Houston Daily Telegraph*, October 15, 1862; Kelly J. O'Grady, *Clear the Confederate Way!: The Irish of the Army of Northern Virginia* (El Dorado Hills, CA: Savas Publishing Company, 2000), 235; Simpson, *Hood's Texas Brigade*, 174, note no. 86.
209. CTSR, NA; Priest, *Antietam*, 66; Harwood Earl Perry, ANMPA; Simpson, *Hood's Texas Brigade*, 174, note no. 86.
210. CTSR, NA; Everett, *Chaplain Davis and Hood's Texas Brigade*, 192–94; Hanks, *History of Captain B.F. Benton's Company*, CRC; Hamilton, *History of Company M*, 14–15; *Palestine Herald-Press*, October 18, 1967; Ralph W. Widener Jr., May 26, 1976, letter to Antietam National Battlefield Site, First Texas File, ANMPA; Henry Waters Berryman to Mother; Simpson, *Hood's Texas Brigade*, 174, note no. 86; Bertram W. Korn, *American Jewry and the Civil War* (Philadelphia: Jewish Publication Society of America, 1957), 1–2.
211. Gregory A. Coco, ed., *From Ball's Bluff to Gettysburg…and Beyond: The Civil War Letters of Private Roland E. Bowen, 15th Massachusetts Infantry, 1861–1864* (Gettysburg, PA: Thomas Publications, 1994), 124; Gindlesperger and Gindlesperger, *So You Think You Know Antietam*, 19; Hanks, *History of Captain B.F. Benton's Company*, CRC.
212. *OR*, vol. 19, pt. 1, 933; Robert C. Cheeks, "Carnage in the Cornfield," *America's Civil War* (September 1989): 35; Otott, "Clash in the Cornfield," 104.
213. *OR*, vol. 19, pt. 1, 933; Work, *1st Texas Regiment*, CRC; Otott, "Clash in the Cornfield," 102; TCSR, NA; Simpson, *Hood's Texas Brigade*, 174.
214. *OR*, vol. 19, pt. 1, 933; Otott, "Clash in the Cornfield," 102; Work, *1st Texas Regiment*, CRC.
215. Williams, *Hood's Texas Brigade in the Civil War*, 109.
216. W.R. Hamby, "Glory of Hood's Texas Brigade," *Confederate Veteran* 18, no. 1. (January 1910): 563.
217. Hamilton, *History of Company M*, 23–24; Work, *1st Texas Regiment*, CRC; Hanks, *History of Captain B.F. Benton's Company*, CRC; TCSR, NA.
218. Hanks, *History of Captain B.F. Benton's Company*, CRC.

219. Otott, "Clash in the Cornfield," 77, 104–5; Henry Waters Berryman to Mother; TCSR, NA; *Houston Daily Telegraph*, October 15, 1862; Eiserman, "We Have Had a Picture Taken," 44–47; Gibbs, *Three Years in the Bloody Eleventh*, 174–77, 184–85; "David King Rice," genealogy.com.
220. Compiled Service Records of Men Who Served from the State of Pennsylvania, Record Group 94, National Archives, Washington, D.C.; Cindy Ekas, "Connellsville's Forgotten Civil War Hero Remembered," *Pittsburgh Tribune-Review*, September 24, 2012.
221. Williams, *Hood's Texas Brigade in the Civil War*, 22.
222. Work, *1st Texas Regiment*, CRC.
223. *Houston Daily Telegraph*, October 15, 1862.
224. Work, *1st Texas Regiment*, CRC..
225. Ibid.; CTSR, NA.
226. Work, *1st Texas Regiment*, CRC.
227. Ibid.
228. Ibid.
229. Ibid.
230. Ibid.; *Houston Daily Telegraph*, October 15, 1862.
231. Ibid.
232. Ibid.
233. Ibid.
234. Otott, "Clash in the Cornfield," 108; Work, *1st Texas Regiment*, CRC; *OR*, vol. 19, pt. 1, 933.
235. Simpson, "Whip the Devil & His Hosts."
236. Ibid.; Glover, "Gaston, William Henry."
237. Simpson, "Whip the Devil & His Hosts"; TCSR, NA; Glover, "Gaston, William Henry."
238. Dempsey and Egen, *Michigan at Antietam*, 34, 36, 75; Simpson, *Hood's Texas Brigade*, 174–75.
239. Bailey, *Bloodiest Day*, 70; Robertson, *Stonewall Jackson*, 613.
240. Hamby, "Hood's Texas Brigade at Sharpsburg," 20.
241. Wert, *Brotherhood of Valor*, 184; Otott, "Clash in the Cornfield," 110; Nolan, *Full Blown Yankee*, 62.
242. Russell Duncan, ed., *Blue-Eyed Child of Destiny: The Civil War Letters of Robert Gould Shaw* (New York: Avon Books, 1992), 240.
243. Polley, *Hood's Texas Brigade*, 128–29.
244. Hamby, "Glory of Hood's Texas Brigade."
245. Ibid., "Hood's Texas Brigade at Sharpsburg," 21.
246. Stevens, *Reminiscences of the Civil War*, 75; CTSR, NA.
247. Cheeks, "Carnage in a Cornfield," 35.
248. Slotkin, *Long Road to Antietam*, 72, 148–51, 236, 264.

BITTER EPILOGUE

249. Gindlesperger and Gindlesperger, *So You Think You Know Antietam*, xvii; Rawley, *Turning Points of the Civil War*, 99–143.
250. McMurry, *Advance and Retreat*, 59; Polley, *Hood's Texas Brigade*, 134; Bailey, *Bloodiest Day*, 79.
251. *Kansas State Journal*, October 2, 1862; Polley, *Soldier's Letters to Charming Nellie*, 85; McMurry, *Advance and Retreat*, 59.
252. Work, *1st Texas Regiment*, CRC.
253. *Houston Daily Telegraph*, October 15, 1862.
254. Henry Waters Berryman to Mother, September 23, 1862, First Texas File, ANMPA.
255. Ibid.; TCSR, NA.
256. Simpson, *Hood's Texas Brigade*, 176–77; Polley, *Hood's Texas Brigade*, 128; Otott, "Clash in the Cornfield," 92.
257. Polley, *Hood's Texas Brigade*, 133.
258. Ibid., 124.
259. Otott, "Clash in the Cornfield," 122, note no. 168.
260. Robertson, *Stonewall Jackson*, 613.
261. "Col. F.S. Bass," CRC.
262. Polley, *Hood's Texas Brigade*, 128; Harwell, *Confederate Reader*, 74; *Houston Daily Telegraph*, October 15, 1862.
263. Everett, *Chaplain Davis and Hood's Texas Brigade*, 139; Gindlesperger and Gindlesperger, *So You Think You Know Antietam*, 221.
264. Widener to Antietam National Battlefield Site.
265. Stevens, *Reminiscences of the Civil War*, 76.
266. Everett, *Chaplain Davis and Hood's Texas Brigade*, 134–35.
267. Heros Von Borche, *Memoirs of the Confederate War for Independence* (New York: Smith, 1938), 234.
268. Polley, *Hood's Texas Brigade*, 133.
269. *OR*, vol. 19, pt. 1, 923.
270. Simpson, *Hood's Texas Brigade*, 181–82; *OR*, vol. 10, pt. 1, 923, 934; Hamby, "Hood's Texas Brigade at Sharpsburg," 20; Rawley, *Turning Points of the Civil War*, 113–14.
271. *OR*, vol. 19, pt. 1, 929.
272. Johnson and Anderson, *Artillery Hell*, 54–55.
273. Robertson, *Stonewall Jackson*, 618.
274. Polley, *Hood's Texas Brigade*, 135.
275. Texas Brigade, First Texas Infantry, Civil War Reenactors, http://texas-brigade.org/frmain1tex.htm; Otott, "Clash in the Cornfield," 110; Christopher Long, "Alto, TX," Handbook of Texas Online,

https://tshaonline.org/handbook/online/articles/hja06; Henry Waters Berryman to Mother.

276. CTSR, NA.

277. Gibbs, *Three Years in the Bloody Eleventh*, 186.

278. Stephen Chicoine, *The Confederates of Chappell Hill, Texas: Prosperity, Civil War and Decline* (Jefferson, NC: McFarland Publishers, 2012), 56.

279. Gindlesperger and Gindlesperger, *So You Think You Know Antietam*, 32; Heller and Heller, *Confederacy Is On Her Way Up the Spout*, 77.

280. Glover, "From Tyler to Sharpsburg," 21.

281. Ibid., 10.

282. Ibid.; Gindlesperger and Gindlesperger, *So You Think You Know Antietam*, 32.

283. Everson and Simpson, *Far, Far from Home*, 150; *Kansas State Journal*, October 2, 1862.

Index

About the Author

Phillip Thomas Tucker, PhD, is an author and historian of numerous acclaimed publications, including *George Washington's Surprise Attack*, *Pickett's Charge*, *Death at the Little Bighorn* and more. After earning his PhD in 1990, he took a position as civilian historian with the U.S. Department of Defense. The author resides in Upper Marlboro, Maryland.

www.ingramcontent.com/pod-product-compliance
Lightning Source LLC
LaVergne TN
LVHW052339100826
845147LV00021B/1118

9781625858658